POLITICAL CHANGE IN TAIWAN

POLITICAL
CHANGE IN
TAIWAN

edited by
Tun-jen Cheng
Stephan Haggard

Written under the auspices of the
Center for International Affairs, Harvard University

Lynne Rienner Publishers · Boulder & London

Published in the United States of America in 1992 by
Lynne Rienner Publishers, Inc.
1800 30th Street, Boulder, Colorado 80301

and in the United Kingdom by
Lynne Rienner Publishers, Inc.
3 Henrietta Street, Covent Garden, London WC2E 8LU

Library of Congress Cataloging-in-Publication Data
Political change in Taiwan / edited by Tun-jen Cheng and Stephan
  Haggard.
    Includes bibliographical references and index.
    ISBN 1-55587-275-1
    1. Taiwan—Politics and government—1975- 2. Democracy.
I. Cheng, Tun-jen. II. Haggard, Stephan.
JQ1522.P65   1991
320.951249—dc20   91-29806
                                                 CIP

British Cataloguing in Publication Data
A Cataloguing in Publication record for this book
is available from the British Library.

Printed and bound in the United States of America

The paper used in this publication meets the requirements
of the American National Standard for Permanence of
Paper for Printed Library Materials Z39.48-1984.

Contents

Part 4
Prospects

Tables and Figures

Tables

Figures

Foreword

SAMUEL P. HUNTINGTON

During the past two decades, two major trends have occurred in the global political-economic environment. East Asia has emerged as the most economically dynamic area in the world. The economic growth of Japan, followed by that of Korea, Taiwan, Hong Kong, Singapore, and now Thailand, Malaysia, and Indonesia, has created the world's most vigorous region in economic terms. The changes that have begun in mainland China suggest that the process of rapid economic growth in this region could well continue into the next century. US trade is shifting from Europe to East Asia. The economic rise of East Asia is clearly one major trend altering fundamentally the balance of world power.

A second major trend has been in politics: the transition to democracy in a large number of countries throughout the world. This process began in 1974, with the Portuguese revolution and the overthrow of the colonels' regime in Greece. It then moved on to Spain, India, the Dominican Republic, Ecuador, Peru, Bolivia, Argentina, Turkey, Uruguay, El Salvador, Guatemala, Brazil, the Philippines, Korea, and, of course, the Republic of China. And this major global democratic surge appears not to have stopped. At the end of the 1980s, an opposition party did unprecedently well in, and indeed may have won, the elections in Mexico; a long-entrenched dictatorship was rejected in a referendum in Chile and fell from power; and an election in Pakistan brought the opposition party, led by a woman, into office. Most dramatically, country after country in Eastern Europe seized the opportunity to end its Communist regime and to introduce a democratic one. Democracy has been and still is on the march around the world.

What factors have been responsible for the remarkable democratic surge of the past fifteen years? One can think of a variety of possible causes. These include, obviously, the economic growth that has occurred in so many parts of the world. They include the failures, economic and military, of undemocratic regimes. They include the increased communication and interaction among societies that has helped the spread of democratic values and concepts of legitimacy. It is worthwhile to note that in a global sense, almost no one is against democracy; in that respect democracy has clearly won the war of ideas. This trend was undoubtedly also encouraged by the influence of the most powerful democratic countries in the world. The attraction of the European Community was a major factor in the movements toward democracy in Spain, Portugal, Greece, and Turkey. The United States under both the Carter administration and the Reagan administration made the promotion of human rights and democracy a key goal of US foreign policy.

This democratic wave swept through southern Europe and Latin America before it reached East Asia. Only in the late 1980s were there significant steps toward democratization in this part of the world, most notably in Korea, the Philippines, and Taiwan, and these have been balanced, one must note, in part by a movement in the opposite direction in Singapore, Malaysia, Burma, and mainland China. Yet the overall trend is obviously clear.

In assessing the future of democracy in Taiwan, three factors may be of critical importance. They are factors that will be familiar to anyone who has studied the process of democratization.

First, as Seymour Martin Lipset has shown, a clear correlation exists between democracy and economic development. The economic and social preconditions for a democratic political order clearly have come into existence in Taiwan. The rapid economic growth of the past two decades has given Taiwan a high-income economy and a complex economy. The per capita income of Taiwan equals that of such European countries as Spain and Ireland, is 50 percent higher than that of Greece, and is double that of Portugal. In the past several years, Taiwan and Singapore have been the only non–oil exporting countries in the world with per capita incomes of $5,000 a year or more that have not had fully competitive democratic political systems.

Thanks largely to the land reform of the early 1950s, Taiwan has maintained throughout the process of industrialization an extraordinarily equal income distribution. A large middle class now dominates the social scene. The population is overwhelmingly urban and literate. Social groups and civic associations exist in increasing numbers. Labor unions and farmers' organizations have begun to assert themselves. In addition, the growth of the economy has created sources of power independent of government control. In 1952 the Republic of China (ROC) government controlled 56 percent of Taiwan's industrial production; in 1972 it controlled 19 percent; today it controls less than 10 percent. Clearly, the economic and social basis for democracy has come into existence here.

Countries, however, do not automatically become democratic when they reach a certain level of material well-being. Institutional and political factors constitute a second influence on the process of democratization. It has been common among scholars to differentiate between transitions to democracy that involve the alteration of a nondemocratic regime by its leaders—a process that I have called "transformation" and that Juan Linz has called *reforma*—and those transitions that involve the overthrow of an authoritarian regime by leaders and groups that have not been a part of that regime—a process that could be called "replacement," or in Linz's term, *ruptura*. The Philippine transition in 1986 was a relatively clear case of *ruptura*: popular forces, opposition elites, and elements of the military combined to overthrow the Marcos government. The movement toward democracy in Korea during the past two years has been a mixed case: major popular forces there pushed for movement in a democratic direction, but the regime itself responded to, and even anticipated, these pressures and kept substantial control of the transition process.

In the Republic of China, the process so far has largely been one of transformation. The democratic movement has, of course, existed for many years, and it took concrete form in September 1986 with the formation of the Democratic Progressive Party (DPP). The government could have crushed this development, which, in a technical sense, was illegal, as somewhat similar movements were crushed earlier. But the government did not do that. Instead, it surprised many people by accepting the formation of the DPP, by announcing that the Kuomintang (KMT) would contest elections like an ordinary political party, and by stating its intention, which became reality in 1987, of terminating martial law. Subsequently, further changes in a democratic direction were made in the structure of the party itself.

It is, I think, widely accepted that democratization in Taiwan is an ongoing process and one that is increasingly irreversible. It is, however, a process the direction and timing of which have so far been largely set by the government. This process of transformation thus bears many resemblances to the somewhat similar processes controlled from above that have occurred in Spain and in Brazil.

There is, however, an additional factor here that distinguishes it from the Spanish and Brazilian cases and puts it in a category with two other cases. This factor involves the nature of the nondemocratic regime. The KMT regime has been one of three non-Communist one-party regimes that came into existence in the third decade of this century. The others were those of the Republican People's Party (RPP) in Turkey and the regime led by what is now called the Institutional Revolutionary Party (PRI) in Mexico. Important differences exist among these countries but in each of them the dominant single party—the PRI, the RPP, and the KMT—was in large part the creation of military leaders and forces. In all three systems, opposition parties were either effectively prohibited or excluded from any significant political role. In all three systems also, the party organization became a key source of power in the regime. The PRI, the RPP, and the KMT were not weak parties like the Falange in Franco's Spain or like the single parties that have existed in so many African countries; they were strong parties. In differing degrees, the military and other social forces shared in power, but the party played a central and usually the central role. Thus these three regimes are distinguished in twentieth-century history by being single-party regimes dominated by strong non-Communist parties.

They are also distinguished by something else. In all three cases, the identity of the state was defined by the ideology of the party. The RPP defined Turkey as a secular, Western, modern, ethnically homogeneous republic. The PRI, boasting that the 1917 Mexican constitution was the first socialist constitution in the world, antedating that of the Soviet Union, defined Mexico as revolutionary, socialist, secular, and corporatist. The KMT defined the Republic of China in terms of Chinese nationalism and Sun Yat-sen's Three Principles.

In recent years, in all three countries, political movements have emerged that have questioned the national identity as defined by the ideology of the dominant founding party. In Turkey, political groups have developed, and acquired some strength, that claim that Turkey should be Islamic and Middle Eastern, not secular and Western. In Mexico, the principal opposition party—which has been the Partido de Accion Nacional (PAN)—argues that Mexico should be a liberal, capitalist society, not a corporatist, socialist one. From the point of view of the traditional leaders of the PRI, that was a subversive ideology. In Taiwan, various political movements have in varying degrees challenged the definition of the state in terms of China and Chinese nationalist identity and have argued for an independent Taiwanese Taiwan.

The appearance of movements challenging the founding myth propagated by the single dominant party poses a central question for democratization. If the identity of the state is defined by the ideology of the dominant party, how can opposition to the party, which in a democratic system is legitimate, be distinguished from treason to the state, which is illegitimate? That question is crucial in the democratization of these regimes.

To date, the problem has been dealt with in two ways. First, those dissident parties challenging the founding myth have been kept out of power or, as once happened in the case of Turkey, removed from power, by both democratic and nondemocratic means. Second, the regime itself has pragmatically adjusted, in effect modified, or even abandoned, the founding myth in practice. The Turkish government supports Islamic groups and builds mosques. The Mexican government under Presidents de la Madrid and Salinas has tried to liberalize the economy and has privatized many state-owned enterprises. The government in Taiwan acts in practice as the government of a highly prosperous, stable, independent nation of 20 million people. Over time, in addition, the founding myth tends to recede into the background. Other issues come forward in political debate, often issues involving economic conflicts and social welfare. It is, however, fair to say that in none of these three countries as yet has the problem of the identity of the state been fully resolved.

Third, there is the question of culture and its impact on democratization. Exceptions exist to any generalization. It is, however, broadly true that democracy developed first in the Protestant countries of Europe and North America. In this century, it has taken root in more and more Catholic countries. It has been largely absent from Islamic societies.

With respect to Taiwan, two issues are relevant. First, some scholars have argued that the emphases in traditional Confucian culture on order, discipline, hierarchy, and the primacy of the group over the individual are obstacles to democratic development. If Taiwan is a Confucian society, then there could be an obvious problem here. But that brings up the second question: Is Taiwan a Confucian society? I do not know the answer to that question, but my colleague Lucian Pye argues strongly that Confucian values and traditions are weak in Taiwan, and he suggests that this creates the basis for what democratization has occurred in Taiwan and that it makes the prospects for further democratization in Taiwan promising.

The question of culture and the impact of Confucian culture on democratization can be approached in two ways. First, the years 1987 and 1988 saw an unprecedented upsurge in protests, demonstrations, strikes, riots, and even scuffles in the legislature in Taiwan. Reflecting, perhaps, traditional Confucian commitments to order, formality, and decorum, many people here expressed concern about these developments that they saw as the unfortunate and disturbing consequences of democratization. I would like to reassure these people. In general, democracies are often unruly, but they are rarely unstable. People will march, shout, confront, and be disorderly; incidents will occur, such as that which occurred in May 1988, but these are superficial events. History shows that in complex and developed societies, democratic governments are very stable. Just as violent social revolutions never produce democracies, democracies never produce violent social revolutions. A study done many years ago by Ivo and Rosalind Feierabend analyzed instability in countries that were democratic, those that were authoritarian, and those that were a mixture, somewhere in between democracy and authoritarianism. The study showed that democracies were the most stable, that the second most stable were the authoritarian systems, and that the least stable were countries that were partly democratic and partly authoritarian. This finding suggests that the events that caused some concern here in Taiwan may be a phenomenon of the transition from what has been a stable authoritarian regime in the past to what will be an even more stable democratic system in the future.

There remains the question of how democracy will develop and survive in Taiwan or other societies that put emphasis on authority as against liberty, that stress the importance of hierarchy, and that elevate the role of the group against that of the individual. It must be recognized that until recently democracy did not develop indigenously in East Asia. With the ambiguous exception of Malaysia, only two East Asian countries have sustained experience with democratic government. In these two countries, Japan and the Philippines, democracy was the product of US presence. It was not just imported from the West; it was imposed by the United States.

The recent movements toward democracy in Korea and Taiwan, in contrast, represent developments that have their origins in the dynamics of those societies rather than in the actions of a colonial or occupying power. The institutions of democracy that prevail in the West are rooted in Western concepts of liberalism, individualism, and human rights. Conceivably, institutions of democracy will develop in East Asia that could take a significantly different form because they are rooted in different cultural traditions and values. To some extent, perhaps, this has already happened. In the West, we think of democracy as normally requiring changes through elections in the parties that control government and hence an alternation in power. East Asia has been different. Malaysia, for instance, has more or less successfully maintained broadly representative institutions in which the key ethnic groups are represented, but there has been no real change of power. No one doubts that Japan is a democracy, but the same party has governed Japan for forty years. Indeed, apart from the Philippines, to the best of my knowledge, no opposition party has ever come to power through elections in an East Asian country. One could cite this as evidence of the absence of democracy, which is obviously the case for many countries. But it may also reflect a different concept of democracy, one that holds that democratic institutions should promote consensus and stability rather than conflict and change.

In any event, as Taiwan moves forward on the democratic path, one should not be surprised to see the possible emergence of new institutional forms of democracy. That brings me to my final point, which may sound trivial, but is not, and which may also sound parochial, and is. A close connection exists between the development of the discipline of political science and the development of democracy. Historically, these two have gone hand in hand. Nondemocratic countries may be outstanding in fields like physics, mathematics, or literature, but they are never outstanding in the field of political science. Taiwan, like Korea, has a healthy and vigorous political science profession. The process of democratization in Taiwan faces many challenges. Taiwan's many talented political scientists, along with their US colleagues, can play a key role in helping to find answers to these challenges and in devising whatever new institutional forms of democracy may be appropriate and required. This volume and the conference on which it was based will, I hope, make a contribution to this important yet difficult task.

Acknowledgments

The chapters in this volume were first presented at a conference at the Institute of International Relations (IIR), National Chengchi University, in January 1989. The conference was jointly sponsored by the Institute of International Relations and the Center for International Affairs, Harvard University. Over two hundred people attended the conference at various times, including a contingent of fifteen social scientists from the United States.

The conference came at a propitious moment in Taiwan's political development and, at the time, was a somewhat novel event. Our purpose was primarily academic: to inquire into the development and prospects of democracy in Taiwan from a broadly comparative perspective. In any country undergoing political liberalization, however, such discussions are never purely academic; moreover, we actively sought to encourage a broader dialogue on the issues at hand.

President Lee Teng-hui of the Republic of China on Taiwan sent a welcoming and encouraging opening message to the conference, and he received the US delegation. The conference was attended not only by leading academics on Taiwan, but also by members of the press, high-ranking officials of the ruling party, and leading figures in the opposition. The result was an invigorating exchange of views not only among academics, but also between government and opposition as well.

Our greatest debt is to Chang King Yu, former director of the Institute of International Relations, who first conceived of this conference. Without his tremendous patience and support, the conference and this volume would not have come to fruition. We would also like to thank Su Chi at the IIR, and the broader community of social scientists in Taiwan who made our stay so stimulating. Samuel Huntington, director of the Center for International

Affairs, Harvard University, gave this enterprise his wholehearted support and has contributed the foreword.

We would like to thank Anthony Westerling for his most competent and meticulous clerical assistance.

Tun-jen Cheng
Stephan Haggard

CHAPTER 1

Regime Transformation in Taiwan: Theoretical and Comparative Perspectives

TUN-JEN CHENG
& STEPHAN HAGGARD

Theoretical Approaches to Democratization

For nearly four decades the authoritarian rule by the Nationalist Party, or Kuomintang (KMT), in Taiwan was stable, continuous, and seemingly unchallengeable. But by the mid-1980s, this steady state could no longer be maintained, and democratic forces advanced. The political space for electoral competition and the scope of political discourse widened as the government lifted various authoritarian restraints, most notably the thirty-seven-year-old declaration of martial law. New civil organizations formed, and new opposition parties appeared. The archaic "Long Parliament" that had lasted more than forty years came under strong pressure to submit itself to fully democratic elections. As civil society reasserted itself, new arenas and arrangements for political contestation gradually began to take shape.[1]

The movement toward political liberalization and democratization in the Republic of China is beyond doubt, but the origins and prospects of democracy are still the subject of debate. Some of these debates center on particularities of the Taiwan case: the KMT is the only example of a Leninist party organization in a capitalist setting, and Taiwan's international political status is unique. Nonetheless, political change in Taiwan also raises important comparative questions. The transformation of the KMT invites comparison with other one-party systems, such as Mexico and the countries of Eastern Europe. Taiwan's political development might also be compared with that of countries that have pursued similar development strategies, including the other East Asian newly industrializing countries (NICs), such as Korea, or Japan in an earlier period.

The Taiwan case also raises broader theoretical issues about the process of democratization. Two theoretical approaches have dominated the burgeoning literature on comparative democratization. The first focuses on the preconditions for democracy. The trend toward democracy in Taiwan can be understood as a consequence of rapid economic growth and social change

1

in a capitalist economy. Virtually all of the socioeconomic correlates of democracy that theorists of modernization have isolated—high levels of urbanization, industrialization, rising per capita income, high literacy rates, and mass communication—are now present in Taiwan.[2] Taiwan is, as Lucian Pye has recently suggested, "possibly the best working example of the theory that economic progress should bring in its wake democratic inclinations and a healthy surge of pluralism, which in time will undercut the foundations of the authoritarian rule common to developing countries."[3]

As Guillermo O'Donnell argued in his classic work on bureaucratic authoritarianism in Latin America, modernization does not necessarily guarantee democratic politics, however, and can under certain circumstances create pressures for political closure. Rapid development can itself be destabilizing.[4] Moreover, there may be an "elective affinity" between certain growth strategies and authoritarian rule. The export-oriented strategy pursued by the East Asian NICs, it has been argued, depended on the political passivity or control of labor and the general absence of leftist or populist political parties, conditions unlikely to hold in a fully democratic polity.[5]

These observations underline a crucial methodological failing of the "preconditions" approach to democratization. Most such studies note the correlation between level of development, or some other social precondition, and regime type. Arguments are then developed as to why such preconditions might be plausibly linked to democratic politics. Yet the analysis of preconditions is necessarily static, and it does not explain how the democratic threshold is actually crossed. The crucial political *processes* that constitute democratization are either not articulated or are assumed to follow a simple model of increasing demand for democratization eventually yielding its supply.

The preconditions approach must also carefully weigh other historical legacies that may offset unfavorable or favorable preconditions. Stable democracy has long existed in the absence of presumably necessary economic conditions in countries such as India, Costa Rica, and Colombia. Conversely, Taiwan's favorable socioeconomic preconditions are matched by several liabilities. First, democratization of a one-party regime might be expected to pose greater difficulties than in authoritarian regimes dominated by militaries. With a powerful organizational reach and a dominant ideology, the KMT's raison d'être is political rule. Democratization thus requires a fundamental transformation of the ruling party from an entity closely intertwined with the state apparatus to an independent political organization competing equally for electoral support. In contrast, military rulers have alternative roles, which may even be strengthened by a retreat from politics.

Second, Taiwan has a colonial legacy that is less auspicious for democratization than that of many other developing countries. The diffusion of political institutions during the colonial era came not from liberal democratic Western powers, as in the case of the Philippines or the British colonies, but from authoritarian Japan. Taiwan's decolonization took the form of a wholesale transfer of power and resources from a defeated Japan to a soon-to-be-defeated KMT. This process occurred without the substantial social and political mobilization of other nationalist movements. Nationalist movements are not necessarily democratic, and they do not necessarily bear a relationship with subsequent democratic politics. But the new political order in Taiwan in the immediate postwar period resembled in many ways a colonial one. An outside power, the KMT, established political control over the domestic politics of a subject people largely excluded from political representation.

The main alternative, or supplement, to the "preconditions" approach to democracy is to focus on the *processes* by which democratic forces in society emerge, grow, and outmaneuver the regime to establish a new institutional framework. First outlined by Dankwart A. Rustow and recently elaborated by Adam Przeworski, this process-oriented approach identifies the agents of political change, examines their reasons for seeking democratic politics, and analyzes the bargaining situations they face with both the state and possible coalition partners.[6] This approach interprets democratic rules and institutions as the result of implicit or explicit bargaining among contending political forces.

This introduction combines the precondition and process-oriented approaches to democratization with comparative analysis of relevant cases. In the second section of this chapter, we consider how the historical role of the KMT in Taiwanese society has affected the prospects for democratization. In the third section of the chapter, we examine the "Lipset hypothesis," which links economic growth to the emergence of democratic politics, and provide some comparative data on Taiwan's modernization. Democratization cannot be fully understood without reference to political processes, however, so in the fourth section of this introduction we analyze the interaction between emergent opposition forces and the state. The fundamental puzzle is why any regime with a monopoly on political power ultimately decides to share it.

One interpretation of how Taiwan liberalized, widespread among supporters of the KMT, focuses on long-standing democratic ideals and the farsightedness of the party leadership, particularly in the person of Chiang Ching-kuo.[7] There is some merit in this approach, and Taiwan's experience has been, in part, a democratization engineered "from above." We argue, however, that weight must also be given to the rise and growth of the political opposition, and pressures for democratization from below. The democratic transition in Taiwan was advanced by the ability of the opposition to set the agenda, to use extralegal methods, to shift bargaining arenas, and eventually to push the ruling elite toward new rules of the game.

A crucial aspect of this process was the effect of the newly emergent opposition on the internal politics of the ruling party, which is essentially a middle-class movement. The leadership of the new opposition consists of a critical mass of social-science-trained intellectuals with professional skills, most notably legal expertise, and social ties to small- and medium-sized businesses. The goals of the middle-class opposition were not altogether foreign to moderates within the party, with which they occasionally formed a tacit alliance. Despite the substantial tensions between the opposition and the ruling party that have surfaced during the transition period, this affinity between the opposition and reformers within the KMT has been a key to the transition.

How unique is the Taiwan experience? In the final section of this chapter, we address this question by comparing Taiwan with other relevant cases. First, we examine Taiwan's transition against that of other non-Communist, one-party systems, including Turkey in the early postwar period and Mexico today. The second set of comparisons locates Taiwan within East Asia, comparing its political evolution with that of Japan and the other NICs, countries with comparable economic trajectories.

Preconditions

The Characteristics of the KMT Regime in Taiwan

With the defeat of Japan in World War II, Taiwan's fate was tied to that of the KMT. In anticipation of its defeat by the Communists, the KMT began to plan for a retreat to Taiwan in 1948. The KMT's flight brought a continental-size administration of 1.5 million people, mostly state employees and military personnel, to a small island with an indigenous population of 7 million.

Several factors accounted for the effective consolidation of the KMT's political power in Taiwan and were to have important effects on subsequent political developments. For one, unlike Korea's postwar experience, the indigenous elite of Taiwan had little access to the state—the government was highly insulated from local social pressures. After decolonization, a large contingent of KMT expatriates quickly displaced the former Japanese administrators. An island-wide revolt caused by the mismanagement of a corrupt KMT governor was brutally suppressed, eliminating key indigenous opposition leaders.

Ironically, the defeat of the KMT regime on the mainland motivated a thorough political reform in 1950–1951 through which the party increased its organizational capacity and developed a semicorporatist structure. The top KMT leadership purged factional leaders within its own ranks and extended its organization throughout all levels of government and into every social organization, both rural and urban.

The KMT's political autonomy from society and its ability to penetrate social organizations and create its own had several consequences for subsequent political development. First, this autonomy permitted a far-reaching land reform. By virtually eliminating the landlord class, the KMT reduced the possibility of the sectoral conflicts and rural difficulties visible in other developing countries. The new farmers may have been squeezed by the KMT's need to extract rice to provision the cities, but they also benefited from the reforms and constituted a tacit base of political support for the regime.

Second, this "preemptive corporatism," the dispersion of industry and intensive linkages between rural and urban society, served to reduce the possibility for an autonomous working-class politics to emerge in the cities (see Chapter 10 for further discussion). In combination, the absence of strong sectoral cleavages and the corporatist organization of the working class foreclosed the populist politics that are characteristic of many Latin American countries and bubble under the surface in Korea. The absence of a strong populist or leftist tradition may also have reduced the threat that democratization posed to both the ruling party and the dominant economic elites.

A third consequence of the internal reform of the party concerns the dog that did not bark—namely, the military. A crucial part of the party reform of the early 1950s was the establishment of a commissar system within the military. It is very difficult for a political party to penetrate an officer corps, because this entails an attack on military autonomy. Once penetrated, however, it is very difficult for the military to overthrow the government. There are a number of other conditions in Taiwan that reduce the threat of military intervention during the period of transition. These include the existence of a genuine external security mission, the government's willingness to meet the corporate interests of the military, and the unlikelihood of the disorder, economic difficulties, and general government ineffectiveness that have invited military intervention elsewhere in the developing world. Nonetheless, the *organizational* relationship between the party and the military reduced, if it did not wholly eliminate, the threat of a military intervention.

The inheritance of colonial properties and the inflow of foreign aid—an economic payoff for political incorporation into the Western alliance during the Cold War—further enhanced the position of the KMT regime vis-à-vis society. In the 1950s, the state controlled all foreign exchange derived from aid and state-managed agricultural exports and monopolized the banking sector. State-owned enterprises accounted for half of industrial production. Usually, such state intervention has been a recipe for inefficiency. On the mainland, the KMT had depended on the support of Shanghai capital, but it severely mismanaged the economy and intervened in ways that reduced the viability of the independent private sector while encouraging rent-seeking and corruption. Why was this experience not repeated in Taiwan? One reason was the link that the KMT leadership drew between economic mismanagement and its loss of China to Communist revolution. Greater attention to the countryside and the pursuit of an extremely conservative fiscal and monetary policy were responses to the rural unrest and hyperinflation that undercut KMT rule on the mainland. A second reason was that US aid gave the KMT greater economic security than they had ever enjoyed, and thus it acted as a partial check on predatory behavior. The combination of economic and political security ultimately allowed the KMT to launch a series of wide-ranging economic reforms between 1958 and 1962 that contributed to the development of the local private sector.

In terms of its political structure, most scholars have treated the KMT regime in Taiwan as an authoritarian one (see Chapters 2, 4, and 5).[8] An authoritarian regime is, in Juan Linz's definition, characterized by a limited but not responsible pluralism, a "mentality" rather than an ideology, and control rather than mobilization. Linz's definition applies only imperfectly to the KMT regime, however. First, because of the KMT's relocation on Taiwan, elections for the three national representative bodies—the National Assembly, which elects the president, the Legislative Yuan (literally, branch), and the Control Yuan that oversees government officials—were suspended indefinitely. Insulated from their mainland constituencies, these representative bodies were exempt from the periodic renewal of their mandate and consequently atrophied. With competing parties effectively banned, national-level pluralism was wholly absent, and intra-elite pluralism was actively discouraged. A limited electoral pluralism was allowed at the local level, however, though under tight KMT control. Although syncretic and vague, a dominant ideology did exist. Sun Yat-sen's Three Principles of the People, or *san min chu i*, included nationalism, democracy, and "the people's livelihood," a moderate form of state capitalism. The regime did impose a consensus on the fundamentals of politics and precluded the advocacy of any alternative ideology. To support specific policies, the KMT also attempted to mobilize the public, often mimicking political campaigns on the mainland.

In terms of party structure and party-state relationships, as Constance Squires Meaney argues in Chapter 5, the KMT regime is more akin to a Leninist party than Linz's authoritarian regime; indeed, Soviet advisers played a role in a crucial reorganization of the party in 1926.[9] The principle of organizational parallelism operated between party and state. Party organs controlled administrative units at various levels of government as well as the military via a commissar system. Party cells penetrated the existing social organizations, which were sole and exclusive. "Opposition parties" were transformed into "friendship parties" of the ruling party. Party cadres were socialized as revolutionary vanguards. The internal decision rules of the party have been "democratic centralist." The KMT can thus be seen as an elitist party using mass organizations to mobilize support from large segments of the population for the national tasks articulated by the regime.

Despite these similarities, three crucial features distinguished the KMT from other Leninist regimes. First, unlike Leninist parties elsewhere, the KMT did not advocate the principle of proletarian dictatorship nor the long-term monopoly of political power by the party. From the beginning, KMT ideology upheld the eventual transition to democracy following a period of "tutelage." Under the 1947 Constitution, the KMT was formally but one of many competing democratic parties and no longer the revolutionary party tutoring the government and society. The 1950 party reform restored the KMT's role as a "revolutionary-democratic" party, a charismatic party with a political role defined in terms of its leadership in the national revolution. Such a redefinition of the party was justified by the historical mission of "retaking mainland China and completing national construction." Nevertheless, the political hegemony of the KMT was not constitutionally enshrined but was based on "temporary provisions" justified by "national emergency." This gap between ideology and practice formed an important opening wedge for the opposition, which could claim that the KMT was violating its own commitment to the 1947 Constitution, and even to Sun's Three Principles of the People.

A second difference is that the KMT regime permitted and organized subnational political contestation. Direct elections for both executive and council positions at the county, township, and village levels have been held regularly since 1950 (see Chapter 7). The provincial senate, composed of delegates elected by county councils, was turned into the provincial assembly subject to periodic direct elections since 1959, although the governor and important mayoral positions (in Taipei and later Kaohsiung) have remained appointive. The encouragement of subnational politics appears as an ingenious political design. It gave elective officials extremely limited power over the budget and negligible regulatory power, but it did indicate the KMT regime's commitment to democracy. Subnational democracy provided a political safety valve. The provincial assembly dissipated the political energy of disgruntled ex-landlords, and local elections provided a mechanism for the KMT to co-opt local elites. Subnational elections should not be altogether dismissed, however, because they may have had some role in contributing to a participatory political culture. Elections were generally competitive and permitted the airing of local grievances, a development unseen in Leninist systems until recently.[10]

The third and perhaps crucial difference between the KMT and other Leninist parties was the promotion of a capitalist economy based on private property and a fairly wide scope of market exchanges. The principle of "people's livelihood," one of the three pillars of *san min chu i*, upheld economic equality as a social goal but did not specify the means through which the goal would be achieved. In the 1950s, the state sector dominated production, and conservatives within the party resisted the transition to a more market-oriented system. This conservative line was partly accommodated, because state-owned enterprises were retained and new ones launched to achieve particular economic as well as political objectives. At the same time, however, the private sector was encouraged. This resulted in a relative, though not absolute, decline in the size of the state-owned sector. The rapid social change that followed the new emphasis on economic growth produced the new political forces that would spearhead Taiwan's political liberalization.

Economic Growth, Social Change, and the Political Sociology of the Opposition

In the late 1950s, economic development became a goal that was to support, and ultimately supplant, the long-term objective of retaking the mainland. Economic development had been important before, but the reorientation of government objectives was probably caused in part by a change in the parameters of national security. Following the 1958 Taiwan Straits crisis, it became clear that US support of Taiwan was strictly limited to the defense of Taiwan.

By the mid-1950s, Taiwan was also experiencing erratic economic performance. The small domestic market was nearly saturated by import-substituting industries. To continue economic growth, the KMT regime, persuaded by the US aid-giving agency, undertook crucial economic reforms between 1958 and 1961 that reoriented the economy toward export markets, limited further growth of the state sector, and granted greater support to private entrepreneurship.

The details of Taiwan's success with export-led industrialization is well known and need not be repeated here.[11] As shown in Table 1.1, between 1960 and 1980, Taiwan's gross national product increased at an annual rate of 9 percent in real terms, more than double the growth rate of other middle-income countries (Table 1.2). Exports expanded at around 20 percent a year and became the economy's leading sector. Industry's share of output increased from 25 to 45 percent. All of this was achieved with remarkably low inflation as well as a steady improvement in the distribution of income. On such social indicators as population per physician, Taiwan was approaching the levels achieved by the advanced industrial states.

With its economic takeoff, Taiwan displayed features common to a modernizing capitalist society (see Table 1.2). The literacy rate increased, mass communication intensified, and per capita income rose. With the rapid movement of labor into manufacturing, a differentiated urban sector developed, including labor, a professional middle class, and business. These new social forces are generally viewed as propitious for the advance of democratic norms (see Chapter 2). Several other specific features of Taiwan's economic development also appeared conducive to the emergence of a more liberal politics.

Table 1.1 Economic Indicators of Taiwan

	1960	1970	1980
Per capita GNP (US $)	130.2	360.4	2,103.0
Ratio of highest fifth's income to lowest fifth's	5.33[a]	4.58	4.17
Industrial origin of net domestic output (%)			
primary	32.8	17.9	9.3
secondary	24.9	34.7	45.3
tertiary and other	42.3	47.4	45.4

Source: Council for Economic Planning and Development, Republic of China, *Taiwan Statistical Data Book*, various issues.
[a]Data are for 1964.

Table 1.2 International Comparison of Taiwan's Socioeconomic Development

Country	Per capita GNP, 1982 (dollars)	GNP growth rate, 1960–82	Higher education: % of age group 1960	Higher education: % of age group 1981	Population per physician 1960	Population per physician 1980
Taiwan	2,290	8.4	5	19	1,553	871
Industrial market economies	11,070	3.3	16	37	816	554
Upper middle-income economies	2,490	4.1	4	14	2,532	2,021
Lower middle-income economies	840	3.2	3	9	17,257	5,414
Low-income economies	280	3.0	2	4	12,008	5,772

Sources: World Bank, *World Development Report 1984;* for Taiwan data, Council of Economic Planning and Development, *Taiwan Statistical Data Book*, and Directorate-General of Budget, Accounting, and Statistics, *Statistical Yearbook*, various issues.

First, businesses in Taiwan are small and unorganized, but therefore they are also beyond the reach of the government. Partly to prevent the concentration of economic power, partly because of the social distance separating the ruling party from the private sector, the regime largely avoided the strategy of politically organizing business or backing large "national champions." As a result, small and medium-sized enterprises dominated industrial production and exports. As major employers and foreign exchange earners, small and medium-sized businesses have maintained their independence from the KMT regime.[12]

Second, the emerging bifurcation of the political and socioeconomic elite overlapped the subethnic division between mainlander and Taiwanese populations. Because national politics was reserved for mainlanders, Taiwanese pursued economic advancement and social mobility. Not only were economic resources diffused in a relatively fragmented private sector, they were largely in the hands of Taiwanese. In many other ethnically divided societies, political and economic power tended to go hand in hand, hardening ethnic divisions into zero-sum political cleavages. Taiwan's ethnic cleavage, by contrast, was muted by the economic opportunities available to the indigenous Taiwanese.

Finally, capitalist development itself undermined the KMT's institutional capacity for mobilization and control. The deficiency of the KMT cadre system provides a notable example. Despite various efforts to reorganize the cadre system along occupational-functional lines, it is still largely based on administrative regions. The rapid growth of civic and economic associations was simply beyond what the KMT could monitor or control.

These changes in and of themselves do not generate demands for democracy; it must still be explained why new social forces have an interest in liberalizing politics. As a number of theorists have noted, the manufacturing sector in the developing world has not generally been at the cutting edge of democratic politics. The same has been true in Taiwan. The KMT regime provided few channels of access for business, yet it also pursued policies that were generally conducive to private sector growth. There were thus few incentives for the private sector to attempt to reshape the political order. Other possible reasons for business quiescence are necessarily more speculative. The absence of a landed class that dominated politics and proved resistant to an industrial project eliminated one motivation for the private manufacturing sector to seek state assistance. In addition, a growth strategy emphasizing low-cost labor and international competitiveness is more likely to be threatened by the labor mobilization that would accompany democratization.

The main agents of political change in Taiwan have been middle-class intellectuals who came of age during the period of rapid economic growth. This new group of elites, predominantly Taiwanese from the countryside, differed from an earlier generation of scholars who had attempted unsuccessfully to push democratic ideas in the 1950s. The earlier opposition led by several scholars and politicians under the banner of intellectual liberalism was crushed in 1960 when it attempted to coalesce with the local elite to form a political party. The leaders of the new democratic movement were trained in the social sciences—notably in political science, law, and sociology. Like their predecessors, these new advocates of democracy were educated elites reacting to ideas and institutions in a foreign "reference society" and seeking to apply them at home.[13] Unlike their predecessors, however, the current opposition elite also adapted political techniques, specific democratic procedures, institutional designs, and legal frameworks from the West. In comparison with earlier dissidents, this new democratic leadership was equipped with organizational skills and was more prone to adopt mobilizational tactics.

As Alexander Ya-li Lu notes in Chapter 6, the detailed empirical study of the political sociology of the opposition has yet to be done. Nonetheless, the middle-class intellectuals that fueled the democratic movement appeared to be connected to small and medium-sized businesses via various social ties based on school, regional, and workplace affiliations. Small and medium-sized businesses, especially those in the export sector, offered political funds and fallback career positions. The numerous small export houses have absorbed college graduates in the social sciences from the major universities, the institutions that supply the political opposition.

Leaders of the democratic movement were first activated between 1972, the year the KMT introduced political reform under new leadership, and 1977, the year members of the political opposition scored their first electoral victory. This first phase in the development of the political opposition started with a political reform movement, which was triggered by diplomatic setbacks. The loss of Taiwan's membership in the United Nations to Communist China and the forced severance of its formal ties with many Western countries were dramatic events. Although the initial reaction to the deteriorating external environment was patriotic, intellectuals soon turned their attention to domestic society and politics. Between 1969 and 1972, young elites conducted several social surveys, notably on the plight of the rural sector. They also questioned the political deficiencies of the regime, especially over the issue of the competence and legitimacy of the "Long Parliament" that never faced reelection and preempted the possibility of Taiwanese participation.

The KMT regime responded to this intellectual challenge on several fronts. Agricultural policy was reversed, and the rural sector was increasingly subsidized and protected. The educated Taiwanese elite were recruited for party and government positions in a classic strategy of co-optation. Supplementary elections were also held to partly replenish the aging national congress (see Chapter 7 for further discussion).

These reforms would not have been possible without the rise of Chiang Ching-kuo, who gained in influence over the older KMT leadership of the Chiang Kai-shek generation after 1972. Yet the reform served to consolidate, rather than transform, KMT rule. Supplementary elections were necessary to reverse the serious decay of the legislature, but by no means did they constitute a genuine political opening. The number of contested seats remained small, and the KMT still dominated the nomination process. Agricultural reforms only consolidated KMT popularity in the rural areas. And the co-optive strategy toward aspiring Taiwanese political elites momentarily blunted the edge of the opposition. As the limits on reform became apparent, an exodus from the KMT began and new centers of opposition emerged. It is to the processes surrounding this third round of opposition that we now turn.

Processes: Strategic Interaction
Between Regime and Opposition

The second phase of the development of the opposition, and the beginning of the democratic transition in Taiwan, can be dated to the formation of an opposition camp—as opposed to the operation of individual independents—in the local elections of 1977. As the opposition sought to establish its legitimacy, both legally and as a credible alternative to the KMT, it became difficult for the ruling party to define the terms of political participation unilaterally. Internal political debates within the KMT were the crucial factor shaping the transition, but these internal political debates were increasingly conditioned by the strategy and tactics of the opposition itself. The most appropriate view of the transition is one that focuses on the strategic interaction between state and opposition yet is careful to remember that neither constitutes a monolithic block.[14]

Disappointed with the limited political reform engineered from above, dissident political elites competed vigorously in the 1977 local elections, registering an astounding success by winning 35 percent of the seats in the Taiwan Provincial Assembly and 20 percent of the gubernatorial positions. As a result of this election, electoral politics became more competitive, and the opposition (called Tangwai, or "outside the party") became a political force. The initial success induced the new opposition to use the islandwide offices of the magazine *Formosa* as an organization to coordinate their efforts for future elections.

Within the KMT, it is useful to distinguish between "hard-liners" and "soft-liners." The hard-liners included party cadres in the internal security apparatus who were concerned with the potential social disorder accompanying political change and the old guard, who defined the KMT's mission in conservative terms: staunch anticommunism abroad, continued commitment to recapturing the mainland, and KMT dominance and "tutelage" at home. The soft-liners included younger cadres in the Department of Organization, a division responsible for conducting elections and intraparty affairs, and newer, Taiwanese recruits throughout the party.

The strategy of political co-optation and the rejuvenation of the party through local recruitment, which had been under way since the early 1970s favored the soft-liners. However, events surrounding the 1977 election tipped the balance back to favor the hard-liners. First, a major riot in the northern county of T'ao Yuan in protest of electoral fraud took the form of an assault by opposition supporters on a police station in Chung-li. Not only was this the first electoral violence in the history of postwar Taiwan, it was also the first popular antigovernment violence. The election also revealed potent social support for the opposition, which was grossly underestimated by the soft-liners. As the soft-liners took the blame for these unanticipated events, the hard-liners argued that the political opposition should be contained before it became uncontrollable.

Ironically, the strong electoral showing of the opposition ultimately had the effect of radicalizing it, opening a split within the opposition that paralleled the hard-liner–soft-liner split within the ruling party. The radicalization occurred because of the frustration that newly elected representatives experienced within the Provincial Assembly. Despite holding one-third of the seats, the opposition had little influence over legislation, and the assembly was in any case a weak body. The frustrated expectations spawned new more-radical opposition tactics centered on social mobilization.

The ascent of the radicals within the opposition and the hard-liners within the party set the stage for confrontation. The radical wing sought to inaugurate a mass movement in defiance of martial law, and the government responded with the deployment of police to deter street actions. The use of police incited additional demonstrations in a self-reinforcing cycle. Seeking to establish a legal basis for its own existence, the opposition emphasized the inalienable nature of human rights and civil liberties, while the regime repeated its obligation and determination to maintain social order and national security. The test of wills between hard-liners and radicals climaxed in December 1979 when opposition supporters and riot police engaged in a bloody encounter in Kaohsiung, a major industrial city in southern Taiwan. Following a carefully orchestrated and highly visible trial, most of the leaders of the radical faction within the opposition were jailed.

The violent showdown in Kaohsiung forced both sides to reassess their strategies. On the opposition side, the jailing of radical leaders enhanced the stature of the moderates, who had argued against futile and costly confrontations with the regime. Within the KMT, the soft-liners gained as the party sought to prevent further direct confrontations. Several signs indicated popular disapproval of opposition violence,[15] thus partly vindicating the hard-liners' advocacy of social order. However, the public also showed widespread sympathy and admiration for the courage of the radical opposition, as evidenced by the astounding electoral support given to the family members of the imprisoned radical leaders in 1980.

The strategy of the KMT, as a compromise between the hard-liner and soft-liner views, was to gradually "normalize" the political process while maintaining various constraints on the activities of the opposition. The regime created more parliamentary seats for electoral competition, enacted electoral laws through which investigative power was vested in a nonpartisan election committee, and initiated a mediated dialogue with the opposition. These measures were intended to incorporate the political opposition into existing political arenas, including the KMT-dominated Legislative Yuan.

However, although the electoral space was expanded, the restrictions on opposition political activity under the martial law regime were not relaxed. Members and supporters of the opposition thus continued to run a high risk of arrest and personal loss for their activities in the extraparliamentary arena and there were even several instances of politically motivated murder.[16]

The hard-liner position weakened, however, after the demotion of the head of the Department of Political Warfare, Wang Shen, in 1984. Evidence of his ambition to succeed Chiang Ching-kuo raised the specter of military intervention. This was deftly managed by Chiang, including through public commitments to constitutional procedure. The gradual ebbing of hard-liner strength did not lead to a lifting of the numerous restraints on opposition activity, but the waning of the "ultra–hard-liners" within the government shifted the dominant mode of interaction between KMT and the opposition toward implicit negotiation.

On the opposition side, the moderate leadership concentrated on rebuilding electoral support, using the Legislative Yuan as an arena for bargaining. To exploit the political thaw and to press for maximum electoral gain, the moderate leadership launched a variety of innovative strategies, including the endorsement of candidates, the building of a campaign corps, and the elaboration of a common platform. Although lacking formal organizational structure or legal standing, the opposition began to function like a parliamentary party.

Shunning activities on the streets, the moderate leadership of the opposition also managed to extend its activities overseas. The most significant overseas arena was the United States, where many Taiwanese had been attempting to influence political development on Taiwan via a variety of methods, including lobbying Congress. In their trip to the United States in 1982, moderate leaders enhanced their visibility, cemented ties with overseas Taiwanese organizations, and highlighted the issue of democratization in US-Taiwan relations.

The very progress that moderate leaders made in the legislative and overseas arenas ironically triggered a leadership crisis. Discounting the incremental gains from either the legislative process or closed-door negotiations with the KMT, Young Turks once again sought street actions to force the pace of concession from the KMT. The Young Turks also opened the touchy issue of Taiwan's international political status, suggesting that Taiwan should move toward "self-determination," a code word for independence (see Chapters 6 and 9). This position was anathema not only to the KMT, which justified its political dominance through its claim to rule all of China, but it was also viewed with alarm by Beijing. Nonetheless, the issue had some appeal to native Taiwanese.

As a result of this "revolt from below," many moderate leaders subsequently lost election bids in the 1983 legislative election. To overcome internal disunity and to recapture the initiative, moderate leaders strove to transform informal groupings of the opposition into a quasi party organization called the Association of Public Policy Studies (APPS). The APPS would allow discussion and also provide an imprimatur for binding members' actions and establishing organizational authority. The APPS would also allow the opposition to accumulate knowledge in substantive policy areas, a factor crucial in negotiation with the performance-oriented KMT. Above all, as a formal political organization, the APPS would provide legal protection for the activities of the opposition.

The APPS was transparently a proxy for a new political party, which the KMT explicitly forbade. The existence and functions of the APPS and its islandwide branches thus became the major focus of conflict between the opposition and the regime in 1984 and 1985. In 1961 the KMT had purged the old opposition when it attempted to form a political association as a prelude to a political party. In light of this precedent, the opposition initially accepted the KMT's invitation for negotiation on the procedure and restrictions to be imposed on the APPS. Eventually the opposition eschewed compromise, announcing its specific demands for democracy and its determination to establish a party. Because the regime controlled all newspapers and broadcasting, the opposition used journal publications to propagate its positions. The dissident journals were banned but continually reappeared under new names.

While threatening to crack down, the KMT regime did not take any punitive action. Absorbed with the question of the political succession to the ailing President Chiang Ching-kuo, the regime appeared on the defensive. In June 1986, Chiang Ching-kuo named a twelve-person blue-ribbon study group to study six crucial political issues: (1) the restructuring of the National Assembly, (2) local autonomy, (3) martial law, (4) civic organizations, (4) social reform, and (6) internal party reform. In September 1986, the opposition regained the offensive by establishing the Democratic Progressive Party (DPP), the first new political party in postwar Taiwan. Instead of suppression, the KMT reacted in mid-October by announcing its decision to lift martial law and the ban on political associations, including parties. The KMT then peacefully competed with the DPP in the December election of that year and promised to accelerate other aspects of democratization, completely reversing its previous stand on political change.

What explains the democratic breakthrough of 1986? It has been suggested that Taiwan's democratization was engineered from above by a liberalizing, though still dominant, elite rather than forced upon the regime by broad social mobilization, as was the case in Korea and the Philippines.[17] This view appears to be plausible in light of late President Chiang Ching-kuo's personal intervention to clear major hurdles to democratization, the comparatively low intensity of confrontation between the regime and its challengers, and the broad continuity in both institutions and personnel during the transition. The events of 1989 in China also suggest the crucial importance of contending political forces within the party itself.

The view that the democratic breakthrough in Taiwan was initiated from above is compatible with the view that the KMT pursued democratization because of external factors, such as US pressure or the diplomatic efforts of the People's Republic of China (PRC) to isolate the country.[18] Although lacking formal ties with Taiwan, the United States could and did continue to supply weapons, offer market access, and support Taiwan's membership in international organizations that have nonpolitical functions. Taiwan did not encounter direct pressure from the United States for the promotion of democracy, as the Philippines and South Korea did. But the KMT regime might have used democratization to preempt such pressure and to shore up an image damaged by various human rights violations.[19] Democratization could also be seen as a response to the mainland's diplomatic offensive to force Taiwan to come to terms for reunification and to isolate Taiwan in the international community (see Chapter 9).

However, these views of democratization from "above" and from "outside" are insufficient to explain the breakthrough in Taiwan. First, in the absence of direct intervention by foreign actors, as in Germany or Japan, or cataclysmic external events, as in Argentina's military loss to Britain, external factors are unlikely to determine processes of democratization.[20] External factors may impinge on the transition because of their effects on the relative bargaining positions of key dominant actors, but the real question is not whether external factors exist or not, but whether domestic actors can exploit the opportunities or minimize the pressures these factors create. Second, one needs to explain why the regime, having shown little interest in political change prior to the emergence of the opposition, suddenly reversed its stand. As Ch'i Hsi-sheng has argued, the KMT has never agreed to the expansion of political participation unless under strong pressure from political opposition.[21]

Yet if Taiwan's democratic transition was not simply engineered from above, it is equally obvious that it did not result from a popular uprising, as was the case in the Philippines. The strategic interaction perspective suggested here sees the transition as a tacit or implicit negotiation. The specific nature of the democratic outcome depended on the ability of the respective sides to set the substantive agenda of the transition and to exploit the arenas open to realize their objectives.

Once the KMT committed itself to some form of political change, it could use that commitment to set limits on the range of tolerable debate. The KMT's initial acceptance of the DPP as a legalized party was contingent on the opposition meeting three preconditions: no use of violence, no advocacy of separatism, and no support of communism. The regime also had the benefit of time, not to mention its control over the media. The KMT could commit to the goal of a democratic transition while keeping that commitment broad and undefined, stressing the incremental nature of the process, and tying the transition to already scheduled events, such as regular elections.

Yet the opposition was not without its own ability to influence the agenda and to force the pace of change. Once the KMT had committed to some form of political change, the opposition gained the advantage of being able to specify alternative transition paths. The opposition's sequence had a particularly compelling logic. The first step was to demand political liberalization, including annulling the martial law decrees and restoring freedoms of speech, press, and assembly. Some have argued that Taiwan's democratization process has in fact not gotten beyond this stage (see Chapters 5 and 10). The next step was reelection of the entire membership of the existing national representatives organs. Only then would the sharper departure take place: direct election of the president and provincial governors. By identifying a logical sequence of measures for the transition, and playing on the government's own commitment to "democracy," the opposition raised the cost of doing nothing and forced the regime to act on some issues.

A second distinct aspect in the process of strategic interaction between government and opposition in democratic transitions is the opposition's use of the available arenas for political action. Learning the lesson of Kaohsiung, the opposition avoided the arena of the street. In the streets, the opposition had the advantage of the initiative but ran two risks. The first, typical of most transitional settings, was simple repression. The second, however, differentiates Taiwan from most of the Latin American transitions. Because of the relatively benign nature of KMT rule, the economic prosperity, and a broad interest in stability, the opposition ran the risk of outpacing a public opinion sceptical of "radical" solutions.

The opposition also avoided the direct, closed-door negotiations sought at various points by the KMT. In this arena, the KMT had distinct advantages. The negotiators for the ruling party came to the bargaining table with strictly delegated authority. Their counterparts, by contrast, formed a loose coalition of forces that had to balance competing positions without the benefit of a hierarchical structure for ultimately resolving them. Thus, unless the regime granted clear-cut concessions, an unlikely prospect, such bargaining ran the risk of being seen as a sellout.

It is interesting that the legislature provided an important third arena of action for the opposition. Active participation in the legislature provided opportunities for gathering information, political learning, and increasing the credibility of the opposition in the substantive formulation of policy. Playing by the rules also enhanced its image as a loyal opposition. Most important, however, the legislature provided an open arena in which the opposition could amplify its advocacy of political change and challenge the government on a variety of substantive issues from pollution to economic management.

Finally, the overseas arena also provided opportunities for the opposition. The opposition managed to get companion organizations to coordinate their activities with events inside the country. Overseas organizations housed dissident politicians from Taiwan and exposed the issue of Taiwan's political change to the US media and Congress. The "Taiwan lobby" on Capitol Hill was divided at best on the issue of Taiwan's independence, but it was unanimous on the value of continued political liberalization and democratization.

Paths of Democratization: Taiwan Compared

Comparative analysis helps shed light on several of the distinctive features of the Taiwan case. One line of comparison is with transitions in other one-party authoritarian systems. In modern Third World history, however, there are only two other cases of political transitions in one-party systems, as most authoritarian regimes have been military in nature: the transformation of Turkey into a two-party system from 1945 to 1951 and the current, and far from complete, transformation of the Mexican political system. A second line of comparison is with the other export-oriented newly industrializing countries of East Asia, particularly Korea. Such a comparison is justified on the grounds that it allows some control, however partial and imperfect, for the influence of economic strategy on political processes. Finally, there is the question of whether the Japanese political system might constitute a meaningful model for Taiwan.

Transitions in One-Party Systems

Like the Republic People's Party (RPP) in Turkey and the Institutional Revolutionary Party (PRI) in Mexico, the KMT was a nationalist party with revolutionary pretensions. The longevity of these three parties can be attributed to their assumption of nation-building and nationalist tasks, both internal and external, at crucial historical junctures. All are cases of "revolution from above."

The RPP transformed a disintegrating Ottoman Empire into a modern republic in 1919 and launched an extensive modernization program designed to turn Turkey into a modern, secular, and even European country. The KMT founded Republican China in 1911, came close to unifying the country and centralizing political authority in the 1920s, laid some foundation for the modernization of the economy in the 1930s, and regained Chinese control of tariffs in the 1940s. The PRI was knit together out of regionally based revolutionary leaders in the late 1920s. Though ultimately conservative, the PRI was heir to a social-revolutionary legacy, which was developmentalist in orientation, and the guardian of the national "patrimony" against external intervention, particularly from the United States. In all three cases, the "revolutionary" history of consolidating the nation and resisting foreign pressures gave the dominant party a privileged position in the political system.

The second distinctive feature of these systems was that political elites used the device of the political party for nation-building, state-building, and modernization rather than a military revolutionary council or plebiscitarian presidency.[22] The specific reasons for this choice vary from case to case: Soviet influence in the case of the KMT, the efforts of contending elites to mobilize support in the case of Mexico, and the necessity for overwhelming the clergy in Turkey. Yet one common thread that runs through the three cases is nationalist ideology itself. Ideologically, nationalism stands in distinct contrast to religious, ethnic, or Communist means of social mobilization, all of which stress underlying social differences and conflicts. Despite the elitist and vanguard nature of the political leadership, all three parties defined the people as their social base, developed encompassing and inclusive corporatist structures, and strove to be catchall parties that cut across various social cleavages. Such an ideological underpinning had the effect of limiting the space for a societal opposition to develop. The superimposition of a party structure on the state apparatus also had the effect of limiting the institutional role of the military, even though many party leaders had military origins. The military might have constrained the party leadership at various points, but it never wholly displaced it during the periods of single-party dominance.

Are there similarities in the transition process in these three cases? In Turkey the RPP's three-decade monopoly of political power during the interwar era gave way smoothly to multiparty competition between 1945 and 1951. Turkey's democratic transition, the first "successful" case of its genre,[23] was attributable to several factors. First, Kemal Ataturk's one-party system had institutionalized the process of elections and legislation. Although elections were noncompetitive among parties, the RPP experimented with an open nomination system and had permitted a number of "independents" to compete. By the end of the interwar period, RPP was less a nation-building party than an electoral machine.

Second, the leadership itself had encouraged the formation of two opposition parties, though within strict parameters set by the government. When the two new parties attracted support from conservative traditional elites opposed to the reform, they were disbanded. Nonetheless, commitment to pluralist politics by the leadership and democratic "trappings," albeit in an authoritarian setting, provided a tradition of electoral party competition and an entry point for the opposition.

Perhaps most important, the making of the first opposition party, the Democratic Party, or DP, which established itself as the principal political competitor in 1946 and successfully defeated RPP in the subsequent election of 1950, was itself a splinter group of the ruling Kemalist elite. From its inception, the DP played the role of a "loyal" opposition. Sharing the Kemalist legacy with the RPP, the DP provided the government no excuses for political suppression and certainly constituted no revolutionary challenge. Mobilizing support from whatever sectors the RPP failed to reach, the DP skillfully advocated a new policy package for electoral gain. As soon as the RPP responded with a competitive policy platform, rather than using the military to persecute the DP leadership, a multiple-party system was born.[24]

Despite numerous other differences, several interesting parallels can be drawn to the Mexican case. From its inception, the PRI has functioned as an electoral machine. Even though opposition groups have been harassed and intimidated by the government, the political leadership has maintained a commitment to the *form* of democratic rule, including local, state, national legislative, and presidential elections. The government has also tolerated the existence of formal opposition party organizations, including most notably the right-wing Partido de Accion Nacional (PAN).

Second, the government itself has shown some commitment to democratizing political reforms, partly to enhance its own sagging legitimacy. During the sexennio of Lopez Portillo (1976–1982), the government launched a variety of institutional reforms designed to increase opposition access to the political system. The response to the opening was a proliferation of new political groupings, mostly on the left, and the beginning of a more vigorous challenge to the government from the PAN.

It is not clear whether the opposition in Mexico is "loyal" or not: the PAN has challenged quite vigorously the legitimacy of the PRI's monopolization of the political system, and the splintered leftist parties have attempted to show the gap between the PRI's revolutionary-reformist rhetoric and Mexican reality. Most strikingly, the son of a former president, Cuahatomac Cárdenas, defected from the PRI in 1988, challenged the handpicked PRI candidate, and scored a significant electoral showing. Nonetheless, neither left nor right poses a revolutionary challenge to the Mexican system, and the PRI continues to benefit from its powerful organization and the splits within the opposition. An old guard favors and has perpetrated the old methods of intimidation and vote buying. But a reformist political current within the government, which appears to include the new president, is willing to treat the opposition as a loyal one in an effort to reconstitute the PRI's political power on a new foundation.[25]

Thus, there are certain broad similarities that might be drawn with the Taiwan case, including the previous existence of some commitment to democratization and democratic forms, important reformist factions within the ruling party itself, and the "loyalty" of the opposition. There are, however, several important differences that deserve underlining. First, neither the PRI nor the RPP developed the kind of cell-like structure or penetration of society achieved by the KMT. As a Leninist type of party, the KMT has relied more on organizational mechanisms and personnel arrangements than on electoral corruption and spoils to maintain its political hegemony (contrast Chapters 5 and 8 on this point). Thus it is difficult for the opposition parties in Taiwan to match the organizational capacity and the skills of personnel control. Moreover, whereas the major opposition was incubated by the RPP or the PRI itself, the Leninist structure of the KMT precludes a spin-off of the single party becoming the core of the opposition. Second, the existence of an external military threat provides the KMT with a powerful weapon in limiting the freedom and the range of political discourse of the opposition. The willingness of the opposition to seek to exploit "dangerous" issues, such as independence for Taiwan, also calls into question the loyalty of the opposition and provides an additional weapon for those within the KMT who are less committed to substantial political reform. These factors may serve to prolong and complicate the transition process.

Political Change in the East Asian NICs

Is there anything in the nature of export-oriented strategy that the East Asian NICs have pursued that affects their prospects for democratization? It could be argued that export-led growth ultimately improved the chances for democracy, or at least hastened liberalization, by contributing to rapid economic growth and social differentiation. Democratization in Korea and Taiwan have come at roughly the same time in the two countries' development trajectories, though Taiwan's per capita income is higher than Korea's. But political developments in Singapore seem to contradict any facile correlation between level of development and democratization and underscore the importance of leadership strategies and political processes. Singapore's rapid growth has, indeed, given rise to new opposition voices, but the government has provided them virtually no room to operate and has moved to make such pluralism more unlikely in the future. The processes that resulted in the democratic transition in Korea and Taiwan are also substantially different. Korea's transition hinged much more critically on street actions by students, workers, and elements of the middle class. The result was a more distinct rupture in the political system, signaled by Roh Tae-woo's dramatic announcement on June 29, 1987, of the government's willingness to accept wide-ranging constitutional reform.

The processes of democratization in Korea and Taiwan appear to contradict the claim that there is an "elective affinity" between export-led growth and authoritarian rule. Economic issues were a factor in Korea's transition, but they were mainly short-run: the government of Chun Doo-Hwan pursued highly unpopular stabilization and structural adjustment measures in the years immediately prior to the democratic transition.

Economic issues do not, at first, appear to play any significant role in Taiwan's transition.

Yet the conclusion that there is no link between economic strategy and democratization is overly facile. First, labor support was an important factor in the emergence of the opposition in Korea, and it is likely to play an important role in defining the possibilities for the opposition in Taiwan. The interests of workers, in turn, have been defined by persistent pressure on the part of both business and government to keep labor costs down in order to compete effectively in international markets. Although concern over labor costs will probably not, in itself, result in a reversion to authoritarian rule, it has pushed the Korean government toward an increasingly restrictive view of the scope of labor's newfound freedom. A similar response could be imagined from the KMT were Taiwan to experience an explosion of labor activity, as Korea did in 1987. Second, and more generally, the opposition in both Korea and Taiwan has sought to exploit economic issues, including the various costs that have attended rapid growth. Thus, if economic strategy does not determine political structure, the opening of the political process will undoubtedly have repercussions for the nature of Taiwan's future economic development.

The Japanese System as a Model for Taiwan?

Of all the possible models of Taiwan's political future, the Japanese model often stands out as an analytical reference (see Chapter 10). The "Japanese model" is a system in which a ruling conservative party dominates the political scene through electoral support garnered on the basis of performance. But the ruling party maintains regular consultation with smaller, fragmented opposition parties. The virtue of having one dominant party ruling in informal consultation with a plurality of opposition parties is that political continuity and stability are maintained but presumably without the "tyranny of the majority." A corollary of this system is pervasive factionalism within the ruling party. Factionalism acts as a check on Caesarian rule and allows representation of diverse social interests.

The institutional innovations the KMT has introduced to regulate political contestation suggest the party's intention to use the Japanese system as a normative model for Taiwan's political development. The qualifications for the formation of new parties are minimal. Thus the entry barriers to political competition are low, resulting in a fragmented opposition. As of June 1989, thirteen new political parties had been formed. The KMT regime has also avoided proportional representation—which allocates seats according to each party's share of popular votes and thus works best for smaller parties. However, the existing single-vote, multiple-seat electoral system does provide space for smaller parties that a single-vote, single-seat district system lacks. Under a single-vote, multiple-seat system, a system practiced in very few countries, including Japan, Taiwan, and Spain, smaller parties can pool their votes to get some seats and therefore are likely to be kept in the electoral game.

The December 1989 legislative election, held simultaneously with the elections for local assembly and county magistrates, was the first election since the lifting of the martial law decree and the legalization of opposition parties. It was not intended to be a "founding election" of a new democratic order. The office of president was not contested. The number of seats in the legislature open for electoral contest was augumented from 94 to 130, but it remained less than those still held by the tenured old-timers (who still hold 167 positions) supposedly elected by mainland constituents. Among 130 new seats, 29 were selected from overseas Chinese, a process also dominated by the KMT. The KMT's share of the votes for all contested seats dropped from 70 percent to 61 percent, while the electoral strength of the principal opposition party, the DPP, increased from 25 percent to 30 percent. The remaining 9 percent of the popular vote went to smaller parties and independent candidates. The KMT still maintained control over 70 percent of the openly contested seats, however.

The KMT construed the results of the elections as "a major setback," and journalists speculated on the advent of a two-party system. For the first time, the number of DPP legislators (twenty-one) exceeded the quorum required for initiating legislation. This gave the DPP a new weapon in its fight with the KMT. Moreover, in 1991 the DPP holds six (a net increase of five) out of twenty-one mayorships and county magistrates, including the crucial and most populated Taipei county. This exposure augurs well for the DPP's chances at capturing the mayoralty of Taipei when that office is made elective.

However, the transition to a two-party system is more apparent than real. First, the KMT continues to dominate the political landscape, outpolling the opposition by two to one, and maintaining a seventy-thirty control of the new seats in the legislature. The continuing institutional linkages between party and state continue to present various obstacles to the opposition. Control of the media, for example, was a controversial issue in the election campaign as opposition candidates charged that the KMT exploited its monopoly over television to unfairly boost its own candidates.

Second, the electoral performance of the DPP in 1989 may well be a onetime gain in the wake of political decontrol rather than a long-term trend. The drop of the KMT's share of the popular vote from 70 to 61 percent was not simply absorbed by the DPP but by independents as well. One can hypothesize that a substantial portion of the KMT's 10 percent loss was a swing vote protesting the slow pace of political liberalization. As political liberalization continues, the opposition will lose a major issue on which it has garnered political support: political liberalization itself. It will then be forced to run on more substantive policy issues, where the KMT has shown itself both relatively competent and extremely capable of responding pragmatically to opposition complaints (see Chapter 8).

The DPP is now in a position to administer at the local level. In future elections, it will be judged by its ability to govern rather than its criticism of the KMT. This may give the DPP a golden opportunity to demonstrate its executive capacity, but its performance also depends on the goodwill of KMT-controlled local assemblies and the resource support from KMT's national government. There is little incentive for the KMT to assist in building up DPP's reputation for political leadership. Nor has the DPP had the opportunity to devote attention to the complex policy issues on which it has rallied political support.

The conflict between the moderate and radical wings of the DPP has also resurfaced as a result of the election and is likely to spill over into the legislative arena (see Chapter 6). The KMT's effort to consult with opposition parties in enacting laws to phase out the authoritarian order has had the effect of placing the opposition in a dilemma, sharpening differences within the opposition on legislative strategy. Constant rejection of negotiation with the KMT is incompatible with the opposition's desired role as a loyal, "responsible" opposition. Taking part in the legislative process does allow opposition parties to influence the content of policy somewhat and provides a crucial platform. A boycott of the legislature would deprive the opposition of political information. On the other hand, the opposition gets no credit for its contribution to the formulation of policy, and it may be hurt by charges of collaboration and selling out. Eventually, the opposition comes to monitor, but also indirectly legitimate, ruling party initiatives, with little hope of ever actually displacing the ruling party.

There seems to be little connection between social cleavages and competition between political parties in Taiwan (see Chapter 8). Both the KMT and the DPP are striving to become catchall parties. The KMT seems to be more successful than the DPP in incorporating and reconciling heterogeneous social interests, as was Japan's Liberal-Democratic Party (LDP) at the turn of the 1970s. The LDP's dominance in Japanese politics has been related to, but cannot be simply reduced to, the manipulation of an electoral system biased toward rural constituencies. Identified with both stability and prosperity, the LDP has been able to build on this base while accommodating demands from overlooked social interests and absorbing constituencies originally "discovered" by the opposition such as environmental and consumer groups. The KMT has, to date, not publicly shown a similar degree of factionalism as the LDP. But the KMT clearly has the capacity and opportunity to transform Taiwan's one-party authoritarian regime into a one-party dominant democratic system.

Organization of this Volume

Part 1 of this volume examines in greater detail the basic social and political changes that have occurred in Taiwan over the past decade. Hung-mao Tien, author of a major new study on Taiwan,[26] provides an overview of many of the central themes that follow. Following the "preconditions" approach, Tien notes that growing differentiation, increased pluralism, and associational activity made it more difficult for the KMT to control politics. Tien underlines the distinction between liberalization and democratization, which is a leitmotif in many of the papers that follow, and provides empirical indicators of both trends. Tien also emphasizes that a third political process is taking place, of equal if not greater significance: the growing participation of indigenous Taiwanese at all levels of the political system.

Sociologist Hsin-huang Michael Hsiao provides basic information on eighteen social movements that have emerged in tandem with the democratization process. Hsiao argues that the locus of these groups' activity has been the state. Groups have organized to confront not only social problems and specific government policies, but also the structure of corporatist control itself. These movements have become more institutionalized, but surprisingly they have not developed close ties with the political opposition. Nonetheless, they have played an important role in forcing the KMT to be more responsive and thus have contributed to more open and democratic politics.

Part 2 examines the party system. Ping-lung Jiang and Wen-cheng Wu argue that the KMT has gradually transformed itself from an authoritarian, exclusionary party into a pragmatic and inclusive one. Examining the internal organization of the KMT, Jiang and Wu trace the development of greater intraparty democracy, inclusiveness, and responsiveness to interest group pressures. They argue that these internal changes have been accompanied by greater interparty democracy as well and that the party system is moving toward a competitive model.

Constance Squires Meaney focuses on the particular difficulties Leninist parties face in democratizing, and she reaches much more cautious conclusions. Squires Meaney draws a sharp distinction between changes internal to the party that do not in themselves constitute a change of the system and the processes of liberalization and democratization. She also notes that any assessment of political change must take into account indicators that run counter to liberalizing trends. She concludes that the process through early 1991 was one of liberalization, but not full democratization, and that a "hybrid regime, neither fully authoritarian nor democratic, can persist for a long time."

Alexander Ya-li Lu provides a detailed study of the development, organization, and ideology of the opposition Democratic Progressive Party, which Lu describes as a "party movement." Lu concludes that the DPP will enjoy a slow but steady growth and expansion and will challenge the KMT at the polls. The DPP is very unlikely to actually rule in the next decade, however—partly because of continuing privileges enjoyed by the KMT and partly because of the factionalization of the DPP itself. Lu suggests that the party system may therefore evolve in the direction of the Japanese system.

Part 3 examines the electoral system. Fei-lung Lui provides useful information on electoral rules, electoral history, and voting behavior. Taiwan's electoral district system—one of the large-size, multiple-seat districts with a single but nontransferable vote—might have worked to the advantage of the opposition. But the KMT neutralized this potential advantage by organizing votes through the "responsibility system," a system that assigned a specific vote-getting duty to each candidate. Regarding voting behavior, Lui argues that its major determinants are not party affiliation or identification, or issues, but rather candidates' qualifications and images and their social networks. One can hypothesize that the distinct electoral system is related to such personalism in electoral behavior.

Fu Hu and Yun-han Chu draw on the results of a large-scale research project at National Taiwan University headed by Professor Hu. Hu and Chu emphasize the independent role of electoral processes in political change. For example, they argue that the increase in partisanship has contributed to the institutionalization of a competitive party system. Through survey data, they identify the most salient political cleavages in the electorate. They find that to date, the issues of democratic legitimacy and national identity have been more salient than social cleavages on public policy issues. As democratization proceeds, however, the utility of the national identity issue will fade, and substantive policy issues and socioeconomic cleavages will become more salient.

Part 4 turns to the critical and fast-changing external environment in the Taiwan Straits and the projected path of political evolution. Andrew J. Nathan analyzes Taiwan-mainland relations and provides an overview of Deng Xiaoping's Taiwan policy. Despite the growing sophistication of Deng's strategy and a number of concessions to Taiwan's concerns, "democratization has so complicated the internal politics of Taiwan that it is now impossible for any deal to be struck with the mainland that does not command wide popular support." Nathan sketches three alternative scenarios for the Taiwan-mainland relationship, the most probable of which is a continuation of the status quo: de facto independence despite continuing official tensions.

In his conclusion, Edwin A. Winckler argues that the "transition" of the 1980s was not to democracy, but from "hard" to "soft" authoritarianism. This transition will not be complete until the mid-1990s, at which point political leadership will reside with a centrist coalition of military, party, and government officials drawing on a combination of the KMT's organizational resources and success at maintaining electoral support. Despite political liberalization, the "Nationalist establishment" will still select the top leaders and basic policies, and the opposition will be too fragmented and structurally disadvantaged to constitute a viable alternative. Beginning in the mid-1990s, Winckler believes, a process of real democratization could ensue, given certain internal and external preconditions, including the development of consultative mechanisms linking state and opposition and a favorable international climate. Winckler suggests that the new Chinese democracy will contain elements of the Japanese one-party dominant system, US interest-group liberalism, and the corporatist structures of the small European states. Winckler concludes by raising some crucial theoretical questions not addressed elsewhere in the volume, including the role of local political networks and sociocultural factors in explaining the outlook for Taiwan's experiment with political change.

Notes

1. Alfred Stepan, *Rethinking Military Politics* (Princeton, N.J.: Princeton University Press, 1988), pp. 3–4.
2. Seymour Martin Lipset, *Political Man*, expanded ed. (Baltimore: Johns Hopkins University Press, 1981); Phillips Cutright, "National Political Development: Measurement and Analysis," *American Sociological Review* 28 (April 1963), pp. 253–264.
3. Lucian Pye, *Asian Power and Politics* (Cambridge, Mass.: The Belknap Press of Harvard University Press, 1985), p. 233.
4. Mancur Olson, "Rapid Growth as a Destabilizing Force," *Journal of Economic History* 23 (1963), pp. 529–558.
5. Stephan Haggard and Tun-jen Cheng, "State and Foreign Capital in the East Asian NICs," in Frederic C. Deyo, ed., *The Political Economy of the New Asian Industrialism* (Ithaca, N.Y.: Cornell University Press, 1987); Stephan Haggard, *Pathways from the Periphery: The Politics of Growth in the Newly Industrializing Countries* (Ithaca, N.Y.: Cornell University Press, 1990).
6. Dankwart Rustow, "Transition to Democracy: Toward a Dynamic Model," *Comparative Politics* 2 (April 1970), pp. 337–363; Adam Przeworski, "Some Problems in the Study of the Transition to Democracy," in Guillermo O'Donnell and Philippe C. Schmitter, eds., *Transitions from Authoritarian Rule: Comparative Perspective* (Baltimore: Johns Hopkins University Press, 1986).
7. Hung-chao Tai, "Shi er nien hou ti Kuo-min-tang shi shen mo yan ti cheng tang?" [Outlooks of Kuomintang Twelve Years from Today], in Michael Y. M. Kau and Hungdah Chiu, eds., *Hai shia nian an fa chan ching yen bi chiao* [Development Experiences on Both Sides of the Taiwan Straits] (Taipai: Twenty-first Century Foundation, 1990), pp. 13–29.
8. Hung-chao Tai, "The Kuomintang and Modernization in Taiwan," in Samuel P. Huntington and Clement Moore, eds., *Authoritarian Politics in Modern Society* (New York: Basic Books, 1970); Na-teh Wu, "Emergence of the Opposition Within an Authoritarian Regime: The Case of Taiwan," mimeo 1980, University of Chicago; Edwin Winckler, "Institutionalization and Participation on Taiwan: From Hard to Soft Authoritarianism?" *China Quarterly* 99 (September 1984), pp. 481–499; Jurgen Domes, "Political Differentiation in Taiwan: Group Formation Within the Ruling Party and the Opposition Circles, 1979–1980," *Asian Survey* 21 (October 1981), pp. 1023–1042; Thomas B. Gold, *State and*

Society in the Taiwan Miracle (New York: Sharp, 1986); Chalmers Johnson, "Political Institutions and Economic Performance: The Government-Business Relationship in Japan, South Korea and Taiwan," in Robert Scalapino et al., eds., *Asian Economic Development—Present and Future* (Berkeley, Calif.: Institute of East Asian Studies, 1987).

9. C. Martin Wilbur, *The Nationalist Revolution in China 1923–1930* (New York: Cambridge University Press, 1983), pp. 33–47.

10. Arthur J. Lerman, *Taiwan's Politics: The Provincial Assemblyman's World* (Washington, D.C.: University Press of America, 1978).

11. Walter Galenson, ed., *Economic Growth and Structural Change in Taiwan* (Ithaca, N.Y.: Cornell University Press, 1979); for data see *Taiwan Statistics Data Book* (Taipei: Council on Economic Planning and Development), various issues.

12. Tun-jen Cheng, "Political Regimes and Development Strategies: South Korea and Taiwan," in Gary Gereffi and Donald Wyman, eds., *Manufacturing Miracles: Patterns of Development in Latin America and East Asia* (Princeton, N.J.: Princeton University Press, 1990).

13. Reinhard Bendix, *Kings or People* (Berkeley: University of California Press, 1978), pp. 12–13, 292.

14. Tun-jen Cheng, "Democratizing the Quasi-Leninist Regime in Taiwan," *World Politics* (July 1989).

15. John Copper with George Chen, *Taiwan's Election* (Baltimore: Occasional Papers/Reprint Series in Contemporary Asian Studies, School of Law, University of Maryland, 1985), pp. 62–63.

16. Parris Chang, "Taiwan in 1982," *Asian Survey* (January 1983), p. 44.

17. Chalmers Johnson, "South Korean Democratization: The Role of Economic Development," *Pacific Review* 2:1 (1989).

18. The demonstration effect of the Filipino people's revolution in 1985 was rarely cited as a factor in Taiwan's democratization. Both the KMT regime and its challenger were aware that the Filipino syndromes—economic failure, an active church, and a politicized military—did not exist in Taiwan.

19. These include events such as the killing of a dissident Chinese-American writer at Daly City, California, in 1985. Government officials were reported to be implicated. See Yangsan Chou and Andrew J. Nathan, "Democratizing Transition in Taiwan," *Asian Survey* 27 (March 1987), pp. 277–299.

20. Laurence Whitehead, "International Aspects of Democratization," in Guillermo O'Donnell, Phillipe C. Schmitter, and Laurence Whitehead, *Transitions from Authoritarian Rule: Comparative Perspective* (Baltimore: Johns Hopkins Press, 1986).

21. Hsi-sheng Ch'i, "Comment," in Yingmao Kau and Hungdah Chiu, eds., *Chung Hua Min Kuo Dan Chien Ge Hsin Ke Ti* [Issues of Current Reform in the Republic of China] (Long Island, N.Y.: China Time Cultural Foundation, 1988), p. 76.

22. Arif T. Payaslioglu, "Turkey," in Robert E. Ward and Dankwart A. Rustow, eds., *Political Modernization in Japan and Turkey* (Princeton, N.J.: Princeton University Press, 1964).

23. One may quibble with this characterization. After all, postwar Turkey has had three military coups and is regarded as the most dubious case of democratic transition in southern Europe. See Philippe C. Schmitter, "An Introduction to Southern European Transitions from Authoritarian Rule: Italy, Greece, Portugal, Spain, and Turkey," in Guillermo O'Donnell, P. C. Schmitter, and Laurence Whitehead, eds., *Transitions from Authoritarian Rule: Southern Europe* (Baltimore: Johns Hopkins University Press, 1986). However, military

interventions were short, never perceived as legitimate, and the military never really ruled as it has in Latin America. Insofar as the process of democratic transition is concerned, Turkey was unquestionably a successful case. It was completed without suppression or confrontation and in a very short period of time.

24. Ergun Ozbudun, "Turkey," in Myron Weiner and Ergun Ozbudun, eds., *Competitive Elections in Developing Countries* (Durham, N.C.: Duke University Press, 1987).

25. Kevin J. Middlebrook, "Political Change in Mexico," in Susan Kaufman Purcell, ed., *Mexico–United States Relations* (New York: Academy of Political Science, 1981).

26. Hung-mao Tien, *The Great Transition: Political and Social Change in the Republic of China* (Stanford, Calif.: Hoover Institute Press, 1989).

PART 1

Social Change, Liberalization, and Democratization: Basic Processes

CHAPTER 2

Transformation of an Authoritarian Party State: Taiwan's Development Experience

HUNG-MAO TIEN

In 1986, Taiwan's ruling Kuomintang (KMT) undertook bold steps to revamp the nation's ailing polity. On April 9 of that year, the KMT Central Standing Committee formed a twelve-member task force to study several major political reforms that included the lifting of martial law, liberalizing political associations, and changing the parliamentary bodies.[1] Following the task force recommendations, the Central Standing Committee passed a resolution the following October 15 to end the thirty-seven-year-old martial law, which was lifted in July 1987 following the adoption of the new State Security Law. Prior to these KMT decisions, the opposition, or Tangwai, forces formed the Democratic Progressive Party (DPP) on September 28, 1986. The government took no repressive measures against the DPP organizers.

The end of martial law plus the revision of the existing laws governing political associations during 1988–1989 set the stage for legalizing opposition parties and for broadening the scope of secondary group autonomy. Meanwhile, in January 1988 the government lifted the previous restrictions on the publication of new daily newspapers. Limited parliamentary reforms followed as the KMT adopted a formula to retire the aging members of the three national representative bodies—the National Assembly, the Legislative Yuan, and the Control Yuan—who represent constituencies on the Chinese mainland and who have not stood for election in Taiwan since 1947–1948. In early 1990, the Council of Grand Justices, with apparent backing of the KMT authorities, exercised its judicial review by setting the end of 1991 as the deadline for involuntary retirement of these members, thus clearing the legal ground for democratic transformation of the parliamentary bodies. These reform measures as a whole indicate remarkable breakthroughs in the nation's political development.

The year 1986 presented the KMT authorities with both a potential domestic crisis and an opportunity for major political reforms. Street protests organized by the Tangwai from May to September were rapidly escalating the level of political conflict.[2] The DPP was formed despite repeated warnings from the authorities. In the face of these critical challenges, plus international pressures from the United States, unresolved succession problems at home, and other problems, the KMT reformists under the late President Chiang Ching-kuo's leadership apparently saw much to be gained by stepping up liberalization and democratization.[3] Reforms offered the advantage of improving the regime's ability to legitimate itself, reducing social conflict, eliciting the confidence of foreign investors and trade partners, and projecting a much-needed favorable image in the international community.[4]

The success or failure of Taiwan's current reform measures may have profound implications not only for the island's internal political life, but also for the future evolution of its relations with mainland China. Since fall 1987 the Republic of China (ROC) government has permitted residents of Taiwan to visit their relatives on the mainland. This represents an official action to legalize direct contacts between Taiwan and the mainland. Liberalization and democratization in Taiwan would put additional pressure on the leaders of the People's Republic of China (PRC) to promote internal political reforms of their own. This is necessitated by the propaganda logic of Beijing's strategy to lure Taiwan residents into accepting the PRC's peaceful unification formula. A more liberal and democratic political system in Taiwan would also complicate the island's decision process with regard to the nature of evolving Taiwan-mainland relations. Views expressed by the opposition political activists as well as the general public in a more open society would have to be taken seriously by the PRC leaders (see Chapter 9).

In light of these recent developments, this chapter will analyze three processes of political change taking place: Taiwanization, liberalization, and democratization. Taiwanization, put in the context of the relationship between the island's subethnic groups, means the creation of a more pluralistic KMT power structure and parliamentary reforms to enhance native Taiwanese participation in the legislative process. Liberalization provides a social and political environment conductive to democratic development. The three processes of political change do in fact reinforce one another. These changes have occurred as a result of the existence of certain socioeconomic requisite conditions, the KMT leaders' normative commitment to representative democracy as a political goal, and the steady growth of political opposition, which has pressured the KMT to make political concessions, though sometimes reluctantly. The combination of these factors has fostered significant political change. These changes involve transforming the corporatist type of authoritarian party-state into one embodying elements of political pluralism and democracy.

Economic Development and Social Change

Taiwan's developmental experience shows a close pattern of intersectoral relationships among industrialization, social change, and political development. Spectacular industrial growth over the past three-and-a-half decades has brought about social change and material improvements quite favorable to political liberalization and democratization.

Industrial Development and Rising Living Standards

Economic development in Taiwan may be divided into three phases. During the first phase, 1953–1960, the government encouraged private investment in labor-intensive light industries. An import substitution policy was pursued to protect domestic industry. Industrial products and consumer goods were manufactured mostly to satisfy domestic demand. The government adopted a series of financial reforms and incentive programs to increase industrial output for both export and the growing level of domestic consumption during the second phase, 1961–1972. Since the early 1970s, the government has adopted measures to promote capital-intensive industries and chemical industries in order to guide Taiwan's transition from light to heavy industrial development.

As shown in Table 2.1, the average annual growth rate of Taiwan's industrial production was 11.7 percent during 1953–1962, 18.5 percent during 1963–1972, and 9.3 percent during 1973–1988. Gross national product (GNP) also grew at an annual rate of 7.5 percent, 10.8 percent, and 8.4 percent, respectively. Apart from the increases in industrial production and GNP, the proportion of industry in relation to the nation's gross domestic product also rose from 18.0 percent in 1952 to about 46.2 percent in 1988.[5]

Industrialization and high economic growth brought affluence and contributed to structural change in the social system. Per capita GNP rose from US $50 in 1952 to an estimate of US $8,400 in 1990.[6] As income rose, so did the material conditions of life on the island. In 1987 there were 204 newspapers and magazines for every 1,000 persons.[7] By 1989, for every 100 homes there were about 26 privately owned automobiles, 94 telephones, 110 color TV sets, 101 refrigerators, 115 motorcycles, 57 air-conditioners, and 88 washing machines.[8] These figures compare favorably with some Western European nations. Popular access to the mass media and to modern transport also helps to bring about social change.

Social Stratification

When the Nationalists arrived in Taiwan in 1949, the island's social structure was relatively simple, but as industrialization and urbanization progressed, it

Table 2.1 Taiwan's Economic Growth: Selected Indicators, 1953–1988 (by percentage)

Years	Industrial Production	Gross National Product
1953–1962	11.7	7.5
1963–1972	18.5	10.8
1973–1988	9.3	8.4

Source: Council for Economic Planning and Development, *Taiwan Statistical Data Book* (Taipei: Executive Yuan, 1989), p. 2.

became increasingly complex and differentiated. This development is clearly reflected in the changing pattern of employment as new jobs and positions are created in urban industrial and commercial sectors at the expense of the rural agricultural and forestry sectors. In three decades, from the early 1950s to the early 1980s, production workers as a percentage of the total labor force grew from about 20 percent to over 40 percent.[9] Meanwhile, only about 18 percent of the labor force remained engaged in farming activities, and 90 percent of these are reportedly part-time farmers.[10] The middle class has grown to include approximately one-third of the total adult population. They include owners of small and medium-sized enterprises, managers in public and private banks and corporations, KMT and government bureaucrats, elected representatives, teachers, and professionals.

As this middle class has broadened, it has had a greater impact on the political process. In general, the middle class supports political reform and democratization.[11] Many of them have supported the opposition movement, as either an expression of their dissatisfaction with the ruling KMT or their desire for political alternatives. As is shown in Chapter 3 of this volume, they stand in the forefront of Taiwan's growing social reform movements, such as those for consumers, the environment, human rights, and women.[12]

Social change has also blurred the subethnic division between the mainlanders and the native Taiwanese. Of the 20 million people in Taiwan, in 1989 slightly over 2.8 million (14.3 percent) were mainlanders who came to the island with the Nationalists in 1949, or their offspring. The remaining are mostly native Taiwanese of Fukien or Hakka origin. Over the years, subethnicity has been a salient factor in Taiwan's political, economic, and social life. But generational change and intermarriage have gradually bridged the ethnic gap. Although the exact figure of intermarriage is not known, it has become quite common among the younger generation. Furthermore, over 1.5 million (55 percent) of those classified as mainlanders in Taiwan were born on the island.[13] This means that approximately 93 percent of the total population are Taiwan-born. Such a demographic change strengthens common identity with Taiwan, particularly among the youth, thus making prospects for a political unification with the mainland on subethnic grounds less appealing. Conversely, this change helps lay a social foundation for Taiwanization of the Nationalist regime.

Social Pluralism

Rapid economic development and social change have also given rise to a proliferation of associations over the past three decades. According to government statistics, in 1952 there were some 2,560 registered associations with over 1.3 million members. By 1988, the number of associations had grown to 12,605, with almost 9.2 million members.[14] The ratio of association membership to the nation's population also increased over time from 16 percent in 1952 to 42 percent in 1988.[15] The flourishing of these associations is a consequence of technological and structural changes in the economy. It reflects the impact of limited political liberalization and social differentiation and shows that Taiwan is fast becoming a pluralistic society.

The KMT regime has adopted a corporatist model of party-state-society relations under which the ruling party maintains organic ties with many of these associations and manipulates the election of their officers. In some instances where political control over large material and human resources is at stake, the KMT has resorted to wholesale intervention in the associations' internal operation and, above all, the appointment of key personnel. The party is particularly keen on maintaining a tight grip over the farmers' associations, the trade unions, the irrigation associations, the associations of industry and commerce, and the teachers' associations. These groups command large resources and can be used for political patronage or mobilized in support of KMT candidates in elections. Thus the processes of both liberalization and democratization involve, among other things, decorporatization of the party-state's relations with the secondary groups.

In recent years, the KMT's ability to control interest groups and other secondary associations has been steadily declining. Many groups and their leaders derive income and resources from the private sector of the economy, thus diluting the leverage stemming from the authorities' patronage. In other words, growth of the private sector plus general economic prosperity have created economic sources of power independent of government control. Between 1952 and 1988, the ratio of privately owned enterprises in Taiwan's economy surged from 43.4 percent to 82 percent.[16] As economic groups become less vulnerable to the party-state's political manipulation, they progressively gain autonomy from political intervention from the party-state.

This is particularly true with regard to the newly formed and issue-oriented public interest groups analyzed by Hsiao in Chapter 3 of this volume. Since the early 1980s, various social movements have been on the rise. Concerned citizens are no longer content with the previous approach of relying on existing institutions and procedures within the party-state to air grievances. Popular consciousness over such matters as the deteriorating environment, consumer rights, equality of women, human rights, and academic freedom gradually assumes the form of social protest.[17] Their emergence has generally coincided with the growth of political opposition, which has provided some social movements with mobilization activists and helped create a liberalized environment for social actions. Even groups traditionally under the party-state's strict corporatist control, such as the trade unions and the farmers' associations, are subject to internal divisions that allow the political opposition to organize countergroups for protest purposes. They are no longer singular, compulsory, and noncompetitive groups that are supposed to serve mainly as the party-state's "transmission belts."

In summary, Taiwan's economic prosperity and industrialization have generated the requisite socioeconomic conditions for progressive political change. A large new middle class has emerged, with strong demands for political participation and institutional reforms. Opposition political activists are largely disenchanted elements of this social strata. In addition, economic prosperity and expansion of the private sector have created abundant private wealth and autonomous sources of income that can be channeled into political activities. With the passage of time, the number of people dependent on state and KMT patronage has been reduced. A growing complexity of social stratification and diversification of interests has fostered the rise of a plural society in which the party-state has become less able to manipulate group activities. These factors plus the general affluence of the citizens, the rising educational level, and broader exposure to mass media have helped set the stage for political reforms since the early 1970s.

Trends in Political Development

As Cheng and Haggard argue in Chapter 1, rapid improvements in socioeconomic conditions generate popular demand for political reform, but there is no guarantee of a causal relationship between the existence of certain socioeconomic requisites and the development of a democracy. Guillermo A. O'Donnell's study of certain South American authoritarian regimes has shown that socioeconomic modernization can enhance the authoritarian regimes' oppressive capabilities or set the stage for praetorian politics.[18] Thus, the ruling elite's decision to pursue democracy can be as important as the existence of requisite socioeconomic conditions. Writing on transitions to democracy, Dankwart A. Rustow has observed that during the preparatory phase following socioeconomic modernization, the dynamic process of democratization itself may be set off by a "prolonged and inconclusive political struggle" between protagonists for and entrenched opponents of democracy.[19] For this antagonism and struggle in the preparatory phase to end, political leaders must accept the existence of "diversity in unity" and take measures to "institutionalize some crucial aspect of democratic procedure."[20] In Taiwan, the KMT regime under Chiang Ching-kuo's leadership since the 1970s has taken measures to accommodate the growing demands for political reforms.

Chiang Ching-kuo's Role

Speaking to a group of visiting editorial writers from the United States on May 15, 1987, Premier Yu Kuo-hwa insisted that political reforms initiated by President Chiang Ching-kuo in 1986 stemmed from a conscious decision to pursue democratization rather than simply a hasty response to external pressures.[21] The premier disclosed that the issue of political reform was fully discussed at the highest circles of the KMT a decade ago. Taiwan's recent political reforms were not conjunctural or accidental. They were pursued by a ruling elite headed by Chiang in a concerted and self-conscious effort to make Taiwan's politics more democratic.

No one will ever know precisely what motivated Chiang's decision to implement the major political reforms in the two years before his death on January 13, 1988, but available information indicates that he played a leading role at critical junctures. It was he who instructed the KMT Central Standing Committee task force, which had dragged its feet, to speed up its study of reform measures. Chiang suspended martial law and legalized the political opposition.[22] During April–May 1986, when tension increased as the Tangwai activists escalated street protests, Chiang authorized a formal channel of communication with the opposition leaders in an effort to fend off serious political disturbance and maintain an orderly reform process.[23] Following the formation of the DPP on September 28, he held meetings with civilian and military leaders to hold off a possible crackdown on the DPP leaders. Clearly, he played a pivotal role in the reform initiatives of 1986 and 1987.

In retrospect, it is clear that Chiang was the leading personality behind Taiwan's steady political reforms dating back to the early 1970s. In 1972 when he became premier, he initiated the appointments of native Taiwanese as provincial governor and vice-premier; he also tripled Taiwanese cabinet members from two to six. Following his succession to the presidency, Chiang steered Taiwan's political development steadily in a reformist direction. At times the military leaders appeared apprehensive about the effect of political reforms on internal security and stability. Through a system of regular rotation among the military leaders, Chiang was able to keep them from overt political intervention. During the critical moment of succession following Chiang's death in January 1988, twenty-four military leaders, headed by Chief of General Staff Hau Pei-ts'un, immediately pledged loyalty to Lee Teng-hui, the new president and a noted reformist.[24] Myron Weiner, a leading scholar on political development, has argued that the success of democratic reform in the Third World depends on the military acquiescing to civilian-dominated democratic rule.[25] Thus, Taiwan's smooth political succession in early 1988 and its continuing commitment to democratic reform was owed in part to the cooperation of the military, another legacy of Chiang Ching-kuo's past leadership.

Taiwanization

Political change in Taiwan also entails alteration of the existing power structure in the party-state, leading to more Taiwanese participation in the elite. The process of co-opting native Taiwanese into the regime's ruling circle began in the early 1970s when Chiang Ching-kuo emerged as a pivotal political figure. Such a change in elite composition, better described as Taiwanization, results in at least two things. One result is interethnic power-sharing through recruitment of more Taiwanese into the upper echelons of the party-state hierarchy and national legislature. Through co-optation, the roles of Taiwanese in decisionmaking are steadily enhanced, which results in raising their common stake in the regime's fortunes. Second, legitimacy of the regime is modified to depend increasingly on its effective governance of Taiwan rather than a fictitious claim of sovereignty over the China mainland.

During the first two decades of Nationalist rule in Taiwan, the KMT was an exclusionary authoritarian party under the mainlanders' domination. Virtually all of the key posts in both the party and the government were held by the mainlanders who had followed former president Chiang Kai-shek to the island in 1949. Twenty years later, the KMT began promoting some Taiwanese party members to the upper-middle ranks. By 1973 three Taiwanese were appointed to the ruling KMT Central Standing Committee (CSC). As shown in Table 2.2, the number and percentage of Taiwanese in the CSC steadily increased from 1973 to 1988. In 1979, Taiwanese received nine seats, or 33 percent of the twenty-seven-member roster. Following the KMT Thirteenth Party Congress held in July 1988, Taiwanese CSC members grew to sixteen, or 52 percent of the total thirty-one members. Meanwhile, Taiwanese representation on the KMT Central Standing Committee roster increased from 17 percent to about 40 percent of the 180 members.[26] Taiwanese membership in the KMT also rose from 60 percent in 1968 to more than 70 percent of the 2.35 million members by the mid-1980s.[27] The party's elite structure is no longer exclusionary.

A similar pattern of change in elite composition has taken place in major governmental appointments. Until the 1970s, only one ministerial post, Minister of the Interior, was held by a Taiwanese. Even the provincial governor was a mainlander. Since then, there has been a steady increase in the number of Taiwanese holding cabinet posts and other key administrative offices. The ministries of Communications and Justice, plus the position of

Table 2.2 Taiwanese in KMT Central Standing Com

	Total Members	Numbe Taiwar
1973	21	3
1976	22	4
1979	27	(
1981	27	
1984	27	1
1986	31	7
1988	31	

Source: Nan Min, "Tui-Kuo-min-tang san-chung-ch'uan-hui ti kuan-ch'a" [The кмт ...
plenum: A commentary], *Chiu-shih Nien-tai* [The nineties], no. 196 (May 1986), p. 43; *Chung-kuo Shih-pao* [China times] (July 15, 1988), p. 2.

vice-premier, went to Taiwanese. During 1988–1990, Taiwanese have headed for the first time the ministries of Finance, Economic Affairs, and Foreign Affairs and the Council for Economic Planning and Development. Taiwanese now hold eighteen of the forty-two cabinet and subcabinet posts and the position of vice-premier. In addition, in 1987, Lin Yang-kang was appointed president of the Judicial Yuan, the highest judicial organ of the state, and Huang Tsun-ch'iu became president of the Control Yuan. Both positions, considered parallel to the premier in official ranking though not as powerful, had been previously monopolized by mainlanders. Taiwanese have also held the governor's office since 1972.

The subethnic composition in the military's officer corps, though still heavily dominated by the mainlanders, shows a similar trend of growing Taiwanization. As indicated in Table 2.3, the percentage of Taiwanese in all categories of military ranks increased during 1950–1987. Although the percentage of Taiwanese generals and colonels rose during the period, the shares of Taiwanese in these two senior officer ranks remain small, particularly in comparison with the lower ranks of soldiers and noncommissioned officers, which are almost 79 percent Taiwanese. Of the nineteen leading posts in the military establishment, only two are held by Taiwanese: those held by General Chen Shou-shan, the deputy-minister of defense, and Admiral Kuo Tsung-ch'ing. Both were promoted to these posts in the 1980s. Clearly Taiwanization at the upper military echelon is slow but definitely happening. As aging generals pass away, Taiwan-born officers are expected to fill in many of these vacancies in the next decade.

Taiwanization also gradually proceeds through changes of composition in the three national parliamentary bodies. This process occurs partly as a result of natural attrition among the old guard elected in 1947–1948 on the mainland and partly through subsequent increases in the number of seats allotted to Taiwan. In 1949, there were 1,576 National Assembly members, 470 Legislative Yuan members, and 104 members of the Control Yuan.

iwanese-Mainlander Composition in the Military, 1950–1987

	Generals[a]		Colonels[b]		Lieutenants[c]		Soldiers[d]	
	M	T	M	T	M	T	M	T
50–1965	97.7	1.3	90.4	9.6	86.2	13.8	47.2	52.8
1965–1978	92.6	7.4	81.2	18.8	65.3	34.7	31.6	68.4
1978–1987	84.2	15.8	67.4	32.6	51.7	48.3	21.3	78.7

Source: Chiang Liang-jen, "T'ai-wan-jen ti erh ke shang-chiang" [The second military general of Taiwanese origin], Hsin hsin-wen [The journalist] 39 (December 7, 1987), p. 9.

Notes: Figures in the table are percentage distribution in that particular category of military ranks.

M = Mainlanders
T = Taiwanese
[a]Includes generals, lieutenant generals, and major generals
[b]Includes colonels, lieutenant colonels, and majors
[c]Includes captains, first lieutenants, and second lieutenants
[d]Includes noncommissioned officers and soldiers

Only a handful of these members were Taiwanese because of the island's small size in proportion to China's national population figure at that time. By 1990, natural attrition had reduced the members of these three representative institutions to 596, 126, and 18, respectively.[28] Meanwhile, members elected in Taiwan rose to 81 in the National Assembly, 100 in the Legislative Yuan, and 22 in the Control Yuan. Because the 1947–1948 cohorts now average about eighty years of age, attrition is likely to increase at a faster pace in the future. Only a few dozen original members remain active in these institutions.

In principle, the KMT authorities have favored an incremental approach to overhaul these three parliamentary bodies by means of voluntary retirements of the 1947–1948 cohorts. Incrementalism, nonetheless, is not acceptable to the majority of Taiwan's residents. The DPP has called for a total restructuring of these bodies that would consist of only members popularly elected in Taiwan. In spring 1990 student protests also demanded the immediate retirement of the members of the National Assembly who were not elected in Taiwan. Such a broad demand has not escaped the attention of the authorities. A KMT task force on constitutional reform, organized in response to a consensus recommendation by the National Affairs Conference held in the summer of 1990, appeared ready to finalize a proposal for a complete reform of these national representative institutions according to the following timetable: 1991 for the National Assembly, 1992 for the Legislative Yuan, and 1993 for the Control Yuan.[29] The reform measures, however, are likely to designate a certain number of parliamentarians as representatives of the mainland and the overseas Chinese communities. At this juncture, it appears certain that a vast majority of future parliamentarians would be elected by Taiwan's electorate.

In short, Taiwanization is a clear and perhaps irreversible trend in the nation's political development. To a large extent, it is a function of generational change as well as the KMT leaders' desire to foster ethnic harmony through political democratization. Generational change weakens political identity with the China mainland among the middle-aged and the youth who have spent most or all of their lives in Taiwan. The proportion of Taiwan's population who were born on the mainland before 1950 has dwindled from approximately 15 percent in 1950 to 5.7 percent in 1985.[30] For the younger generation, even those of mainlander parents, identification with a China that includes the mainland is becoming an abstract notion; their primary concern is their own welfare on the island.[31] This change of identity has gradually chipped away the basis of political loyalty toward a much larger China—a loyalty perpetuated for almost four decades by the Nationalist authorities.

Meanwhile, the KMT leaders, particularly the late President Chiang Ching-kuo, have tried to promote political unity between Taiwanese and mainlanders by expanding the scope and level of elections. This provides legitimate channels for politically ambitious Taiwanese to pursue upward mobility in ways that lead to identification with the regime. But at the same time, in a game of numbers such as an election, the Taiwanese, being the majority, clearly possess a natural advantage. So, having more officials subject to popular election—a process of democratization—also means increasing Taiwanese political power in the government.

Liberalization and Democratization

Liberalization and democratization are separable processes of political development, but they have mutually reinforced each other in Taiwan's political transformation. Liberalization refers to the trend of rising autonomy in such matters as citizens' associations, freedom of speech and the press, transmission of information, and social and political movements. The party-state progressively reduces its intervention in and restrictions upon the citizens' activities in general. Democratization, in contrast, rests on the ideals of popular sovereignty and political equality. Such a political change entails both broader political participation and democracy within the KMT itself. Taiwan residents have demanded that more public officials be subject to open and competitive elections and that they be held accountable to the electorate for their conduct. This change requires a fair electoral system with open competition among legalized opposition parties. In Taiwan, liberalization and democratization are two distinct processes, with the former coming first and the latter moving somewhat slowly.

Taiwan had made steady progress in liberalization and democratization even before the major breakthrough in 1986–1988. This development can be illustrated by the emergence of progressively stronger opposition political forces, the proliferation of journals critical of the authorities, more open and fairer coverage in daily newspapers, greater tolerance of protest movements, and the enlarged scope of electoral activities. To be sure, progress has come at a cost and development is not always smooth. In fact, severe setbacks have occurred periodically. But taking the changing events as a whole, one sees a positive trend over time. Whereas the authorities have resorted to certain oppressive acts in recent years, actions taken have been less brutal than in the past. Let us examine briefly the trends of liberalization and democratization.

Political Opposition

The development of the opposition movement in Taiwan may be divided into three major phases of development (see Chapter 6 for further discussion). During the initial phase in the 1950s, political opposition, cast in the form of intellectual liberalism, was promoted mainly by a group of disenchanted mainlander intellectuals, many with KMT ties. Supported by a handful of local Taiwanese politicians, they made an unsuccessful attempt to form the China Democratic Party. The effort completely failed before it could even get off the ground. Lei Chen, the principal organizer, and some of his followers were arrested on September 4, 1960, on a dubious charge of patronizing Communist agents.[32] In the subsequent years, the opposition continued to exist, but it never posed an organized challenge to the ruling KMT. Individual opposition leaders did score impressive victories in local elections, for instance in Ilan (Kuo Yu-hsin), Taipei (Kao Yu-shu), Yunlin (Li Wan-Chu), and Kaohsiung (Kuo Kuo-chi and Huang Chin-fu), but coordination for a nationwide opposition movement was not seriously contemplated for fear of political reprisals. Opposition politicians tended to settle for localized activities and were generally reluctant to raise issues regarding legitimacy of the regime or to challenge the government's fundamental policies.

The turning point came in 1977 when a mass protest in Chungli against an irregularity in KMT vote counting touched off a serious clash between angry voters and the police.[33] Since then, the opposition forces, mainly consisting of indigenous elements, have pursued more confrontational tactics and have attracted an activist strata fundamentally different in age and political outlook from their predecessors. In local elections that year, opposition candidates won one-quarter of the magistrate and mayoral posts as well as 30 percent of seats in the provincial assembly. A new era of nationwide opposition movement was dawning.

In the subsequent decade, the opposition movement showed two interrelated developmental tendencies. First of all, it made relentless efforts to become organized. Operating under the common label of Tangwai, it began to recommend candidates and to coordinate interconstituency campaigns in the 1981 parliamentary election. Three years later, a group of elected Tangwai officials formed the Association of Tangwai Public Officials for the Study of Public Policy, which was later renamed the Association of Public Policy Studies (APPS). The APPS, never fully accepted by the authorities as a legally constituted organization, exercised quasi-party functions in electoral and other political activities.

The third phase of opposition development came in September 1986 when the DPP was created by Tangwai activists (see Chapter 6). In December 1986, it formally nominated party candidates for the parliamentary election, ran a nationwide coordinated campaign, and scored impressive gains in both legislative seats and popular vote.[34] It adopted a party constitution and a party platform and established a nationwide organizational structure with headquarters in Taipei. But the DPP remains at the early stage of party development. With a membership of slightly more than 20,000 in late 1990 and party activists factionalized, the DPP's future prospect as a major party is still uncertain.[35]

In addition, at least forty other parties have registered with the government. All of them are rather tiny in membership base. Among them is the Labor Party, launched in December 1987 by a group of intellectuals and labor activists, which has a potential social base in some of Taiwan's more than 5 million industrial workers. But the party failed to realize its potential in the 1989 election. Moreover, a group of left-wing intellectuals and militant activists split from the party in 1988 to form the separate Worker's Party, thus undermining the Labor Party's political potential. In the light of growing labor unrest, the KMT has paid closer attention to workers' grievances. Meanwhile, the DPP is also becoming involved in some of the workers' organized activities.

The opposition forces have pursued street protest actions in an effort to pressure the KMT authorities into making political concessions. The KMT leaders' strong desire for internal political unity and political stability makes it possible for the much weaker opposition to obtain political leverage for democratic reforms. In recent years, the late President Chiang Ching-kuo and other reformist KMT leaders sought to avoid blatant political suppression in order to win popular support for the regime both at home and in the international community. Any outbreak of extensive political confrontation in the streets between the authorities and the opposition could seriously undermine the legitimacy of the KMT regime and its ability to govern, particularly in the face of the Communist threat across the Taiwan Straits. The Tangwai and now the DPP fully understand this political logic and look upon street protests as useful vehicles for advancing political demands. Nonetheless, the DPP's protest activities have been relatively mild and visibly self-restrained, especially in comparison with opposition action taken in neighboring South Korea.

Proliferation of the Dissenting Press

The press in Taiwan has been put under heavy restriction by the use of elaborate laws and by the KMT's media sanitation policy. Principal sources of legal regulation were found in the National Mobilization Law, the Marital Law, and the Publications Law. The authorities applied any or all of these legal restrictions to penalize publications considered undesirable. The KMT also guided the mass media along the party's policy lines. Party offices and state agencies responsible for the mass media frequently scrutinize the media and other publication activities.

During the 1950s and the 1960s, censorship by the authorities was tightly executed, with severe penalties for violators, including stiff jail terms. Since the 1970s, the authorities' scope of tolerance has broadened somewhat. Even the newspaper published by individual members of the KMT has printed articles critical of officials and public policies. Penalties for violators have been reduced.

The best illustration of press liberalization is the way that opposition journalism has flourished. Before early 1988, when law and government policy restricted the publication of daily newspapers, political journals— published either weekly or monthly—were the most popular format for the opposition press. They are financially manageable, and they can provide the antigovernment activists with avenues to criticize the party-state and to publicize their views on issues and policies. In addition, they offer opposition activists important sources of income by contributing articles or by editing. In recent years, these journals have broken several taboos, including fierce attacks on the personal lives of several KMT leaders. The extent to which opposition journalism sought to exercise freedom of the press often exceeded the limits of official tolerance.

The authorities responded by suspending publication, banning selective issues, or confiscating copies ready for circulation. As shown in Table 2.4, the number of confiscations and bannings increased from 9 in 1980 to 295 in 1986. Censorship escalated during 1984–1986 as a reflection of the authorities' growing vigilance. The number of magazines suspended remained about seven per year except in 1984 and 1985, when the number of cases jumped to thirty-five and fifteen, respectively. The increase of censorship during 1980–1986 partially reflected the fact that more political journals were published. But the harsh censorship activities of the Garrison Command took their toll as even respected moderate opposition journals—*The Asian* and *The Eighties*—ceased to exist in 1986. At the end of 1986, there were five weekly and four monthly opposition publications left, with a combined monthly total of approximately twenty-five issues.[36]

These censorship figures raise a paradoxical question. Are they indicative of liberalization or its opposite? Statistics alone would support the thesis of counterliberalization. However, such a view is simplistic at best. To be sure, censorship results in financial loss for the publishers. But, in recent years,

Table 2.4 Press Censorship in Taiwan

	1980	1981	1982	1983	1984	1985	1986
Total number of actions	16	19	27	33	211	275	302
Confiscations/bannings	9	13	23	26	176	260	295
Suspensions	7	6	4	7	35	15	7

Source: International Committee for Human Rights in Taiwan, *Taiwan Communiqué* 29 (March 28, 1987), p. 20.

very few publishers have actually served prison terms for alleged violations of laws and regulations governing publication. The content of some opposition journals can be outlandish and provocative. The most sensitive political topics—the Chiang family, Taiwan-mainland relations, self-determination for Taiwan residents, and lately even Taiwanese independence—have found their way into publications. The fact that the number of censorship incidents kept increasing during 1980–1986 reflected the Garrison Command's desperate efforts to enforce existing rules that were rapidly becoming outdated. Since the lifting of martial law in 1987, press censorship has significantly declined, although statistical data are not available. Taiwan's newspapers and popular journals have since openly reported activities and discussed issues that had previously been sanctioned by the authorities. In brief, the mass media are becoming significantly liberalized, despite the fact that electronic media remains fully under the control of the KMT and the government.

Social and Political Movements

Mass movements express the effects of social mobilization and politicization of the populace (see Chapter 3). Such movements—in forms such as mass rally, street protest, strike, and demonstration—were restricted by martial law and other legal instruments. They were rare events in the 1950s and the 1960s except for campaign rallies during elections. In recent years, mass movements have intensified, and activists are more willing to take risks. Possible confrontation with the police and even jail sentences are losing their deterrent effect. The authorities are now willing to tolerate mass activities so long as they do not constitute serious threats to security. With an ever-present potential for subethnic conflict on the island and possible intervention from Beijing, the Nationalist authorities seem reluctant to apply harsh oppressive measures to mass activities. They have grown accustomed to rallies and street protests.

The new social movements are discussed in detail by Hsiao in this volume. The focus here is on several elements of the new social activism that are of particular political significance to the process of democratization.[37]

Political demonstrations and rallies. These are mostly organized by the oppositionist groups. The frequency and scale of such activities have steadily increased since the 1977 Chungli Incident. In 1979, the Tangwai, under the pretext of establishing "service offices" for *Mei-li-tao* ("Formosa," a political journal), held antigovernment rallies in many cities. On December 10, a Tangwai rally in Kaohsiung resulted in a serious street confrontation between rally participants and the police and exploded into an unexpected riot known as the Kaohsiung Incident.[38] Scores of policemen and civilians were reportedly injured. Forty-one Tangwai activists were subsequently charged and sentenced to jail terms. The incident has since served as a constant reminder of possible consequences of holding mass political rallies. Both the oppositionists and the KMT authorities have consciously tried to avoid similar outbreaks in subsequent years.

Although the Tangwai approach political demonstrations with more caution and better planning since the Kaohsiung Incident, they have not abandoned street protests. On the contrary, protest rallies occurred with higher frequency during 1981–1989. In 1986 alone, there were about twenty such rallies throughout the island, mostly protesting against martial law, unfair trials, and the sentencing of some leading Tangwai activists on libel charge. Although statistics are not available, closer observation of Taiwan's political science would indicate a significant escalation of demonstration and rally activities during 1987–1989. Protest issues have become substantially broader in their variety.

The labor movement. Taiwan has over 5 million industrial workers; only about 1.6 million of them belong to trade unions.[39] Tightly controlled by the KMT, unions are not free to articulate the workers' common interests effectively; they lack autonomy in the political process. One result has been rapid increases in wildcat strikes and worker-management disputes. In 1963, there were only 20 such disputes, involving 550 workers. By 1981, the number of disputes had grown to 1,000, involving about 7,000 workers.[40] Between 1971 and 1982, a total of 6,398 disputes were reported, involving about 123,000.[41] The annual number of disputes has escalated since 1987 as movements toward free unionism have picked up momentum.

At issue are worker rights to collective bargaining, working conditions, social insurance, retirement benefits, job security, and the controversy surrounding the government enforcement of labor laws. As Taiwan becomes highly industrialized, problems faced by the workers multiply. In recent years, the plight of Taiwan's workers has received considerable attention from the mass media and in the influential academic community. In April 1987, thirty-nine leading scholars and legislators issued a declaration that listed twelve basic rights for the workers.[42] This well-publicized action came on the heels of a government decision to create the Labor Commission in the Executive Yuan to address mounting labor grievances.

During 1987–1988, independent trade unions were organized in various industrial regions on the island, mainly among workers of larger corporations and state enterprises. The Brotherhood unions, under the leadership of Lou Mei-wen, a militant factory activist, are gaining support among disenchanted industrial laborers who refuse to affiliate with the KMT-controlled trade union federation.[43] The labor movement received a big boost when the Labor Party was created in December 1987. The party's manifesto proclaims its hope of becoming the main political instrument for Taiwan's industrial workers.[44] Lou Mei-wen became the party's vice-chairman. In June 1988, Lou and other activists split from the party to form a new Worker's Party. Efforts were also made in 1988 to form a national federation of independent unions.[45]

Church and political issues. Religion has taken on a new life in Taiwan as the pace of social change quickens and the society grows affluent. Buddhist and Taoist temples are multiplying. The total number of religious believers has risen to 2.6 million, and there are close to eighty religious associations.[46] The Council of Presbyterian Churches is the most politically active.

Although there are only 210,000 Presbyterians, virtually all of them are native Taiwanese. Over the years, the churches, particularly those in central and southern Taiwan, have battled the authorities on a number of sensitive issues. The most serious confrontation occurred in August 1977 when the council issued "A Declaration of Human Rights," which urged the government to take effective measures "to turn Taiwan into a new and independent state" in the face of changing international reality.[47] Many church leaders also have been actively involved in the opposition political movement, speaking out frequently on democratization and civil rights issues. Eight Presbyterian ministers were implicated in the 1979 Kaohsiung Incident and were sentenced to jail terms. More recently, in March 1987, the Presbyterians in south Taiwan staged a street demonstration to protest the government's confiscation of official church publications.[48] The publications contained an article that discussed the "February 28 Incident" of 1947 in which at least thousands of Taiwanese were killed by the KMT troops under the command of General Ch'en Yi. As a result of the protest rally, the seized publications were subsequently returned. In November 1987, 120 Presbyterian ministers and 300 believers demonstrated in Taipei to protest the arrest of two political activists who publicly advocated Taiwan independence in a gathering of former political prisoners.[49]

In summary, since the 1970s there has been a steady escalation of social and political movements. As the number of these movements multiplied, the authorities became reluctant to suppress them by coercive force. Governmental tolerance of these activities, already evident in some cases, is likely to be extended further as the new laws governing group activities, including demonstration and assembly, are now in place. Nonetheless, the future development of liberalization probably will encounter periodic setbacks as some activities are perceived as threats to further economic development as well as to the fundamental political stability and security of the nation.

Elections

Under Nationalist rule, elections were first initiated at the township, county, and city levels. In 1954, the first election of provincial assemblymen was held. Popular election at the national level first occurred in 1969 when a handful of national parliamentarians were elected for life tenure. Since 1972, the president has authorized additional seats for the National Assembly and Legislative Yuan through supplementary popular elections.

As the Nationalist government suffered growing diplomatic isolation and the members of parliament gradually died off, the KMT authorities look to popular elections as an additional important source of legitimacy for the regime. The opening of more posts for popular election indicates a trend toward democratization of Taiwan politics.

But Taiwan's democratic evolution still faces serious limitations. The government's powerful executives are not subject to popular election. The president and vice-president of the republic are elected by the National Assembly, a majority of whose delegates have never been elected by Taiwan voters. The premier is appointed by the president, with the consent of a Legislative Yuan still controlled by members elected on the mainland during the 1947–1948 period. Even the governor of Taiwan and the mayors of the two largest cities—Taipei and Kaohsiung—are appointed by the president. Popular elections of government executive officials occur only at the local levels.

Despite these limitations, political liberalization achieved thus far is likely to greatly impact electoral politics. It will make Taiwan's elections more competitive and fair as the authorities are put under close scrutiny by both the media and the opposition. The KMT will find it less able to count on pocket votes traditionally delivered by the party-controlled secondary associations—such as farmers' associations, trade unions, and military residential complexes—which have mobilized their members to support the KMT candidates. In order to win elections fair and square, the ruling party must also adopt a more democratic procedure in selecting party candidates who are popular among its rank and file and are thus more electable. The role of party bosses in candidate selection will be gradually weakened. The opposition parties, in contrast, began to launch coordinated campaigns with a nationwide organization network in the election held in 1989. With a freer media, they have a more open environment to mobilize their potential supporters at a level that would have been impossible only a few years ago.

Conclusions

The Republic of China's political system in Taiwan is undergoing significant change. The one-party system has clearly come to an end, although the ruling KMT will probably continue to dominate the political scene in an emerging "dominant-party system." Already the power structure of the party-state has shown a remarkable trend toward Taiwanization that permits Taiwanese to share power. This trend, coupled with current proposals to overhaul the parliamentary bodies and to hold popular elections for Taiwan's governors and mayors of Taipei and Kaohsiung, points to a possible new era of political development in Taiwan.

Looking immediately ahead, one can still see elements of uncertainty regarding the nature of the evolving political system. Much depends upon the roles of the military and the painful process of redefining the relationship between the KMT, the government, and society. Given popular demands for institutional reforms and democratization, there is a growing pressure for separation of the state from the party, a task that will be difficult to implement so long as the KMT remains in power. Both the party and the state may also be compelled to lessen their control over and manipulation of social and economic groups on the island. But the party-state may be most reluctant to allow autonomy for groups that hold large human and material resources, such as the trade unions and the farmers' associations.

Whether political development now under way can proceed on a steady course is closely tied to four major political events. The first is consolidation of civilian leadership under President Lee Teng-hui, who took over Chiang Ching-kuo's remaining 1984–1990 presidential term and was reelected in April 1990 for another six-year term. He was also elected chairman of the party by the KMT Party Congress in July 1988. In the initial post–Chiang Ching-kuo period, Lee Teng-hui gained important backing from both the leading party bureaucrats, such as Li Huan, and the military establishment headed by Chief of General Staff Hau Pei-ts'un. However, Lee lacks an institutional base of power, and he appears to have received only reluctant endorsement from the old guard and party politicians. The underlying power struggle between Lee Teng-hui and his political rivals—including Li Huan and Hau Pei-ts'un—came to the surface in spring 1990 when competition for the offices of president, vice-president, and premier intensified. President Lee's reform initiatives have since encountered serious opposition from within the KMT and the military (see Chapter 5).

Second, the roles of the military in politics have become increasingly important since the appointment of General Hau Pei-ts'un as premier in May

1990. Hau has been perceived as the only man capable of bringing stability to a social system riddled with protest movements and growing social crimes stemming from the breakdown of authoritarian structure. The middle class, particularly in the business-industrial circles, has shown serious concerns over the sociopolitical instability that has undermined the foundations for continuing economic growth. Although further political liberalization and democratic reform are viewed as a necessity by a majority of the general population, both the conservatives and business elites favor a slowdown of the reform process. Premier Hau, the pivotal person in the military-security establishment, has considerable reservations about the pace and the direction of ongoing political reform. He is particularly irritated by the Taiwan independence movement, which has become more assertive. The opponents to democratic reform naturally rally behind him, creating a strong coalition of antidemocratic forces.

Third, the ROC government's decision to permit its citizens to visit their relatives on the mainland and to tolerate investments in the mainland have substantially altered the nature of Taiwan-mainland relations (see Chapter 9). If the new open-door policy is continued, the expected increase in civilian contacts, investment ventures, and higher trade volumes will create new conditions for closer ties between the two sides. The PRC will want to use these new opportunities to push for its self-proclaimed goal of peaceful unification with Taiwan. Taiwanization and democratization also could bring forth a Taiwan political elite that views informal contacts and trade more pragmatically. Paradoxically, the Taiwanese and the second- or third-generation mainlanders now gaining more power may have less feeling of ethnic affinity with their mainland "compatriots" and thus have little use for the idea of national unification in the absence of fundamental changes in the PRC's political and economic systems. In this case, more contact will not necessarily lead to more trust or more affection. Nevertheless, Taiwan's recent initiatives toward the mainland will certainly have a great impact on the island's internal political development.

Finally, conflict between proponents of Taiwan independence and those in favor of eventual unification with the mainland is likely to intensify. Advocates of Taiwan independence are becoming more vociferous in public statements and bolder in action, and activities that used to be regarded as treasonous are finding their way into Taiwan's media and street rallies. They fear a potential KMT-CCP (Chinese Communist Party) deal to determine Taiwan's political future. Growing contacts with the mainland have made such fear more credible in the eyes of Taiwan independence proponents. Some leaders of the influential Presbyterian church openly lend their support to Taiwan independence, as do many overseas Taiwanese political activists. In fall 1990 the DPP, under pressure from its radical wing, adopted a resolution that declared Taiwan's de facto independence from the mainland.[50] The party subsequently formed a committee called the Independence of Taiwan

Sovereignty to counter the Council for National Reunification, which was created by the KMT government. Thus the issue of Taiwan independence versus reunification with China has formally entered the political agenda with a strong potential of sharpening political conflicts between the KMT mainlanders and the opposition radicals. Such a political polarization is deemed to complicate Taiwan's future transition to a democratic polity.

In short, democratic transformation of the KMT's authoritarian system has clearly entered a critical phase of intensifying political conflicts between the proponents of and the opponents to fundamental reform, and its future is uncertain. If the pro-independence radicals do not exercise self-restraints, the conservatives backed by the military-security forces could resort to political suppression in a cycle described by Cheng and Haggard in Chapter 1. Once that happens, the course of democratic evolution could be reversed. The outcome of current political polarization depends on maintaining dialogue between the opposing camps as well as timely concessions made by both sides. Only with renewed dialogue and compromise can the moderate reformers be expected to continue pressing for orderly reform at a steady pace.

Notes

1. See interview with KMT secretary-general Ma Soo-lay, *The Central Daily*, November 9, 1986, p. 1.

2. Hung-mao Tien, "Taiwan in 1986: Reforms Under Activity," in John Major and Antony Kane, eds., *China Briefing 1987* (Boulder, Colo.: Westview Press, 1987), pp. 11–14.

3. Yangsun Chou and Andrew J. Nathan, "Democratizing Transition in Taiwan," *Asian Survey* 17 (3) (March 1987), pp. 283–285. President Chiang Ching-kuo died on January 13, 1988. Dr. Lee Teng-hui, vice-president and a Taiwanese, succeeded him as both the president and the KMT acting chairman, thus completing a smooth transition of power.

4. Ibid., p. 299.

5. Council for Economic Planning and Development (CEPD), *Taiwan Statistical Data Book* (Taipei: Executive Yuan, 1989), p. 41.

6. Ibid., p. 29; and *The Free China Journal*, October 22, 1990, p. 7.

7. RDEC, *Annual Review of Government Administration, Republic of China, 1988* (Taipei: Executive Yuan, 1989), p. 169.

8. *The Free China Journal*, October 22, 1990, p. 7.

9. Wen Ch'ung-i, "T'ai-wan ti kung-yueh-hua yu she-hui pien ch'ien" [Industrialization and social change in Taiwan], in *Taiwan Ti-ch'u She-hui Pien-ch'ien yu Wen-hua Fa-chan* [Social change and cultural development in the Taiwan Area] (Taipei: Chung-kuo Lun-t'an, 1985), p. 17.

10. Ibid.

11. Hsin-huang Michael Hsiao, "The Middle Classes in Taiwan: Formation and Implications" (Paper presented at the China Council's Deliberative Conference on Taiwan Entering the 21st Century, April 23–25, 1987, The Asia Society, New York), p. 9.

12. Ibid.

13. Hungdah Chiu, "Prospect for the Unification of China," *Asian Survey* 22 (10) (October 1983), p. 158.

14. CEPD, *Taiwan Statistical Data Book*, p. 303.

15. Ibid., pp. 4, 303. Calculation of percentages is made according to the official figures of population and association membership.

16. CEPD, *Taiwan Statistical Data Book*, p. 89.

17. See Chang Mao-kuei, "Pa-shih mien-tai T'ai-wan she-hui yun-tung feng-ch'ao yu cheng-chih chuan-hua" [Taiwan social movements and political change in the 1980s] (Paper presented at the Conference on National Policy and Social Order, Institute for National Policy Research, Taipei, January 22, 1989); and Sheldon R. Severinghaus, "The Emergence of an Environmental Consciousness in Taiwan" (Paper presented at the annual meeting of the Association for Asian Studies, Washington, D.C., March 18, 1989).

18. Guillermo A. O'Donnell, *Modernization and Bureaucratic-Authoritarianism: Studies in South American Politics* (Berkeley: Institute of International Studies, University of California, 1973).

19. Dankwart A. Rustow, "Transition to Democracy, Toward a Dynamic Model," *Comparative Policies* 1 (April 1970), pp. 352–354.

20. Ibid., p. 355.

21. *Min-chung Jih-pao* (May 16, 1987), p. 1

22. Chang Shu-ming, "Chieh yen chueh-ts'e nei-mu" [Decision to lift the martial law: An inside story], *Shih-pao hsin-wen chou-kan* [Times news weekly] 21 (October 17, 1986), p. 14.

23. Chou and Nathan, "Democratizing Transition in Taiwan," p. 287.

24. Ssu-ma wen-wu [Chiang Ts'un-nan], "Han Pet-ts'un pu tsai cho ch'iang ien?" [General Han Pei-ts'un, no longer a strongman?], *Hsin hsin-wen* 49 (50) (February 15, 1988), pp. 44–45.

25. Myron Weiner, "Empirical Democratic Theory and the Transition from Authoritarianism to Democracy," in *PS* (American Political Science Association Newsletter), Fall 1987, pp. 861–866.

26. Hung-mao Tien, "Origins and Development of Taiwan's Democratic Change" (Paper delivered at the annual meeting of the Association for Asian Studies, Washington, D.C., March 17–19, 1989), p. 3.

27. Wen Man-ying, "Ch'ung cheng Kuo-ming-tang ku-fen yu-hsien kung-szu [Restructure the KMT LTD., Inc.], *Yuan-chien* [Global views monthly], no. 21 (March 1988), p. 16. Many party members have neither paid dues nor attended party meetings, thus are technically inactive. The figure for inactive members is not available.

28. Figures provided by *Chih-yu-Shih-pao* [The liberty times], July 20 and 22, 1990, p. 1.

29. *Chih-yu Shih-pao*, November 7, 1990, p. 1.

30. Li Wen-lang, "Social Change in Taiwan and a Solution for Ethnic Problems," *International Daily News* (Chinese), May 19, 1987, p. 2.

31. This acute observation is by Prof. Yang Kuo-shu, who has done studies on this subject. See Wun Ying-ts'un, "Ch'uan-wei yu shui hueh pa-ho" [A tug of war between power and generation change], *Tien-hsi* [Common wealth], no. 70 (March 1, 1987), pp. 76–77.

32. Lei Chen, *Lei Chen Hui-i-lu* [Lei Chen's memoirs] (Hong Kong: Ch'i shih Nientai She, 1978), pp. 28–29; and Pan Chia-chieh, "Lei Chen an chung yu ta pai" [The Lei Chen case is finally brought to the open], *Shih-pao Chou-kan* [China times weekly], no. 212, March 18, 1989, pp. 52–55.

33. Lin Cheng-chieh and Chang Fu-chung, *Hsuan-chu Wan shui* [Long life election!] (Washington, D.C.: Taiwan Monitor Reprint, 1978), pp. 240–279.

34. Nicholas D. Kristof, "Opposition Party Strong in Taiwan Vote," *New York Times*, December 7, 1986, p. 3; and Patrick L. Smith, "Taiwan's New Opposition Party Becomes Force to Be Reckoned With," *Christian Science Monitor*, December 8, 1986, p. 15.

35. Figure given to me by Huang Hsin-chieh, the DPP chairman.

36. International Committee for Human Rights in Taiwan, *Taiwan Communiqué* 29 (March 28, 1987), p. 19.

37. See Chen Che-ming et al., "Tang-ch'ien wu ta she-hui yuntung ti tung-li, tsu-li, ya-li" [Five major social movements: The dynamics, obstacles, and pressures], *Times News Weekly* 46 (April 14, 1987), pp. 37–51; and Wen Manying, "K'an ch'un-chung hsi yung-tung" [A close look at the mass movements], *Yuan-chien* [Global views monthly] 9 (March 1987), pp. 28–36. For a detailed chronological account of movements and organizations related to consumer rights, ecology, trade unionism, women's rights, aborigines' rights, and farmers' interest, see Chang Mao-kuei, "Pa-shih mien-tai," pp. 9–14.

38. John Kaplan, *The Court Martial of the Kaohsiung Defendants* (Berkeley: University of California, Institute of East Asian Studies, 1981), pp. 16–14 and 34–38.

39. Wang Li-hsia and Chang Hsiao-ch'un, "Kung-hui yu kung-yun, ta'i-wan lao-kung yung-tung ti hsien-chai yu wei-lai" [Trade unions and labor movements—Taiwan's current labor movements and their future prospects], *Lien-ho yueh-kan* [The united monthly] 70 (May 1987), pp. 85–86.

40. Hsu Ya-yuan, "Lao-kung li-fa pu jung hu-shih" [Labor legislation should not be ignored], *Shih-pao tsa-chih* [Time magazine] (July 10, 1983), p. 45.

41. Hung Chin-chu, "Ch'eng-chang chung ti lao tzu chiu-fen" [The growth of worker-employer disputes], *Shih-pao tsa-chih* [Time magazine] (June 27, 1984), p. 7.

42. *Min chung jih-pao* (April 26, 1987), p. 2.

43. *Chung-kuo pao* (January 9, 1988), p. 3.

44. Ibid.

45. *Chung-kuo shih-pao* (January 24, 1988), p. 3.

46. *Statistical Abstract of Interior* (Taipei: Ministry of Interior, 1984), pp. 191–192.

47. Chu Hai-yuan, "Chen chiao kuan-hsi ti szu-ka'o-T'ai, wan chi-tu-chang-lao-chicago-hui" [A reflection on church-state relationship—Taiwan Presbyterian Church], *United Monthly* 6 (January 1982), pp. 47–48.

48. Chang Ch'un-hua and Chi-Hui-jung, "Pei-ch'i shih-tzu-chiam, tso chai shih-tsu-lu" [March on the crossroad with the cross on their backs], *Time News Weekly* 46 (April 4, 1987), pp. 64–65.

49. For details see Chen Min-feng, "Tso ch'u chiao-tang, tso shang chieh t'ou" [Out of the church and into the street], *Hsin hsin-wen* (October 26, 1987), pp. 18–23.

50. *Min-chung jih-pao* (October 8, 1990), p. 1.

CHAPTER 3

The Rise of Social Movements and Civil Protests

HSIN-HUANG MICHAEL HSIAO

This chapter sketches the general background of the various social and protest movements that have emerged in Taiwan during the 1980s. The purpose here is not to theorize about these movements in any major way, but to analyze the historical origins and social, political, and economic contexts in which they arose. I examine the commonality as well as the uniqueness of their objectives and goals and discuss the character of their activities. Finally, I elaborate tentatively on the developing relationships between a "soft authoritarian state" and a "demanding civil society" that is manifest in these emerging social movements.

The Political Context

Based on the available survey evidence compiled since 1980, it is apparent that the people of Taiwan have developed a new collective consciousness that reflects a more autonomous conception of civil society. Public attitudes toward the government have also changed. People now demand that the state face new social issues, such as worsening public safety, environmental quality, economic crimes, income distribution, obscenity and prostitution, and traffic conditions, instead of concentrating exclusively on those problems that have long occupied the government, such as national security, political stability, and economic growth.[1]

It is useful to think in terms of the political, economic, and social forces that have affected state-society relations in postwar Taiwan. Three periods can be distinguished. The first period, from 1947–1962, was one of *political forces in absolute command*. Beginning in 1947, when the tragedy of the February 28 Incident erupted and the Nationalist troops brutally massacred local Taiwanese, the KMT regime established an unchallengeable authoritarian regime on the island. All aspects of public life were placed completely under the control of the party-military state. Political considerations overruled all economic and social factors, and economic rehabilitation and stability were given high priority not for any developmental reason but simply for the political survival of the regime.

No recognition was granted to any indigeneous social forces. Taiwanese civil society fell under the complete control of the mainlander-dominated central state apparatus. Suppression and coercion were immediately applied to any autonomous demands from society that might threaten the power of the party-state.

The defining feature of the second period, from 1963 to 1978, was *economic forces in relative command*. During this period of state-society relations, new economic forces emerged as the KMT state made economic growth a priority. A shift from an import-substitution industrialization (ISI) strategy to an export-oriented industralization (EOI) strategy produced private capitalists (both mainlanders and Taiwanese), booming small and medium-sized enterprises, a new urban middle class, and a growing industrial working class.

Economic considerations were taken very seriously, which allowed new interests to articulate and exert their influence on the state. However, the KMT regime was still very much in command of most aspects of the economy. The private sector exchanged political loyalty to the KMT state in return for the opportunities provided by EOI development strategy.

Toward the end of this period, efforts were made by various sectors of the previously pacified and coerced civil society to "return to their roots." The social sciences assumed a new significance, as did the indigenous literature, music, and dance. A new kind of "Taiwan consciousness" emerged among many intellectuals.[2] Yet these social and cultural efforts to redefine the nature of Taiwan's social reality were confined to the intellectuals and not evident among other social groups and economic classes. Civil society had not yet been mobilized to challenge the power of the authoritarian state directly, although the political opposition had already gained wider support from the populace.

During the third period, from 1979 to the present, we see *social forces in mobilization*. In the past ten years, industrial development has created a new civil society. This new civil society, which cuts across subethnic and class lines, started to press for change in the existing system of state-society relations.

One means of change was to voice grievances about the serious social problems facing Taiwan. With the class structure of Taiwan still in a formative phase, no distinct class-consciousness has yet developed. Collective action to date has not been mobilized along clear class lines; rather, the common target has been the state. Recent social movements have directly questioned state-society relations, particularly the mode of state control over civil society, and have sought to acquire autonomy from the domination of the authoritarian state.[3] Reform has been sought not only in specific public policies, but also to transform the power relations between state and society.

The state in Taiwan has long exercised dominance over the economic and social spheres; the explicit coexistence of authoritarianism and capitalism is also evident.[4] This coexistence became particularly evident during the second period. As emerging economic interests began to articulate their influence, other sectors of society also benefited and made claims on the state for greater autonomy. These combined forces contributed to what has been conceptualized as a transition from "hard" to "soft" authoritarianism.[5] This process did not come about "naturally," as some local observers assert, but was the result of a conscious effort by the KMT to manage demands from the civil society. Nonetheless, emerging social movements have played a significant role in accelerating the transition process.

The Emerging Social Movements: Commonality and Uniqueness

By the end of 1989, at least eighteen social movements had emerged to make claims on the state.[6] Their claims were varied, but four distinct types can be delineated: The first were those protesting the state's inaction in the face of new issues such as consumer protection, pollution, rising housing costs, and conservation. A second type of movement focused on state policies regarding ethnic groups and minorities' language rights, land control, and cultural identity and preservation. Protests have also risen against inadequate policies in caring for disadvantaged groups, such as the elderly, the handicapped, and veterans, and the treatment of certain religious groups. A third group of movements has challenged the state's corporatist mode of control over key social groups, such as workers, farmers, students, women, and teachers and intellectuals. Finally, groups have emerged to change the established rules governing politically sensitive issues such as the ban on contacts between people in Taiwan and the mainland and human rights violations. This section provides a brief description of these emerging social movements in terms of their stated objectives, major participating organizations, and methods used for making claims.

Consumers' Movements

The consumers' rights movement emerged in 1980. The Consumers' Foundation, the first active grass-roots consumer organization, was established by middle-class intellectuals and professionals. Up until 1987, the Consumers' Foundation was still the most active social movement in Taiwan. The consumer movement served as an important model for other social movements in mobilizing to make demands on the state. The methods used by this movement have been a mixture of sounding alarms to the public through effective media coverage, engaging in policy dialogue with officials, consumer education via seminars, meetings, and publishing monthly consumer reports and granting legal assistance to consumers injured by negligent manufacturers. Although the consumer movement remained apolitical in its initial years in order to survive, it has very successfully pressed the state to respond.

A key element in the relative success of this movement is the active participation of a large number of liberal scholars and professionals who, in the eyes of the government, do not threaten the existing power base of the regime. The same liberal scholars who supported the consumer movement later extended their support to other newly emerging social movements, however. It can thus be said that the success achieved by the consumer movement helped to legitimize subsequent social movements.

Local Antipollution Protest Movements

Even though environmental pollution problems were worsening during the 1970s, and local pollution victims voiced their grievances before 1980, local antipollution protests did not become widely known to the public or covered in the media until the early 1980s. Local residents who had fallen victim to pollution organized these antipollution protests, with some external support provided more recently by scholars, university students, and concerned journalists.

A study using media coverage of such protests found that there were 108 such protest campaigns in various localities around the island from 1981 to 1988.[7] The protestors showed a willingness to threaten violence and coercion to force polluters to comply with the demands of the victims, usually after long and drawn-out petitioning of local government agencies failed to produce any results. Taiwan has no specific or effective law governing the methods for dealing with pollution disputes, but past experiences of local victims in dealing with the government have convinced them to take direct action. This government action has generally proved satisfactory and effective, with the polluting factories being forced to make improvements or even to close down. In some cases, where stopping a proposed industrial facility was the major objective, plans to construct the new plant were eventually canceled because of strong and persistent resistance.[8]

Even though the direct objectives of such localized protest movements were usually restricted to a single pollution case, the cumulative result has been the growing public distrust of the state's determination to address worsening pollution problems. Another significant consequence is the permanent establishment of local antipollution organizations as well as the formation of several nationwide environmental organizations such as the Taiwan Environmental Protection Union and the Taiwan Greenpeace

Organization. These local and nationwide environmental groups exert constant pressure to strengthen environmental policy.

The Conservation Movement

Beginning in 1980, a few concerned scholars and writers began campaigning for the conservation of select geographic areas where wildlife or natural scenery was endangered. The initial efforts attracted neither a great deal of public attention nor government response, but in 1982, the Society for Wildlife and Nature (SWAN) was founded with the active participation of conservationists and academics. This newly established conservation movement takes a soft-line approach, using newspaper articles, magazine publications, education, and arranged visits for concerned people to natural conservation sites such as national parks. In comparison to the antipollution movement, the conservation movement does not have a mass base and few demonstrations and protests have been mounted. Conservation of nature continues to be a concern limited mainly to middle-class intellectuals.

The Women's Movement

The first wave of Taiwan's women's movement was initiated in the early 1970s by a few progressive women intellectuals led by Lu Hsio-Lian, an active opposition leader involved in the Kaohsiung Incident in 1979. At this initial stage, the movement did not gain much social support, and it aroused suspicions of a different political motivation among KMT leaders.

The women's movement revived when a new women's group, the Awakening, was organized by a later generation of feminist intellectuals. This new women's group, which received a broadly sympathetic response from the public, breathed life into Taiwan's feminist movement by posing controversial feminist issues that challenged established male-dominant beliefs and social mores.

In the past few years, many other women's organizations have been established for various women's causes, such as protection of teenage prostitutes, child welfare, the enhancement of women's status in society, and the environment. The movement challenges bias in the legal system, organizes study sessions on women's issues, holds rallies and demonstrations for specific purposes, and educates the public via the mass media.

The Aborigine Human Rights Movement

This movement started as a cultural consciousness campaign by a group of young tribal aborigines who had been educated in urban Taipei. The Aborigine Human Rights Promotion Association was founded in 1983, advocating legal and social rights for Taiwan's minorities, who comprise about 2 percent of the total popoulation. Several challenges were made to the state's policies on aborigine land rights: against demeaning comments about aborigines contained in primary school textbooks, against a nuclear waste site constructed on Orchid Island, where the Yami tribe resides, and in support of a call for using indigenous names rather than the sinicized names imposed on the aborigines.

Demonstrations and protests have been the major tactics used in this movement, and an alliance was recently formed to push the movement's current objectives on land rights for the aborigines. The movement is minority oriented but predominantly elite, and it receive considerable support from educated aborigines and sympathetic church groups.

The Student Movement

Keeping the campuses quiet, especially university campuses, has long been a major objective of the KMT, which effects state control by means of various corporatist tools, "hard" and "soft" alike. It has been very effective in keeping university campuses isolated from external political activism. Until recently, university students were quiescent. A short period of student activism in the early 1970s, caused by Taiwan's worsening diplomatic situation, resulted in demands for more vigorous political and social reforms. However, it was quickly and effectively defused as the government channeled the students' enthusiasm and energies into a depoliticized social service campaign. The active operations of the China Youth Corps also consumed students' attention and energies in various recreational and social activities.

In the early 1980s, some university students began to pay attention to and even support opposition candidates in elections; some engaged in campus reform efforts. However, this student activism was never fully organized into a large-scale student movement. Since 1986 this situation has changed, starting at National Taiwan University, where a demand for liberalization on the campus was made by a group of student activists. The campus reform movement began by challenging the university authority and the KMT's campus security rules. The stated objectives of the student movement included a democratic form of students' self-governance and campus autonomy from KMT influence. The students also questioned the legitimacy of the presence of military officials and the inclusion of military and political education in the curriculum. Between 1986 and 1988, the student movement spread to many university campuses and a cross-campus alliance has been formed to apply more effective collective pressure on educational policy.

New Testament Church Protests

These single-issue protests, undertaken by a religious group, erupted when a government agency and the Garrison Command Force banned this church group from settling in a remote mountain area in southern Taiwan. Several violent conflicts have occurred between the church followers and police forces during the past few years. The situation became more complicated when the government refused entry permits to a group of international New Testament visitors to Taiwan. This protest movement relies upon street rallies and demonstrations to promote its cause.

Because of the unique nature of the religion, the cause has not been widely supported by the general public, and the protest movement is confined to church followers alone. No sign of a coalition with any other movement has been observed. Its internal cohesion and ability to mobilize is exceptionally strong, however, and its denunciations of the government are both forceful and direct. Through the mediation of scholars, settlement in the particular mountain area has been permitted recently and protest action from church followers has gradually disappeared.

The Labor Movement

The KMT state's labor policy has been quite regressive in terms of granting labor unions autonomy and protecting labor welfare. Workers have been a prime target for state controls. The unions have been dominated by management, strongly aided by the KMT machine. Workers tended to be quiescent, particularly the first generation of the industrial working class, which was largely recruited among the migrant small farmers who still had strong ties to the countryside and had inherited a conservative outlook.

The second-generation working class is further removed from its rural background and tends to be more questioning of pro-management policies. Since the late 1970s, labor-management relations in the workplace have gradually changed. During the 1980s, increasing labor disputes and scattered efforts to mobilize workers in some workplaces were observed, but not until the end of 1987, when the year-end bonus problem became a source of labor-management conflict, did a large-scale islandwide labor movement begin to take shape in Taiwan.

In the 1986 election, labor voters demonstrated their dissatisfaction toward the KMT by casting votes for two opposition Democratic Progressive Party (DPP) candidates for seats in the Legislative Yuan and the National Assembly. However, such voting behavior cannot be viewed as evidence of a direct connection between the DPP and the labor movement, as the DPP had not paid serious attention to the labor issue. Nevertheless, signs of political revolt from the working class were clearly visible to the KMT government, and a series of compensational moves were made, in particular by establishing a new Labor Commission in the central government to deal with growing labor demands.

Meanwhile, the labor movement is becoming more aggressive and better organized and can make stronger claims regarding the economic and political conditions suitable for labor as a whole. In the late 1980s, strikes became more frequent because of failed negotiations between labor and management. The Labor Commission has not been effective in responding to the expanding demands from workers. New independent unions are being formed by labor activists and are directly challenging the representative nature of existing unions. Cross-regional, cross-factory, and industry union federations have also been established. A Labor Party was established in 1988 but split shortly thereafter. One faction left the Labor Party and formed a Worker's Party in early 1989. The politicized inclination of the labor movement is increasingly evident, though its history is short.

The Farmers' Movement

Since land reform (1949–1953), Taiwan's small family farmers have been the backbone of conservative support for the KMT regime. They, like the laborers, have long been deprived of political power, however. The farmers' associations have been manipulated by local political factions and, directly or indirectly, controlled by the KMT. They do not have any substantive political bargaining power with the state.

The sociopolitical character of the small farmers changed somewhat over the 1970s because of the deterioration of Taiwan's agricultural sector. Farmers have expressed their grievance with the state's pro-urban industrial development policies in elections since the late 1960s. However, no expressive rural social actions took place in Taiwan; even organized grievances limited to market concerns were absent. The absence of a "commodity reform movement" before the 1980s can be accounted for by the conservative character of the small farmers and the state's absolute domination in the countryside.

But in a surprise to many observers, including government officials, political observers, and economic specialists, more than 3,000 fruit farmers from central Taiwan protested for the first time in December 1987 in front of the Legislative Yuan and demanded that the government take immediate action to reverse a drastic decline in domestic fruit prices caused by imported fruit, mainly from the United States. Among the protesters were Taiwanese, aborigines, and mainlander veterans who were specialized fruit farmers. This spontaneous protest was initiated and organized by the farmers themselves. No direct involvement from the opposition Democratic Progressive Party or other political forces was found. Since that occasion, there have been several other large-scale farmers' protests and demonstrations in Taipei that challenged the state's squeezing agricultural policies.

The participants have gradually increased to include not only full-time specialized farmers, but also the largely part-time rice farmers. The objectives have also expanded to include the complete revision of existing agricultural policy, expansion of farmers' insurance, democratization of the farmers' associations, and establishment of a Ministry of Agriculture. The independent Farmers' Rights Promotion Associations have been formed in many counties by farmer activists, and two nationwide unions have been established to coordinate organized collective actions among those local associations.

After recent protests, particularly the demonstration of May 20, 1988, by rice farmers from the southern counties that ended in large-scale urban violence in Taipei, the KMT began to take farmers' demands seriously. The chairman of the Council on Agricultural Development and Planning was replaced by an agricultural economist-turned-technocrat who was also a favorite of President Lee Teng-hui. A provincewide farmer insurance scheme was implemented on a trial basis. The procedures for selecting the farmer associations' general secretary were changed to involve less party interference, and a national meeting on agriculture was held to determine what future actions should be taken to solve Taiwan's agricultural problems.

The government is the prime target of this farmers' social movement. Economic concerns, particularly commodity reform, are the major appeals at the present time, but it is clear that the demands have expanded to include more autonomy for farmers' organizations vis-à-vis the domination of the KMT.

The Teachers' Rights Movement

Teachers, as Chinese intellectuals, enjoy a great deal of social recognition and respect. Yet they normally have no direct political influence on campus policy, and their own employment security has no proper legal protection, particularly in high schools and some private universities.

As indicated earlier, the campus has been one of the critical social sectors that the KMT felt impelled to control. The KMT rulers clearly believe that education should be guided by political ideology through informal sanctions on employment and control of curriculum. As a result, Taiwan's teaching faculty has tended to be passive and conservative in expressing its political opinions. No organized efforts have ever been made to protect teachers' employment security, academic autonomy, or teaching environment.

In 1987, however, demands were voiced by a group of high school teachers who were fired for controversial reasons. They formed a Teacher's Rights Promotion Association. In the beginning, it was a very small organization, but then it quickly developed into an influential nationwide movement backed by large numbers of liberal university professors. As a result, school administrators came under pressure. The association also openly challenged the presence of military personnel who conduct military and political training for students. At several universities, quasi-unions were organized for the purpose of enhancing professors' input into administrative policymaking. A draft University Law has now become a battleground between educational authorities and liberal academic activists.

The long-standing presence of the KMT apparatus at schools, which exerts nonacademic influence on various decisions, is the prime target of this middle-class social movement. The association put up its own candidates to compete for seats in the Legislative Yuan in the election held at the end of 1989.

Handicapped and Disadvantaged Welfare Group Protests

In Taiwan, welfare policies for caring for the elderly, handicapped, and disadvantaged have been regressive and inadequate. They are the marginal groups in Taiwan society, with no resources or power to influence the state's welfare policies. Their condition was made worse when the government decided to terminate the circulation of government-run lottery tickets that the handicapped and the elderly poor had relied on for their livelihood. This neglected minority, for the first time, went into the streets to protest and present their petitions. This resulted in several other demands being pressed on the state from needy people.

Many meetings and discussion sessions have been organized by existing welfare associations urging amendment of the welfare laws for the elderly, the handicapped, and those on social relief. New welfare laws for children, adolescents, and women are also called for by the various concerned groups.

This social movement is basically a humanitarian movement largely devoid of broader political motivation. The methods used are mild, and so far no direct threats have been used against the government. To maintain its human rights record abroad and to present itself as a humanitarian and caring regime, the government has been responsive to these welfare demands.

Veterans Welfare Protests

Senior veterans have long been loyal supporters of the KMT regime, holding strong emotional and patriotic sentiments that are similar to those of the senior elites who came to rule Taiwan after the defeat on the mainland. In the past, very few complaints were heard from these veterans, who had long been discharged from the service and who, with meager retirement pensions, have had to be largely self-supporting.

In 1987, thousands of senior veterans were mobilized in a protest rally in front of the Executive Yuan, demanding that better subsidies be provided by the Commission on Veterans. Such drastic and unprecedented protest struck a politically sensitive nerve, and an immediate increment of the monthly compensation was promised by the government. Another even more sensitive problem remains to be solved: that of the land certificates given to veterans entitling them to a piece of farmland in their respective hometowns on the mainland after reunification with the mainland is achieved. Under current circumstances, reunification seems a long way off, and as veterans doubt it will be fulfilled in their lifetime, they demand that the state convert the certificates into cash. The KMT is now seriously considering that possibility as political pressures have built up considerably from various veteran groups.

By the end of 1988, several veteran groups had been organized, and some ideological cleavages and conflicts emerged. The KMT has been mobilizing among the veterans to form a pro-KMT group in order to establish a balance against the more radical veteran factions. The radical factions are now engaging in various protest actions for institutional reform, such as the demand for an overall reorganization of the aging legislative bodies.

To the KMT regime, the protests of the veterans present an acutely embarrassing problem. The party, the military, and the administration are likely to make substantial consessions to pacify veterans.

The Human Rights Movement

The issue of political prisoners has long been a politically sensitive one. In legalistic terms, all the prisoners who were convicted of crimes on political grounds were not considered political prisoners. In reality, they were all dissidents who had mobilized against authoritarian rule in Taiwan. It is not surprising that some of those political victims were jailed without due process.

In 1987, a group of these political victims, having been released from jail, formed the Human Rights Promotion Association for both emotional and social support. They demanded fair treatment from society and full civil rights. Recently this movement has become more and more politicized, with one faction joining the DPP in waging a political campaign calling for a "new and independent Taiwan." Such a change in the nature of this movement is not difficult to understand.

The Mainlanders' Home-Visiting Movement

In order to break the ban on contacts between the two separate Chinese societies, a group of senior mainlanders, most of them veterans, organized a group demanding permission to visit the mainland after forty years of separation from family members. This campaign was greeted with sympathy and support from both the general public and the reform-conscious political elites of the KMT and DPP. In October 1987, the announcement to lift the ban was made, allowing those mainlanders with relatives on the mainland to visit on an individual basis.

The KMT decision to permit the mainlanders to visit their homeland should be seen as a strictly humanitarian gesture and should not be viewed as a change in the established policy toward the PRC. It was a welcome move, though, and it enhanced the KMT's reputation for being more sensible. Because its single objective has been achieved, this movement is now dormant.

The Taiwanese's Home-Visiting Movement

In 1988, some of the key individuals of the mainlanders' home-visiting movement turned their attention to a call to grant permission to Taiwanese on the mainland to return to the island. Those trapped on the mainland had either been soldiers drafted by the KMT to fight against the Communists on the mainland during the civil war period between 1945 and 1949 or those who, for political reasons, had been exiled to the mainland after the February 28 Incident in 1947. Establishment of a philanthropic foundation is being considered by a group of concerned individuals and by the private business community to financially assist those Taiwanese on the mainland who wish to return to Taiwan but cannot afford to do so. This appeal is also being seriously considered by the KMT government.

The Antinuclear Power Movement

By 1988, Taiwan had constructed three nuclear power plants with four reactors. The Taiwan Power Company (Taipower), strongly backed by the government, expected to have a total of twenty reactors by the year 2000. But in recent years, this aggressive target has come under severe criticism by concerned scholars and environmentalists. A heated debate took place in 1985 between the Taipower officials on one side and scholars and environmentalists on the other on the issue of whether or not the already planned fourth plant should be built. That debate was organized by the Consumers' Foundation and established an antinuclear public opinion. However, despite capturing public attention, no organized movement was formed to resist Taipower on nuclear power policy.

In early 1988, the local residents near the newly designated plant site organized an Anti–Fourth Nuclear Plant Committee with support from some environmental activists. In April, a group of professors and activists waged a hunger strike for the antinuclear cause in front of the Taipower headquarters. The resistance is growing among local residents, and nationwide environmental groups are also taking a strong antinuclear stand. The controversy is expected to continue. For the economic officials, and Taipower particularly, it will be one of the most difficult problems they have had to face. Under strong pressure from the media and public opinion, the government will probably modify its established policy on nuclear power development and adopt a lower profile on this issue in order to avoid the expected conflicts.

The Hakka Rights Movement

Since the February 28 Incident, the Hakka, a distinctive local dialect group, has been caught in the middle of the Taiwanese-mainlander ethnic conflict. They constitute about 15 percent of the total population yet have taken no stand in the political struggles between the mainlander-controlled KMT regime and the Fukienese-dominated DPP opposition. They demand instead that both political parties take the Hakka seriously. On December 28, 1988, 5,000 Hakkas, from almost all counties where the Hakka reside, gathered in Taipei to demonstrate. The immediate appeal was what they called "Return My Mother Tongue." They asked for increased Hakka language programs on radio and television, which had not been allowed by the current KMT's Radio and Television Law. The Hakka movement also has direct implications for changing the KMT's national language policy in the public media and schools.

It is expected that the Hakka Right Promotion Association, which has generated much support from the Hakka elites and intellectuals, will continue such campaigns in the future. A new foundation is also being set up in order to promote the culture of the Hakka and to enhance its social and political recognition in Taiwan.

The Nonhomeowners' "Shell-less Snail" Movement

This most recent protest movement to take place in Taiwan was led by a group of primary school teachers, graduate students, and professors of urban planning and was helped by wide and sympathetic coverage in the media. A crowd of more than 10,000 people gathered in the eastern business district of Taipei on September 28, 1989, to protest the worsening housing problems and skyrocketing housing prices. Carnival-like protest activities were also arranged, emerging as an alternative to the hard-line approaches of other social movements.

The Nonhomeowners Solidarity Organization, established in the summer of 1989, has since been the key organizer of this movement, voicing specific demands for housing policy changes. The concerned state agency has responded to demands by agreeing to formulate more effective housing programs for needy lower- and middle-income families. This movement is unique because, as a middle-class movement, it has been able to mobilize extensive support in the public.

Concluding Remarks

The most striking characteristic of the social movements that have emerged in Taiwan in the 1980s is that each movement demanded reforms by the

KMT in the fundamental nature of state-society relations so as to grant more autonomy to civil society.

A second feature of these movements is that conflicts between classes have not been a basis for social mobilization. The common target of all the social movements has been the state. Even in the labor and farmer movements, the state and the government policy were the critical targets to which participants made strong appeals.

Third, most of the emerging social movements have adopted an apolitical strategy by avoiding any obvious connection with the political opposition. The opposition DPP has not played a significant role in leading social movements, certainly not in an organized way. Though DPP politicians appeared to be supportive of many of the protests, there is still no clear sign that the DPP has formulated a concrete political stand in relating to most of the social movements. Moreover, the social movement leaders have apparently seen no advantage in aligning openly with the DPP.

Fourth, the most significant collective sentiment expressed in most of the emerging social movements has been a feeling of "victim consciousness," the feeling of being ignored and excluded. Most participants in the new social movements subjectively identify themselves as victims. They feel that they have not been treated fairly even though they are not necessarily isolated from society. Collective action has reflected efforts to create new channels for participation and inclusion in the system.

Fifth, in a short period of time, most of the social movements discussed here have coalesced firmly and some have begun to institutionalize. There are even attempts to extend coalitions and alliances *across* movements. Some common goals are being developed across social movements that have a sufficient commonality of interests to generate broader movements. By so doing, their combined strength and visibility will increase and the state will come under stronger pressure to respond.

A new kind of participatory political culture rooted in a "demanding civil society" is gradually appearing in Taiwan, emerging slowly but surely from the social movements of the 1980s. Taiwan's civil society is no longer passive in the face of state domination; instead it has been mobilized through a learning process engendered by these protest movements. As a result, civil society as a whole, not just those active in the movements, has learned how to make wider claims on the state. These observations on the changing character of Taiwan's civil society are supported by empirical studies of people's political behavior and political culture.[9]

The urge to participate in the existing system by way of collective action has not resulted in revolutionary changes, however. Rather, it has provided opportunities for a new kind of loyal opposition. Although some participants in the protest movements feel deprived by the system, most activists appear to understand that they have more to lose if the existing political and economic system is weakened drastically.

The new social movements now confronting the KMT state have, to a certain extent, accelerated the state's move to transform its rule from a "hard" to "soft" authoritarian posture (see Chapter 10). Liberalization is not the same as democratization, but liberalization can more easily proceed toward democratization once the rules of the game between civil society and the state have been changed. In various policy realms, the KMT has begun to liberalize in order to meet the challenge from a demanding civil society.

The state has permitted citizens to visit the mainland and permitted the New Testament church to settle in a remote mountain in southern Taiwan. Measures have also been taken to respond to demands from consumers' movements, the labor movement, the farmers' movement, the student movement, and the Taiwanese's home-visiting movement by changing administrative agencies and reforming related legal arrangements. The Labor Commission is to be upgraded to a ministry, and a Ministry of Agriculture is also being seriously considered. A Consumer Protection Act, University Law, and Regulation Governing Civic Relationships in Taiwan and the Mainland are all now pending passage by the legislative body. Though these responses from the state are not necessarily sufficient to meet the demands from civil society, the state has taken steps to respond to pressures that could no longer be ignored.

What has emerged is a restive civil society that will increasingly exert direct pressure on the conduct of the state. The emergence of social movements has forced liberalization and responsiveness on the part of the KMT state, though not necessarily through an acceleration of democratization per se.

Democratization requires institutionalized political changes, not just a relaxation of authoritarian control over society. But without such concessions to society on the part of the state, the restructuring of political institutions cannot be realized. Once liberalization becomes a reality, and is firmly guarded by a newly awakened civil society, learning the rules of the game of democracy will be the next goal.

Notes

1. Hsin-huang Michael Hsiao, "Analyzing the Changes of Social Paradigms of Taiwan in the 1980s," *China Times* (October 10, 1984), and "On Affluence, Pluralism, and Social Forces: Reflections on the Social Transformation of Taiwan in the Past Ten Years," *China Times* (April 5, 1985).

2. Hsin-huang Michael Hsiao, "The Taiwan Consciousness of Taiwan's Intellectuals: A Sociological Assessment," in *The Taste of Sociology* (Taipei: Dong-Da Books, 1988), pp. 185–212.

3. Alain Touraine, "Social Movements and Social Change," in *The Challenge of Social Change*, ed. Orlando F. Borda (Beverly Hills, Calif.: Sage Publications, 1985), pp. 77–92.

4. Chalmers Johnson, "Political Institutions and Economic Performance:

The Government-Business Relationship in Japan, South Korea, and Taiwan," in *Asian Economic Development: Present and Future*, ed. Robert Scalapino (Berkeley: IEAS, University of California, 1985), pp. 63–89.

5. Edwin Winckler, "Institutionalization and Participation in Taiwan: From Hard to Soft Authoritarianism?" *China Quarterly* 99 (September 1984), pp. 481–499.

6. Hsin-huang Michael Hsiao, "The Newly Emerging Social Movements in Taiwan: Structural Causes, Typology and Development Stages" (Paper presented at the Conference on Taiwan's New Social Movements, Tsinghwa University, Hsin-chu, February 10–11, 1988).

7. Hsin-huang Michael Hsiao, "The Structural and Processual Analysis of the Anti-Pollution Protests in Taiwan in the 1980s" (Republic of China: Environmental Protection Administration, 1988).

8. Ibid.

9. Fu Hu, "Attitudes Toward Political Participation in Taiwan," in *Taiwanese Society in Transition*, ed. Kuo-shu Yang and Hei-yuan Chiu (Taipei: Institute of Ethnology, Academia Sinica, 1988), pp. 327–354; and Soong-hsi Yuan and Teh-yu Chen, "Political Culture in Taiwan," in *Taiwanese Society in Transition*, ed. Yang and Chiu, pp. 299–326.

For further coverage of these issues, see Mau-kuei Chang, "Social Protests and the Reorganization of the Political System" (Paper presented at the Conference on Chinese Modernization, Taipei, July 1988).

PART 2

The Transformation of the KMT and the Party System

CHAPTER 4

The Changing Role of the KMT in Taiwan's Political System

PING-LUNG JIANG
& WEN-CHENG WU

Gradual political changes in Taiwan, especially those that took place over the past two decades, culminated in the dramatic reforms that took place in 1986–1988, including the lifting of the Emergency Decree that activated martial law, which allowed the formation of opposition political parties and lifted the bans on strikes, demonstrations, and publication of new newspapers. One of the key changes during this time has been in the ruling party itself, the Kuomintang (KMT, or the Nationalist Party of China). This chapter assesses the transformation of the KMT, especially as it has changed in conjunction with the rest of the political system. The main thesis is that the KMT has gradually transformed itself from an authoritarian and exclusionary party into a pragmatic and inclusionary party, and that it has done so in response to the changing demands of the electorate. As a result, the authoritarian one-party system has moved to the threshold of a democratic and competitive party system.

Samuel P. Huntington hypothesizes that because of socioeconomic modernization, a revolutionary and exclusionary party may transform itself into an established and inclusionary party. He divides the evolution of a revolutionary one-party system into three periods: (1) transformation, characterized by strong ideological commitments and an autocratic leader; (2) consolidation, characterized by pragmatism and institutionalization; and (3) adaptation, characterized by greater reliance on technocrats and by more room for the play of interest groups, a critical intelligentsia, and popular participation.[1] The evolution of the KMT more or less followed this model. The KMT entered the period of adaptation in 1968 and has gradually become an inclusionary party.

Huntington's classification scheme is broadly in line with Giovanni Sartori's division of ruling parties in single-party systems into three types: totalitarian, authoritarian, and pragmatic. The authoritarian party is a control system bent upon exclusionary policies. It impedes subsystem autonomy but tolerates, at least de facto, some subgroup autonomy. It is unrestrained, but confined within predictable limits of arbitrariness. A pragmatic party is characterized by inclusionary or aggregative policies. It may be quite open to subgroup autonomy and may also allow room for some peripheral subsystem autonomy. With regard to arbitrariness, it is bounded by the constellation of forces with which it must bargain.[2] In Sartori's framework, the KMT has gradually transformed itself from an authoritarian party into a pragmatic one.

Huntington and Sartori are concerned primarily with the transformation of individual parties.[3] Yet such change has implications for the party system as a whole. Sartori makes the distinction between a noncompetitive party-state that denies the validity of dissent and impedes opposition and a competitive party system that recognizes dissent and institutionalizes opposition. However, after examining the historical record, Sartori concludes that there is a discontinuity, a break or a boundary, between being a noncompetitive party-state and a competitive party system. Whereas a party can be transformed from totalitarian into authoritarian and from authoritarian into pragmatic, the step that follows—crossing the boundary into a competitive party system—is a most difficult one.[4] However, we argue that the political system in Taiwan is now undergoing precisely this transition: from an uncompetitive party-state to a competitive party system.[5]

The Authoritarian Party-State: Structure and Operation

The Kuomintang was founded by Dr. Sun Yat-sen as a secret revolutionary society called Hsing-chung Hui (Society for Rebuilding China) in 1894 in Hawaii. In 1905, Hsing-chung Hui was reorganized into Chung-kuo Ke-ming T'ung-meng Hui (Chinese Revolutionary Alliance) in Tokyo, Japan. The goals of the revolution were "to drive out the Tartars [Manchus], to restore the Chinese nation, to establish a republic and to equalize land ownership."[6] During the seventeen years after 1894, Sun and his followers made ten abortive uprisings to topple the corrupt and despotic Ching Dynasty. Tens of thousands of revolutionaries sacrificed their lives in these attempts before they succeeded on their eleventh try on October 10, 1911, and the Republic of China was born. Thus, the KMT was created and conceived as a revolutionary party. The nature and structure of the Kuomintang have been profoundly influenced by its revolutionary and extraparliamentary origin.

In 1912, T'ung-meng Hui merged with four other parties and was reorganized and renamed the Kuomintang. At this point, the KMT became a parliamentary political party instead of a revolutionary party.[7] However, in the republic's early years, China was torn among competing, regionally based warlords. The parliament was soon dissolved and the KMT disbanded and persecuted by Yuan Shih-k'ai, who later proclaimed himself emperor. In 1914, Sun reorganized the KMT and renamed it Chung-hua ke-ming-tang (Chinese Revolutionary Party) in Tokyo. Some party leaders were dismissed and "false revolutionaries" were weeded out. New members were rigidly screened and required to sign an oath to obey the directives of Tsung-li (president of the party) and abide by strict party discipline.[8] Therefore, the KMT once again became a clandestine revolutionary organization.

Prior to 1924, the KMT remained weak and loosely organized. It had neither a unified party structure nor an army to carry out its revolutionary programs. In 1924, the Kuomintang was completely reorganized along Leninist lines. In that year, the KMT held its First National Congress in Canton and established a military academy in Whampoa, with Generalissimo Chiang Kai-shek as commandant. The Whampoa Academy trained national revolutionary forces, a "party army" with an internal control system similar to the Soviet commissar system. Since then, the KMT's structure, composed of units pyramiding upward through subdistrict, district, county, and provincial levels to a national congress, took definite and permanent shape.

The basic unit of the KMT is the cell, which is generally organized on an occupational rather than geographical basis, though some area cells exist side by side with workplace cells.[9] The size of the cell is limited. The nature and size of the cell give it a much greater hold on its members than have the branches of other Socialist parties. The branch allows for only a superficial and intermittent discipline. The cell, on the contrary, is characterized by tight discipline and is organized not only for electoral mobilization, but for agitation, propaganda, discipline, and, if necessary, clandestine action.

According to the KMT's party constitution, the cells meet once a month, the subdistrict plenary meetings every six months, and the district congresses or plenary meetings once a year. The county or city congresses meet every two years. The provincial congresses meet every three years. Finally, the national congress is convened every four years at the seat of the Central Party Headquarters. Except at the local level, delegates to congresses are not elected directly by members but are elected indirectly by congresses or plenary meetings at the next highest level. Indirect representation is a way of guaranteeing control while appearing nominally democratic. Every additional stage of delegation increases the gap between the interests of those at the base and the decisions of the apex.

However, congresses are seldom convened in line with the schedule called for by the party constitution. The KMT's Thirteenth National Congress, for example, was convened seven years after the Twelfth National Congress. At each level except that of the cells, a party committee is elected by the plenary meeting or congress at the corresponding level to represent the plenary meeting or congress when it is not in session. The indirectly elected committee members are the titular leaders of the party; in fact, they have little power. The committees meet infrequently and usually only for a short time. The committee members may have other jobs outside of the party; they are not paid, permanent party cadres.

At each level except those of cells and subdistricts, the party also maintains a secretariat consisting of departments and commissions. In theory, these are appointed by and responsible to the corresponding committee; actually, they are appointed by the higher party headquarters. Every department and commission at the Central Party Headquarters has a director and three deputy directors. Every provincial, city, and county committee has a chairman and three vice-chairmen. The Central Party Headquarters (secretariat) is headed by a secretary-general and three deputy secretary-generals. These high-ranking party leaders are appointed by the party chairman. They in turn appoint all party cadres working in secretariats at the various lower levels. These appointed cadres run the day-to-day party affairs and are paid, permanent party functionaries. These party leaders and cadres exercise real power in practice.[10]

In principle, the National Congress of the KMT is the highest organ of the party. Its principal duties include the adoption and approval of government and party affair reports, the revision of the party constitution and platform, the discussion and passage of new resolutions and policies, and the election of members to the Central Committee and Central Advisory Committee. Between sessions of the National Congress, the Central Committee (the total membership is now 180) constitutes the highest authority of the party. Its main functions include the execution of resolutions passed by the National Congress, organizing and administering party and political affairs, training and appointing party cadres, and enforcing party discipline.

However, the plenary session of the Central Committee is in principle held only once a year; in fact, it sometimes meets less frequently. It elects from among its members a certain number to form a Central Standing Committee (CSC), which functions during its recess. Thus, the CSC (its membership is now thirty-one) is the highest and most important decisionmaking body in the Republic of China. It forms an inner circle that has vast power to screen and approve all important government and party policies and the power of nomenclatura—to name political appointees to important government and party posts.

Chapter 4 of the KMT party constitution designates Sun Yat-sen as president (Tsung-li) of the party and stipulates that "members of the Kuomintang shall follow Tsung-li's instructions and strive for the realization of his principles." The president of the party serves concurrently as chairman of the National Congress, the Central Committee, and the Central Standing Committee (called Central Executive Committee in the mainland period). The president also has the right to return resolutions to the National Congress for reconsideration, and to make final decisions on resolutions of the Central Committee and the CSC. Generalissimo Chiang Kai-shek was elected director general (Tsung-tsai) of the party in 1938, but he was in fact endowed with the same powers that Sun had enjoyed. Chiang Ching-kuo was elected chairman of the party in 1975 and assumed the same rights and

Figure 4.1   Organizational Structure of the Kuomintang

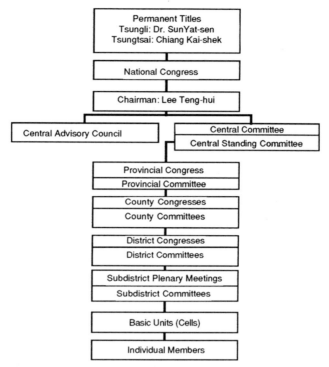

Source: Chung Kuo Kuomintang Chien Chieh [An Introduction to the Kuomintang], (Taipei: The Central Committee of the Kuomintang, 1984), P. 4.

responsibilities; the titles of Tsung-li and Tsung-tsai were reserved in the party constitution out of reverence. President Lee Teng-hui was elected party chairman in July 1988 at the Thirteenth National Congress. According to the party constitution, Chairman Lee has the same formal powers as his three predecessors, because the party leader dominates the Central Standing Committee and the party secretariat and makes all important policy and personnel decisions. Of course, the party leader's actual power in the recent period has depended less on constitutional provisions and to a greater extent on the balance between the conservative and liberal forces within the party.

As this organizational structure suggests, the KMT's guiding principle of organization is democratic centralism. According to Article 4 of the party constitution, "free discussion is to precede decisions and all members have to obey decisions once they are reached through free discussion so as to assure democracy within the organization and freedom with discipline." In other words, party members elect party leaders to higher echelons through indirect representation, whereupon those leaders are endowed with powers of command and the right to be obeyed. Theoretically, the mandate of power flows upward from the base of the pyramid; in reality, control comes downward through the party hierarchy. Because most important positions in the party are appointed by the higher echelon, whoever controls the central organization of the party actually controls the party.

However, with an anti-Communist stand and an ideology that espouses democracy as one of its final goals, the development of the KMT regime has been quite different from the Communist countries. After the KMT moved to Taiwan in 1949, it adopted a pro-capitalist domestic policy and a pro-West foreign policy and opened itself to Western ideas and influence. In short, it was, in Sartori's terminology, more like an authoritarian party than a totalitarian party to begin with. A crucial difference between Communist parties and the KMT was the willingness of the KMT to allow the development of the private sector; this was crucial, because it meant the defense of private property separate from the state, and thus the emergence of an independent middle class not dependent on the state. The KMT did mobilize support for party programs, such as land reform and local self-government, but its mobilization has never reached the extent of that launched by the Chinese Communist Party during its various political campaigns. Except for limitations on the expression of political dissent and the formation of opposition parties, citizens enjoyed a much broader scope of freedom in their daily lives, including economic activities in particular.

The KMT's Thirteenth National Congress held in July 1988 broke with several past practices and moved the party in a somewhat more democratic direction. First, an overwhelming majority of the 1,209 delegates were democratically and freely elected by, and from, the rank and file of the party, without direction or interference from the hierarchy. Second, election of Central Committee members was changed. The chairman nominated one-half of the candidates, but the other half were freely nominated from the floor by the delegates themselves. Of the 180 successful candidates, 33 were *not* nominated by the chairman, a fact further indicating the emergence of competition within the party. Third, it was decided in principle that the new committee members should participate more actively in the "areas of responsibility" of their own choice, either at the central or at the local level. Fourth, it was decided that chairmen and vice-chairmen of local party committees would be elected from among committee members rather than by appointment from above. The new spirit of intraparty democracy did not extend to the subsequent election of the party chairman, and a number of CSC members were nominated from the top. Nonetheless, these changes had a profound effect in opening the party to grass-roots influences.

The Transformation of the Kuomintang:
The Development of Intraparty Democracy

Political analysts have long been fascinated with the evolution of one-party regimes as they adjust to a changing environment—particularly the processes of industrialization and urbanization (see Chapter 1). There are a number of characteristics of the KMT that reflect the larger process of party transformation. These include greater inclusiveness, an increase in technocratic power, greater participation, changes in the party-government relationship, and a greater role for interest articulation.

Inclusiveness

In its mainland period (before 1949), the KMT used to recruit almost exclusively from among elites. Even though the KMT's membership had increased substantially in Taiwan during the 1950s and 1960s and an effort was made to broaden its political base by recruiting members from other sectors of society, including the local Taiwanese elite, party membership amounted to only 6.9 percent of the population in 1968. A full 60 percent of these members were politicians, civil servants, and military officers, and 61 percent of all KMT members were mainlanders.[11] Thus, in the first two decades, the KMT in Taiwan remained elite oriented and predominantly a mainlanders' party. However, in the 1970s and 1980s, the party's membership increased rapidly, with an average annual growth rate exceeding 20 percent. People from all walks of life were recruited. By the end of 1983, KMT membership had reached 2,121,000, or 11.37 percent of the population and 19.45 percent of the electorate, with more than 70 percent of them Taiwanese. The makeup of the membership has become younger, better educated, and more balanced in terms of provincial origin.[12] In short, the KMT has transformed itself from an exclusionary party into an inclusionary party, and from an elite party or cadre party into a mass party.

The Thirteenth National Congress of the KMT passed a "Guideline for Party Reform" in July 1988. The guideline consists of many reform measures that, if fully carried out, will change the nature of its organization. First, all special party headquarters that are organized on an occupational basis, including parliamentary party headquarters, will be changed into party caucuses. All party members, including parliamentarians, will be affiliated with local party headquarters, which will be organized on a geographical basis. Second, the cell system will be transformed into a subdistrict branch system, which will constitute the basic unit of the party. Third, a drive has been launched to double the membership of the party. However, the "detailed implementation measures for party reform" passed by the Central Standing Committee stressed the first measure listed. The other two measures, which have not yet been implemented, would make the party more democratic.

The KMT has also opened other channels of political recruitment. Of these, the most important has been elections. In the past four decades, hundreds of thousands of people have been recruited into official positions through the electoral process. Other channels of political recruitment, such as civil service examinations and the military, have reinforced the expansion of party membership and elections by making the political system more inclusive.

Technocratic Power

The members of the KMT's Central Standing Committee (CSC) and other decisionmaking bodies in the 1950s and 1960s were mainly revolutionary party elite and generals who specialized in ideology, propaganda, and mobilization. They were most concerned with ideological purity, national security, and social stability.

But along with rapid economic development and social change, the national political elite has undergone a structural transformation. Technocrats who specialized in management and climbed up through the governmental bureaucratic ladder began to emerge in the late 1960s. They became mainstream in the CSC in the mid-1970s and have dominated the political scene ever since. The technocrats first captured the cabinet (the Executive Yuan), then the CSC and other decisionmaking bodies. They are development oriented and concerned mainly with transforming Taiwan into a modern industrialized society.

The second most important structural change in the makeup of the political elite is the trend toward "Taiwanization" (see Chapter 2). In the 1950s and 1960s, Taiwanese were encouraged to participate in local elections and politics, but they were virtually excluded from national politics. Only a few Taiwanese who had ties with the KMT during the mainland period were allowed to join the national elite. Even in the Taiwan Provincial Government Council (TPGC), Taiwanese formed a minority of its membership.

Sweeping changes came in the 1970s and 1980s. The number of Taiwanese members in the CSC (now 16 out of 31) and the Cabinet (currently 9 out of 19) gradually increased. Moreover, the TPGC members and national-level representatives elected in the supplementary elections since 1972 have been mostly Taiwanese. More significantly, more than half of the TPGC members have been former county magistrates, city mayors, and other elected officials. Successful Taiwanese politicians with voter support owe their political prominence to various elections, and it is only natural that they have found it politically expedient to respond to the demands from the electorate and favor a faster pace of democratization and liberalization.

In addition, some prominent young social and natural scientists have been co-opted into the elite circle and are now positioned in the second echelon of the national leadership. Because most of them have studied abroad and have been influenced by Western democratic theories, they also tend to favor democratization and liberalization. The last two groups are still a minority in the CSC. Six of the 16 Taiwanese members are technocrats who have never gone through electoral politics, four of them are former elected officials, and only six of them owe their present position to electoral success. But their influence is expected to become greater in the near future.

Technocrats, being pragmatic in mentality and oriented toward efficiency, cannot repress participation and tolerate inequality for long. In contrast with ideology-oriented party cadres and security-conscious generals, technocrats are development oriented. Because their main concern and responsibility is the economy, they favor peaceful and gradual steps toward democratizing and liberalizing the political system so that the economy will grow in a free and open society. But they are against drastic and swift political changes because the economy will be rocked if social stability is greatly disturbed.

Participation

The KMT has gradually expanded political participation in Taiwan by its decisions to hold various elections. Although the Republic of China (ROC) government began to implement local self-government and to hold elections in 1950, political participation for the majority of Taiwanese in the 1950s and 1960s was limited because of the KMT leaders' concern for political stability and their mentality of "political tutelage." Only the provincial assembly and local governments were open for Taiwanese participation; national elections were suspended for two decades (1948–1968). Political participation during the 1970s and 1980s gradually expanded and is now much more comprehensive. In 1968 the KMT decided to hold a supplementary election for the National Assembly, Legislative Yuan, and Control Yuan, thus broadening electoral participation to the national level. Five more national elections have been held since then, and the seats being contested have greatly increased. (For electoral data, see Chapter 7). Election regulations have also been drafted for every kind and level of elections. Some of these regulations (not laws) for local elections were drafted by the Taiwan Provincial Government and approved by the Taiwan Provincial Assembly. But the regulations governing central-level elections in 1969, 1972, and 1975 were initiated by the party and drafted by the National Security Council (NSC), an extraconstitutional institution set up according to the Temporary Provisions and bypassing the legislature. A Public Officials Election and Recall Law, which governs all elections, was promulgated in 1980 and revised in 1983; it was drafted by the Ministry of the Interior and enacted by the Legislative Yuan. In this case, the due process of enacting laws has been followed respecting the position of the legislature.

The rate of political participation in terms of the number of candidates to the number of contested seats, both within the KMT and among the nonpartisans, has increased manifold. Electoral turnout has steadily climbed, as people have become intensely interested in the electoral process and election results. Campaign rallies, complete with rousing speeches, have drawn huge turnouts, and campaign literature is eagerly sought out and read voraciously.

The KMT has also changed its nomination policies and processes. Originally, all KMT candidates were designated by a higher echelon. Later, the evaluations made by local cadres were taken into consideration. Beginning with the 1983 elections, "party members' opinion response" became the determining factor in nominating party candidates. Finally, the party held primary elections to nominate party candidates for the general elections of 1989.

The explosion of political participation has occasionally erupted into social unrest accompanied by violent demonstrations, such as the Chungli Incident (1977) and the Kaohsiung Incident (1979). These destabilizing events, however, did not deter the KMT from further broadening the scope of political participation. Since the lifting of the Emergency Decree in July 1987, many new social movements have emerged, street protests and demonstrations have become commonplace, and a participatory political culture has risen in the civil society (see Chapter 3).

Party Versus Government Role

While the KMT was still in control on the mainland, the guiding principle of the party-government relationship was to rule the state with the party, meaning the party's position was above the government. In the 1950s and 1960s, the principle was to guide politics by the party, as the party receded to the role of behind-the-scenes policymaking even though its dominant position over the government remained fundamentally the same. Since the Tenth National Congress held in 1969, the KMT has accepted the principle of separation of party and the government, and as a result the party has gradually become a policy coordinator rather than a policymaker. Members from the government sector and representative bodies have become the majority in the CSC and members from the party sector have become the minority. The institutionalization of the constitutional arrangement with a strong Executive Yuan (Cabinet) responsible to the Legislative Yuan has gradually taken shape.

It is beyond the scope of this chapter to explore the growing role of the legislature in policymaking (see Chapter 5). But one example is typical: The Labor Standards Law promulgated in 1984 was the result of protracted drafting, revising, and other legislative processes. KMT legislators representing management and KMT legislators representing labor argued vehemently for their points of view in the Legislative Yuan. In addition, the

Ministry of the Interior championed the cause of labor, and the Ministries of Economic Affairs and Finance spoke for the interests of management. During the whole process, the party played the role of coordinator or mediator between the two sides. The final law was a result of compromise. It is apparent that the party is gradually giving the legislature more leeway and more say in the decisionmaking process.

Interest Articulation

In the past, special interest groups were created, licensed, and subsidized by the KMT and the government. Gradually, their formation has become more spontaneous and their functions more autonomous. As economic development leads to further social change, new interest groups have mushroomed, such as those interested in consumer and environmental protection and in the prevention of public hazards (see Chapter 3). Many existing groups, including Chambers of Commerce and the Lion's and Rotary clubs, have become more assertive in articulating their interests.

These new and old interest groups have now become more active in their lobbying activities. As a result, the KMT and the government must provide additional channels for the articulation of these interests. The time is past when the KMT could claim to be the sole representative of diverse interests. In fact, the KMT has gradually been transformed from a corporatist system, in which major interest groups are incorporated into the system only to be controlled and mobilized to achieve the overall goals set by the party, to a pluralist system, in which the party's main functions are the representation and aggregation of diverse social interests.

In response to pressure from rank-and-file union members, as exemplified by the 1986 elections in which two KMT candidates were defeated by Democratic Progressive Party (DPP) candidates, the KMT and the government have adopted many liberal policies toward labor unions. For example, the ban on strikes was lifted, the four-level indirect election system for choosing union officials was changed to direct elections, and the formation of new unions, the unionization of workers, and the merger of small and weak unions into larger and stronger unions have been encouraged to make the unions more self-sufficient.

The governmental agency in charge of labor affairs has been elevated from the Department of Labor Affairs under the Ministry of the Interior to the Council for Labor Affairs directly under the Executive Yuan in order to provide better service to labor. It will soon be elevated again to the status of a full-fledged ministry. When all these changes are put into effect, labor unions will certainly become more independent and autonomous.

In response to a series of spontaneous student movements and protests that occurred recently at National Taiwan University, the KMT and the university authorities have adopted new policies toward student associations.

The president of the United Student Association will be directly elected by all students. The Regulations on Training and Guidance (which regulate extracurricular activities) will be revised to ensure the rights of assembly and association for teachers and students. Articles in student magazines will be reviewed only by teachers, and students can have original articles printed without revision. A Taiwan University Forum has been set up to allow students to deliver speeches on any issue without censorship. Finally, the KMT party office at the university has moved off campus. With many of these liberal policies already enacted, the university campus has already become much more free and democratic.

The Transition to a Competitive Party System: The Development of Interparty Democracy

The KMT's policy toward opposition has gradually changed from repression to toleration. In January 1989, it finally came to accept the legitimacy of new political parties through enacting the Law for Civic Organizations, under which political parties are subsumed.[13] As of March 1991, sixty-one old and new parties are reported to have registered with the Ministry of the Interior and have already received their certificates.

During its mainland period, the KMT adopted the policies of "no party outside the party" and "no faction within the party." It did not recognize the legal status of any other party until the war against Japan, and the country was organized as a noncompetitive party-state system. Before the lifting of the Emergency Decree on July 15, 1987, in Taiwan, only three political parties were admitted by the government, namely the ruling KMT, the Young China Party (YCP), and the China Democratic Socialist Party (CDSP), which came over to the island with the government in 1949. Although the latter two parties managed to have a few of their members elected in the first nationwide general election of 1947 to all three central representative organs (the National Assembly, the Legislative Yuan, and the Control Yuan), their combined strength came to less than 10 percent of the total membership in each of these organs. They were therefore unable to play an effective parliamentary role. Presently the YCP claims to have a membership of more than 10,000, while the membership of the CDSP is estimated at around 6,000. From 1960 on, they practically ceased nominating candidates for local, and later national, elections, and they seem to be perpetually troubled by factional infighting. The ruling party used to call them "the friendly parties," while critics have nicknamed them "flower vases in a latrine." Impartial observers doubt that these two parties can be successfully reinvigorated.

In the summer of 1960, a group of liberal-minded intellectuals headed by Lei Chen, a mainlander and former KMT high official who also published the *Free China Fortnightly* to bravely propagate liberal democratic ideas for some ten years, collaborated with some local politicians in attempting to organize a new political party, to be named the China Democratic Party. Even before the new party was officially born, Lei was arrested, arraigned on charges of harboring a Communist infiltrator and of propagating pessimistic ideas about the recovery of the mainland, and given a long prison sentence.

The institution of the supplementary elections for the national representative organs, starting in 1969, provided the stage for local dissidents to gradually combine and generate a new political force. Calling themselves the Tangwai (literally, "outside the party"), the opposition targeted one-party rule during election campaigns. When the 1978 supplementary elections were abruptly called off because of President Jimmy Carter's announcement of the US decision to terminate diplomatic relations with the ROC, the radical wing of the Tangwai movement, the Formosa Magazine Group under the leadership of legislator Huang Hsin-chieh, staged a series of anti-administration rallies across the island, culminating in the Kaohsiung Incident, or the Formosa Magazine Incident, of December 10, 1979. Some sixty participants in the riot were arrested, and eight of them, including Huang himself, two brilliant provincial assemblymen, and two female human rights activists, were subsequently tried in the military tribunal on charges of sedition and sentenced to prison terms of twelve to fourteen years. One of the eight, Shih Ming-teh, was given a life term.

The opposition movement seemed to have suffered a heavy blow with the cream of its leadership in jail. Yet when elections were resumed in 1980, the wives of the imprisoned politicians stepped in as candidates for the various offices and all experienced landslide victories. The stiff measures employed by the government unexpectedly turned out to be a great bonus for the opposition movement as a whole.

In the spring of 1984, those oppositionists who held elective offices formed the Association of Public Policy Studies as the coordination center of their movement. This was pronounced illegal by the government on a legal technicality.[14] And when the association decided in early 1986 to set up branches in the various cities of the island, the authorities became worried and declared several times that such action would not be tolerated. For a while it looked as though another serious political incident could erupt, but President Chiang adopted a more conciliatory attitude. In April 1986, he instructed the party's Central Standing Committee to study the ways and means to implement reforms in six critical political and social areas, and he hinted at the possibility of lifting the Emergency Decree and legalizing new political parties. In May he ordered his party's functionaries to "sincerely communicate (consult) with people from different segments of society."

Encouraged perhaps by the new atmosphere of liberalization and conciliation, the opposition began secretly to make the preparatory steps for the formation of a new political party. This they did, christening it the Democratic Progressive Party (DPP) on September 28, 1986, in a meeting in the Taipei Grand Hotel. For a moment the political atmosphere in Taipei was electrified with possibilities. But the authorities, although they claimed the new party was illegal, decided to do nothing drastic. (For more detail on the formation of the DPP, see Chapter 6).

Of the other newly formed parties, the Worker's Party has attracted the most newspaper coverage. It was organized on November 1, 1987, by legislator Wing Yu-hsiung, a former member of the DPP's central control board. It claims to represent the interests of Taiwan's 5 million workers, but it is doubtful whether it enjoys as much support as the KMT or the DPP among this important sector of the society. Recently some farmers have become restive and have hinted at the possibility of forming a party of their own. So far this has not yet materialized. Chu Kao-cheng, a famous former DPP "Rambo star," formed the Chinese Social Democratic Party in March 1991. Of the other fledgling parties, some may quickly disappear, and some may survive to decorate the facade of a multiparty system, but none is able to pose as significant a challenge to the KMT as the DPP.

As the standard carrier of the mainstream of the opposition movement, the DPP can count on around 25 percent of the popular support to win about 15 percent of the seats contested in national elections. The 1986 supplementary elections sent twelve DPP members to the Legislative Yuan and eleven to the National Assembly. But as these bodies are still manned mainly by old representatives elected forty-two years ago in the mainland, the DPP representatives come to only about 4 percent in the Legislative Yuan and a little more than 1 percent in the National Assembly.

Political scientists generally postulate that for the smooth functioning of competitive politics, a political system should not be bedeviled by unbridgeable cleavages. A certain acceptance of the system and some degree of consensus on the basic constitutional order should be secured among contending groups before they engage in presenting competitively their policy alternatives to the electorate. The situation in Taiwan is just the reverse. There are no significant social or economic policy differences between the KMT, especially its locally elected representatives, and the DPP. The cleavage pertains to a much higher political terrain. First, the current constitutional and legal structure that seems to warrant the continued rule of the KMT is relentlessly assailed by the DPP. Second, looming large in the consciousness of every concerned citizen is the potentially highly explosive issue of whether Taiwan must permanently remain a part of China (the KMT's unification stand) or perhaps become a de jure independent state if the majority of the inhabitants so prefer (the DPP's self-determination doctrine) (see Chapter 9).

On the structural level, the DPP demands prompt action in the following areas:

1. The Temporary Provisions During the Period of Communist Rebellion, which have the effect of suspending the working of certain articles of the republic's Constitution and greatly enlarging the discretionary power of the president, must be abolished immediately.
2. Immediate and total reelection for the central representative organs needs to take place. In other words, all old representatives elected in 1947 must retire within a definite time schedule, not on a voluntary basis, as the KMT had insisted.
3. The government should stop appointing overseas Chinese, who are not taxpayers, to the central representative organs.
4. The governorship of Taiwan Province as well as the mayoralties of the two metropolitan cities, Taipei and Kaohsiung, should be subject to popular elections.
5. Political neutralization of the civil service, the judiciary, and the military should take place.
6. There should be strict separation between the party (namely the KMT) and the government in personnel and finance.

The self-determination principle has been written into the DPP's political platform. But since open advocacy of Taiwan's independence is still illegal and subject to prosecution, this touchy issue is rarely debated in the legislature. It is reserved mainly for stump oratory during campaign times.

Over the past two years, many KMT high officials, including its chairman, President Lee Teng-hui, have repeatedly proclaimed that the party hereafter will play the role of a competitor, and no longer that of a dominator. In and out of the legislative hall, it has shown an admirable spirit not only of toleration but also of positive willingness to accommodate at least some demands of the opposition, as shown in the legislation of the recently amended Law of Election and Recall. Several times after stormy outbursts in the Legislative Yuan, leaders of the caucuses of the two parties are soon seen sitting together in a side room or over a hotel dinner to iron out their differences. If the steps taken so far to provide fair ground rules for a truly democratic and competitive system are deemed by some people as too cautious and tardy, the blame is not solely attributable to the KMT. If the opposition purposely or inadvertently continues to raise the cost of toleration for the ruling party, by threatening to jeopardize its survival and to undermine the very foundation of the system, it should also bear part of the blame.

The Future Role of the Kuomintang

The KMT completed an internal reconstruction program in 1950, labeling itself a "democratic revolutionary" party. Thereafter it gradually penetrated every sector of the society and has since maintained a firm rule over Taiwan. When the KMT convened its Thirteenth National Congress in July 1988, it resolved to keep the party's characterization intact in spite of repeated advice from more liberal circles to drop the word "revolutionary." How sincere then is the KMT in saying it opts to become a democratic party and a competitor? If the KMT decides, or is forced, to play the game fairly and honestly, how long will its present dominant position last? In the meantime, the internal structure of the party as well as its relations with the opposition, other social groupings, and the general populace have undergone substantial changes over the past two years. What will be its likely profile in the future?

In a purely formal sense, when new political parties can be formed freely and are free to engage in the normal activities of a democratic party, the system has already become competitive. Yet as long as the central representative organs are controlled by members who do not need to renew their mandates, and such powerful executive positions as the provincial governorship are not subjected to popular elections, the so-called free contest is a much circumscribed one indeed. The Legislative Yuan passed the Law on Voluntary Retirement of Senior Parliamentarians in early 1989. This law allows those senior parliamentarians elected four decades ago a dignified retirement after long service to the nation and ushers into Taiwan elected parliamentarians. The KMT soon after proposed a plan to urge their voluntary retirement in three stages within two years. The Council of Grand Justices also issued constitutional interpretation no. 261, which stipulates that the term of those senior parliamentarians shall expire by the end of 1991. From then on, all parliamentarians will be elected by the electorate in Taiwan and subject to reelection at regular intervals. The government also has announced that the governorship of Taiwan and the mayoralties of Taipei and Kaohsiung will be subject to popular election soon after constitutional reform is completed by the middle of 1992.

The KMT used to exercise tight control over all organized groups. However, this control has begun to crack recently. In the 1986 national elections, some of those seats reserved for and voted by the union members fell for the first time into the hands of the opposition. Also for the first time, KMT candidates for the reelection of union leaders of governmental enterprises tasted the bitterness of defeat. The workers now have their own party. Meanwhile farmers have staged a number of street demonstrations in Taipei, violently clashed with the police, and set up their own associations aside the government-controlled Taiwan's farmers' association. Liberal-minded college students compete in organized form against KMT protégés for student union offices. Teachers in most of the universities have inaugurated their own associations without prior approval from the KMT and independently of the administration. Party cells that used to be set up in every civic organization have gradually disappeared or stopped functioning. Evidently the KMT no longer enjoys a monopoly of power over the various functional groups in the society, and it has to assume the more modest role of a competitor.

In its inception the KMT was a revolutionary party. It created its own armed forces to achieve power and to stay in power. In the training program for the cadets in the military academies, the leader, the party, and the nation are purposely made conceptually indistinguishable from each other. At every hierarchical level of the military command, military leadership and party leadership are closely fused. The military always has representatives sitting in the highest organ of the party, the Central Standing Committee. This complete integration of the military within the ruling party accounts very much for the absence of military coups in Taiwan. This is a good thing in itself, but as long as this state of party-military relationship remains unchanged, the opposition has reason to be suspicious of the KMT's sincerity in implementing genuine democratization. Yet, when the DPP repeatedly trumpets its self-determination slogan, thus casting a long shadow on the all-important issue of national identity, how can one expect a military that has been incubated in a long nationalistic tradition to become politically neutral? Without a solid consensus on national identity, when the status of the nation itself remains unsettled, to which nation can the military be nationalized? We can thus predict that as long as the DPP harbors or is suspected to harbor the scheme of creating a de jure independent state of Taiwan, the KMT will cling to its intimate relationship with the military, and the military will do likewise.

Political parties in the democratic states, whether presidential or cabinet systems, after deciding on the planks and nominating candidates for elections, generally give the elected officials and representatives a free hand in carrying out their respective duties. Political power, for almost all practical purposes, resides in the hands of elective officials and party caucuses in the legislatures. But in the case of the KMT, all important and not-so-important policies (for example, the amount of annual income tax deductions) have to be decided first by the Central Standing Committee, the membership of which was handpicked by the party's chairman and is composed mainly of high-ranking political appointees. If legislation is required, party members of the Legislative Yuan are asked to fulfill the formalities. But now an increasing number of the locally elected members of the Legislative Yuan have begun to express objection to this customary arrangement. They organized themselves in small factional groups with the view of gaining greater influence and policy discretion through the legislature. They have justified their actions on the grounds that they had to face stiff competition periodically from other candidates and could not, therefore, disregard the sentiments and interests of their constituencies.

The party decided that it would employ US-style primaries in the 1989 supplementary elections for the members of the Legislative Yuan and local elections for the county magistrates. The elections were looked upon as of critical importance in view of the enlarged number of seats contested and the growing mobilization capability of the DPP. The party's intention is to progress further toward internal democratization, but this will undoubtedly affect party discipline. Some people speculate that the new practice of primaries may lead to the development of a factionalized dominant party like the Japanese Liberal Democratic Party. But from the perspective of party histories of other developing nations, it is possible that giving up the power of centralized nomination will result in weakening the party substantially.

In sum, the KMT has changed substantially since 1989. It has finally conceded the dissidents the legitimacy of an organized opposition, albeit some people may say its eagerness to appear as a competitor far exceeds its willingness to undertake the necessary structural modifications required for fair play. It has taken a conciliatory attitude toward all parties and has shown a high degree of toleration of sometimes caustic criticisms. The protection of citizens' constitutional rights, such as freedom of speech, assembly, and association, have been given more concrete form. Internally, the leadership is more responsive to the needs and suggestions of the rank and file, and hierarchical control has relaxed somewhat.

The transformation of the Kuomintang has confirmed both Huntington and Sartori's theories on the evolution of one-party regimes. The KMT has indeed transformed itself from an authoritarian and exclusionary party into a pragmatic and inclusionary party, and it has done so in response to socioeconomic development and the changing demands of the electorate. In association with the KMT's transformation, the political system has been gradually democratized (expanded participation) and liberalized (increased competition), and the one-party system has come to the threshold of a democratic and competitive party system.

As for political competition, the KMT elites have gradually come to accept it as not only inevitable but also desirable. As Taiwan's society has become more complex and diverse interests and groups have mushroomed, conflict, negotiation, and compromise have gradually become accepted values. In fact, the KMT has gradually become a party primarily concerned with electoral victory like an ordinary democratic party. It has gradually changed its view of itself; it has begun to act more like a competitor than a dominator in various elections.

The DPP has strong communal consciousness and local sentiment, thereby posing a real problem of integration. It appears as though the KMT leadership thought it better to channel the activities of the opposition forces toward electoral and parliamentary competition than to force them to street protests and demonstrations. As a result, the KMT has changed the emphasis on participation from its educative function to its integrative function. The KMT may also have thought that by giving the opposition a legal status its activities could be regulated by consensus as backed by legal procedures, and that the liberalizing and democratizing reforms could in the long run lead to a more stable political system.

The general elections held December 2, 1989, ranked as the most free, open, and fair election in China's history as a nation-state. It was the first election held after the lifting of the Emergency Decree and it was the first time that legally constituted political parties were pitted against the ruling party in a truly competitive, multiparty election. The electorate was quite well informed because of the robust state of the mass media in Taiwan. And the people made their voices heard; voter turnout was a high 75 percent of all eligible voters. As the result of the election, the KMT remains unmistakably the majority party, winning 60 percent of the popular vote and 70 percent of contested seats. The DPP secured its position as the major opposition party by winning about 30 percent of the vote. Independents running without party affiliation divided up the remaining 10 percent. All other minor parties failed the contest, with the exception of the Labor Party, which captured a city council seat.

Of the many democratic practices adopted in recent years by the KMT, perhaps the most significant was to hold primary elections in July 1989 for the December 1989 general election. The decision to hold party primaries for the first time in its ninety-five-year history shifted a large measure of its decisionmaking power from the upper echelons to the grass roots. Despite some shortcomings, by and large the primaries held by the ruling party were a successful test of intraparty democracy, a test that will help to transform the nature of the party from an authoritarian structure into a more democratic one. However, because the votes for the KMT candidates were reduced from its usual share of 70 percent to 60 percent, the KMT leaders considered the general election results the KMT's worst setback in forty years, and part of the blame was placed on the primary system. John Kuan, the chief architect of the primary system, was relieved of his posts as deputy secretary-general and director of the organizational department. Whether the KMT will continue to use a primary system in the future remains to be seen.

It must also be recalled that many of the vestiges of an old revolutionary party, which at one time hardly made any significant distinction between the state and the party, still remain discernible (see Chapter 10). Nor has its profile as the predominant political force in Taiwan been substantially changed. With its great socioeconomic-political resources garnered over the past forty years, one may safely predict that the KMT will be able to retain this predominance for at least a couple of decades, even as it gradually sheds its revolutionary mantle and as the society becomes increasingly pluralistic.

Notes

1. Samuel P. Huntington, "Social and Institutional Dynamics of One-Party Systems," in Samuel P. Huntington and Clement H. Moore, eds., *Authoritarian*

Politics in Modern Society: The Dynamic of One Party Systems (New York: Basic Books, 1970), pp. 32–40. Huntington makes a distinction between a revolutionary and an exclusionary party. The KMT demonstrated both characteristics of a revolutionary party and an exclusionary party in its inception period. Therefore, this chapter does not make the distinction.

2. Giovanni Sartori, *Parties and Party Systems* (Cambridge: Cambridge University Press, 1976), pp. 226–227.

3. The transformation from an "exclusionary party" to an "inclusionary party" that Huntington talks about is similar to a transition from Sartori's "one-party authoritarian" regime to a "one-party pragmatic" regime.

4. Sartori, *Parties and Party Systems*, pp. 43, 217, and 273–282.

5. The KMT is not the only party to make such a transition; Turkey has done so as well. But Sartori argues that the RPP underwent the transition because of external pressure—it did not transform itself spontaneously.

6. See "Inaugural of the Hsing-Chung Hui in Honolulu, Nov. 24, 1894," "Manifesto of the Hsing-Chung Hui of Hongkong, Feb. 18, 1895," and "Road of Progress—Dr. Sun Yat-sen's Message to *Min Pao* [People's Journal], Nov. 26, 1905," in the *Kuomintang Selected Historical Documents, 1894–1969* (New York: St. Johns University, 1970), pp. 1–12.

7. See "Manifesto on the Organization of the Kuomintang, Aug. 13, 1920," in ibid., pp. 35–39.

8. See "Manifesto of the Chung-hua ke-ming-tang, Sept. 1, 1914," in ibid., pp. 53–55.

9. For the differences between the cell and other basic elements of a party, see Maurice Duverger, *Political Parties* (London: University Paperback by Methuen, 1982), pp. 17–40.

10. For the distinction between titular and real leaders, see Duverger, *Political Parties*, pp. 146–151.

11. "Party Affairs Report," made by Secretary-General Chang Pao-shu at the KMT's Tenth National Congress (April 9, 1969). See *Ge Min Wen Hsien* [Revolutionary Documents], a compilation of important reports and resolutions passed by national congresses of the KMT (Taipei: KMT Party History Committee, 1978), no. 77, p. 313.

12. *Kuomintang Chien-chieh* [The Kuomintang: A brief introduction] (Taipei: Central Committee of the Kuomintang, 1984).

13. The only restrictions for the formation of political parties are now stipulated in Article 2 of the recently enacted Law for Civic Organizations: "Civic groups in their organization or activities may not violate the Constitution, advocate communism or separation of the national territory."

14. Under the old law of civic organizations, not more than one organization of the same kind was acceptable in an administrative district. Some KMT academicians, on learning the intention of the Tangwai politicians, promptly formed their own public policy study association and registered it with the Ministry of Interior, thus forestalling the action of the Tangwai and making it illegal.

CHAPTER 5

Liberalization, Democratization, and the Role of the KMT

CONSTANCE SQUIRES MEANEY

A large body of scholarly literature has developed on the topic of transitions from authoritarian rule.[1] The cases studied have largely been bureaucratic-authoritarian regimes in Latin America and southern Europe. Most typically these involve the removal or exit of military juntas and the restoration of civilian rule. The single-party rule of the KMT distinguishes Taiwan from these cases. It distinguishes Taiwan from Spain, a frequent subject in the study of democratic transitions, which had an entrenched civilian dictatorship but lacked a well-organized political party to survive the dictator.[2] It is not a case where the old regime's organizations retreat from political life (the military in Latin American cases) or dissolve altogether (franquist organizations in Spain). It is not a defeated power, as were Italy and Japan. The KMT expects to remain on the political scene, transforming itself into a competitive party that holds power via the ballot box.

What kind of an organization is the KMT? Throughout this chapter I use the terms "quasi-Leninist" or "Leninist-type party" to refer to the KMT. The party's structure and its relations with other organizations and the society resemble that of Leninist parties in the Communist bloc, despite obvious ideological differences. The party interlocks with the government at the top: the KMT party chairman and the president of the country are the same person. The Central Standing Committee (CSC) of the KMT, like a politburo, includes the top government officials. The party maintains cells within the main branches of the central government consisting of key administrators, who report to the KMT CSC.[3] Nomenklatura-like, all responsible officials in the bureaucracy belong to the party. The party maintains "transmission-belt" organizations such as labor unions and businessmen's and farmers' associations guided from the top down. As with true Leninist parties, the KMT's ethos is (or has long been) that of an elite leadership organization, not a representative party. In the words of one scholar, the KMT "may be second to none in the noncommunist world in its horizontal and vertical penetration" of state and society.[4]

Having noted this parallel, there are two aspects in which the KMT does not represent a true Leninist party. First and most obvious is the ideological difference. Not having a Marxist-Leninist ideology has political consequences (no doctrinal disposition against bourgeois democracy), economic consequences (absence of a commitment to a mixed economy and a central planning apparatus), and organizational consequences (absence of a party apparatus, on the scale of true Leninist regimes, that deals with cadre appointments). Second, the KMT has a strong "leaderist" orientation: an exalted leader-figure personally dominated the party throughout its history until the death of Chiang Ching-kuo in 1988.[5] Although this may represent an "un-Leninist" characteristic, it is one that has been exhibited to varying degrees by genuine Leninist parties in the Soviet Union, China, North Korea, and Cuba. Although the KMT has been as leaderist as any of these countries, the fact that there is no question of the party dissolving upon the passing of the Chiangs (unlike, for example, franquist organizations after Franco) suggests that a quasi-Leninist rather than leaderist designation for the party is appropriate. The leaderist qualities it does exhibit also make the KMT more comparable to a Leninist party than to a party like the PRI in Mexico that does not produce, or allow, such dominant figures.

The question I pose in this chapter is how a single-party regime of this sort complicates the transition from authoritarian rule. To address this question, I review some characteristics of transitions from authoritarian rule and make a distinction between the processes of liberalization and democratization, establishing indicators of both. On the basis of this I distinguish among (1) changes within the KMT that are progressive but not in themselves indicators of system liberalization or democratization, (2) indicators of system liberalization, (3) indicators of democratization, and (4) counterindicators to liberalization and/or democratization.[6] I argue that the existence of a single party as ruler increases the potential for the emergence of a hybrid regime, neither fully authoritarian nor democratic, that may persist for a protracted period.

Liberalization and Democratization in a One-Party State

A transition from authoritarian rule begins, Philippe C. Schmitter and Guillermo O'Donnell argue, when the authoritarian rulers "announce their intention to extend significantly the sphere of protected individual and group rights—and are believed." The announced intent to liberalize must be "sufficiently credible to provoke a change in the strategies of other actors."[7] Spaces for liberalized action then emerge. In these spaces, the "rules of the political game" are contested: "Actors struggle not just to satisfy their immediate interests and/or the interests of those whom they purport to represent, but also to define rules and procedures whose configuration will determine likely winners and losers in the future . . . which resources can legitimately be expended in the political arena and which actors will be permitted to enter it."[8] Liberalizing moves by the authoritarian regime and responses by other actors open the door to democratization. But power remains concentrated in the hands of the regime and a transition to democratic rule is not inevitable; indeed, at this stage liberalization may well be reversed.

When considering a chain of events that suggests the presence of a transition from authoritarian to democratic rule, a distinction must be drawn between processes of liberalization and democratization.[9] Some draw the distinction thus: liberalization refers to the loosening of restrictions on political activity and expression within an authoritarian regime, whereas democratization implies the construction of new institutions.[10] A slightly different emphasis appears in the analysis of Schmitter and O'Donnell, who define liberalization in terms of civil rights (such as freedom of speech and petition, privacy of correspondence, right to a fair trial, and freedom of press and association) and democratization in terms of political rights (the rights to vote and run for office). They note that historically there is a close relationship between liberalization and democratization, but they can exist separately.

This distinction between processes of liberalization and democratization accounts for the occurrence of hybrid regimes that are neither authoritarian nor democratic, which the authors attempt to capture with the terms "liberalized authoritarianism" (*dictablanda*) and "limited democracy" (*democradura*).[11] Liberalized authoritarianism (also known as "tutelary democracy") occurs when authoritarian rulers promote liberalization believing that "by opening up certain spaces for individual and group action, they can relieve various pressures and obtain needed information and support without altering the structure of authority, that is, without becoming accountable to the citizenry for their actions or subjecting their claim to rule to fair and competitive elections."[12] Limited democracy occurs if, after the institution of political competition has begun, old or new restrictions on the civil rights of particular individuals or groups are maintained.[13] In addition, there are degrees of democratization. For instance, conditions can be set that "restrict party competition and electoral choice, as with the banning of certain parties or fixing prohibitive standards for their formation, restricting admissible candidacies, rigging constituencies, or limiting means of party finance." Or, a "second tier of consultative and decisional mechanisms, such as autonomous parastate agencies, corporatist assemblies, and/or consociational arrangements" can be created to "circumvent accountability to popularly elected representatives by placing certain issues out of their reach."[14] In another formulation, Giuseppe Di Palma refers to both *dictablanda* and *democradura* as "halfway houses," the key feature of which is that in neither has a "democratic agreement" been reached by regime elites and their opponents. This lack of agreement can arise from resistance to the notion of democracy on the part of the regime and/or the opposition forces.[15]

These categories are especially useful when dealing with change in a one-party regime. Although a military junta may intend to create a "halfway house," a strong single-party organization makes it more probable that such an arrangement will be envisioned. A political party apparatus by definition would be more likely than the military to see itself remaining as a political actor in whatever system emerges from a transition. Thus there is an organization highly inclined to "restrict party competition and electoral choice" and/or to maintain a "second tier" of mechanisms that places issues out of the reach of popularly elected representatives. The second tier concept is particularly important when dealing with a Leninist-type party because the essence of such an organization is that it *is* a "second tier" or "parastate agency."

What Constitutes a Full Transition to Democracy?

Because liberalization and democratization are not so much successive phases but partially independent processes, it may be difficult to ascertain a point where both have progressed and merged sufficiently to constitute a decisive system shift. This would be especially true in the case of an authoritarian political party transforming itself into a more democratic one. When does it make sense, politically and analytically, to say that a qualitative transformation of an authoritarian regime has occurred? A useful perspective on this problem is offered by Adam Przeworski, who defines democracy not as a laundry list of attributes but as "a form of institutionalization of continual conflicts" in which "outcomes of conflicts are not uniquely determined . . . by the institutional arrangements."[16] He notes that in an authoritarian system, some groups (typically the army) can intervene whenever some outcome contrary to their interests or their program threatens to emerge. Thus, the process of establishing democracy becomes a process of "institutionalizing uncertainty, of subjecting all interests to uncertainty. . . . It is this very act of alienation of control over outcomes of conflicts that constitutes the decisive step toward democracy."[17] When the case involves a political party, and particularly a Leninist or quasi-Leninist party, it is especially critical to concentrate not only on the usual indicators of democratization, such as contested elections, but also on the broader constellation of formal and informal political arrangements that may indicate that the party has not "alienated its control over outcomes of conflicts."

Indicators of Liberalization and Democratization

Liberalization (following the Schmitter and O'Donnell definition) involves the creation of political space in which group and individual rights are exercised. It does not involve the ruling party "alienating its control over outcomes." For indicators of liberalization within the authoritarian regime, we would at least look for the relaxation of press censorship; allowance of meetings, protests, and demonstrations; and tolerance of criticism from citizens and opposition politicians. De facto and legalized forms of this both indicate liberalization; the latter of course implies greater commitment on the part of the regime. Departing somewhat from Schmitter and O'Donnell's civil rights/political rights distinction, I would also include under "liberalization" elections that permit choice among candidates but are structured to assure the ruling party's hegemony at the national level (thus no "introduction of uncertainty" for the regime). I will also include freedom to form political associations or parties under these circumstances.

For indicators of democratization one would, at a minimum, look for contested partisan elections. Actual alternation of parties in power obviously would be the best indicator that no party can be assured that undesired political outcomes will not come to pass. But alternation is not an absolute necessity for classification purposes, at least if one uses standards applied to other countries generally classified as democratic, such as Japan. In the absence of alternation in power, there would have to be elections in which the possibility of the dominant party losing is not institutionally prevented by various rules and limitations. One would want to be alert as well for informal practices that prevent regime defeat such as intimidation of voters and candidates and corrupt practices such as stuffing the ballot box, tampering with vote counting, and so forth.

Equally important, elected officials must have access to or influence over the real locus of decisionmaking. Otherwise the nonelected sector can still effectively put issues out of reach and prevent unwanted outcomes as it sees fit. One fairly obvious indicator that elected officials are in fact relevant political actors is an active rather than rubber-stamp legislative body. Another would be the removal of military and/or security-related organizations, by nature prime sources of veto power over outcomes, as occupants of key roles in domestic politics. Finally, in a Leninist-type party-state, we would look for disengagement of party and state organizations and officials. Two good indicators of this would be (1) transformation of important decisionmaking bodies from party or quasi-party status into state institutions, accountable to the legislature, and (2) elimination of the practice of officials occupying key party and state roles simultaneously.

In summary, for purposes of this chapter I will follow Przeworski and define democratization as the "alienation of control over outcomes for all groups and organizations." Indicators of such a condition are

1. political arrangements that permit party alternation in power at the national level (even if this has never actually happened)

2. an active legislative arena at the national level
3. an end to veto power over the domestic political process held by military, security, and/or leaderist elements
4. disaggregation of party and state organs and personnel

Transitional Politics and Liberalization in Taiwan

Against a background of the slow softening of the regime and increasing electoral activity by the opposition, a major departure occurred in September 1986, when the Democratic Progressive Party (DPP) was organized by the Tangwai politicians. This development came in the wake of indications that the KMT was considering major political reforms. Although such organization was still officially proscribed by the regime, the KMT did not crack down (as many expected it would) on the new party, which fielded candidates as a political party in the legislative elections later that year. Following these developments, in July 1987 the KMT lifted the martial law that had been in effect throughout its tenure on Taiwan. This event can be considered the equivalent of an announcement by the authoritarian regime that it intends to modify its own rules to provide a larger space for the exercise of individual and group civil and political rights.

The lifting of martial law opened the way for a further interactive process of liberalizing moves on the part of the regime and responses by politicians and public. These actions included the relaxation of restrictions on the founding of new newspapers and magazines and a glasnost policy toward formerly unmentionable topics. As Hsin-huang Michael Hsiao documents in Chapter 3, numerous groups took to the streets to air grievances—an activity that would have been quickly suppressed in the past. Meanwhile, the KMT began drafting legislation to govern political activities no longer prevented by martial law. This program included bills covering public demonstrations, election and recall, civic organizations (i.e., political parties), and retirement of old parliamentarians. The bill governing demonstrations was passed in January 1988 and the other three bills in January 1989. Much of this legislation was a focus of negotiations as well as heated confrontations between the KMT and the opposition, as would be typical of politics during a transition where the rules of the political game are being contested.

The formation of the DPP, the ending of martial law, the livelier press, the public demonstrations, and the KMT's legislation concerning rights and freedoms (as well as the battles over it) are all indicators of transitional politics and a process of liberalization. In short, the authoritarian regime announced an intent to liberalize, which was sufficiently credible for actors to change their political behavior.

Limitations to Liberalization in Taiwan

Although the KMT lifted martial law, it retained its "Temporary Provisions" (the Provisional Amendments for the Period of Mobilization Against the Communist Rebellion), which grant virtually unlimited authority to the president. At the opening of 1991, President Lee was planning to submit a proposal to lift the temporary provisions to a special meeting of the National Assembly in April. The end of martial law also saw the retention of some rather harsh provisions regarding sedition, which included advocating Taiwanese independence. The government was not loathe to act on these kinds of provisions in the ensuing period, which in turn kindled protest in varying forms. Two individuals were sentenced to ten- and eleven-year prison terms on sedition charges in January 1988. In December 1989, the editor of a dissident magazine, the *Freedom Era Weekly*, published a proposed new constitution for Taiwan; as a result, a warrant was put out for his arrest for sedition. When the arrest was attempted, he apparently committed suicide by torching the building. During a memorial service for the editor, attended by 6,000–8,000 people in front of the Presidential Palace, a DPP member committed suicide by setting himself on fire.[18] On Christmas Day 1990, 4,000 people marched peacefully to protest a ten-year sentence given to Huang Hua, a DPP leader and independence advocate, for committing violent acts during a demonstration earlier in the year.[19]

Protest appeared in a different form during 1990 than earlier, when relatively small demonstrations had expressed particular grievances. Huge protests took place that targeted more fundamental political issues, including a massive student sit-in protesting manipulations by aged parliamentarians and calling for constitutional reform in March and violent mass demonstrations against the appointment of retired general Hau Pei-ts'un to the premiership in May, which produced a major police reaction. These protests suggested growing impatience on the part of a large segment of the public with liberalization that fell short of full democratization, on the one hand, and growing willingness on the part of the police to crack down, on the other.

Other limits on liberalization include continuing KMT dominance of the media, despite the relaxed rules governing the press. Of Taiwan's three TV stations, one is linked with the KMT's Cultural Affairs Department, one with the military, and one with the Taiwan Provincial Government.[20] With respect to print journalism, the KMT directly controlled several major dailies and the owners of two of the principal privately owned daily papers were KMT-connected figures.[21] With the advent of the new "glasnost" policy, dissidents published weekly magazines with apparent ease, but leading DPP politician Kang Ning-hsiung's efforts to launch a daily in 1989 encountered difficulties in hiring and finding advertisers because people feared KMT retaliation.[22] With respect to retaliation in a different context, a Taiwan scholar notes the "personal inconvenience" that people in key professions may suffer as a result of joining the DPP and cites the case of a military officer who was "transferred to Quemoy after he had been discovered to be a member of the DPP."[23]

All of these limits suggest that liberalization is not unproblematic in Taiwan. Spaces for the exercise of political freedoms have emerged, but limits remain. On a behavioral level, the KMT and opposition changed their political behavior following the initial liberalizing steps, but neither could be said to exhibit a high level of trust in the other's intentions. Meanwhile, significant segments of public opinion appeared fed up with the government and/or with demonstrations, which contributed to a negative view of democratization as a threat to public order.[24]

Progressive Changes in the KMT

Before proceeding from liberalization to a discussion of democratization, I should note that concurrent with the systemic liberalizing measures of 1987–1988 was a process of internal liberalization in the KMT and a renewal of its higher organs. The party's Thirteenth Party Congress, held in 1988, was considerably more democratic than past practice. For example, for the first time in KMT history, nominees for the Central Committee (CC) were not all proposed by the party chairman. Instead, President and Party Chairman Lee Teng-hui proposed that half of the 180 members of the CC step down and nominated a slate of 180 candidates for the new CC. As a result, as many as 180 other candidates entered the race, "lobbying furiously for support among their colleagues in a way unheard of in the normally staid party parleys."[25] The congress also saw a shift toward young, Taiwan-born reformist and technocrat members in the KMT's top organs, detailed by Hung-mao Tien in Chapter 2 of this volume.[26]

Such trends in the composition of KMT organs and internal political processes were often mentioned in the same breath with democratization but properly should not be counted as indicators of liberalization or democratization of the system. Invigorating the membership of top party organs by the new party head after the death of a long-ruling leader is common in one-party regimes: it serves to rationalize or revivify the party organization and consolidate the new leader's position by surrounding him with his own supporters. Taiwanization in itself says nothing about the shape of systemic political institutions. With respect to a ruling party becoming more technocratic, such trends characterized the Communist party in the Soviet Union for years, long before the Gorbachev period, and in general need have nothing to do with democratization; indeed, the worldviews of the technocrat and the democratizer are often quite incompatible. With respect to democratic procedures within the ruling party, these also do not touch systemic political institutions.[27] Neither Taiwanization, technocratization, or "youthification" in themselves imply that the ruling party is disposed to alienate its control over political outcomes. Thus we must look elsewhere for indicators of system democratization.

Democratization in Taiwan

The December 1989 elections for seats in the legislature and various local offices were a milestone in that this was the first time that the KMT had competed at the polls with legalized rival parties. The DPP won twenty-one seats in the legislature, a gain of eight and enough to propose legislation, with an additional eight seats going to non-DPP opposition parties. The KMT won seventy-two seats. The opposition also made significant gains in contests for the Provincial Assembly and Taipei and Kaohsiung city councils and won some important county posts, including the executive of Taipei county. The KMT's vote count fell below its target 70 percent in all of the elections. Foreign poll-watching teams judged the elections to be reasonably free of irregularities.[28] That the KMT won a majority in the national election that was solid but not as large as the overwhelming victories often recorded by ruling parties in dictatorships suggests movement toward a genuinely competitive party system in which the KMT would participate as a democratic player. However, the situation remained "movement toward" democracy as distinct from the genuine article, which is defined as alienation of control over outcomes. This was so because of the continued occupation of parliamentary seats by aged officials elected on the mainland in 1948.

Party Alternation in Power

As stated previously, party alternation in power is a basic indicator that a democratic rule has emerged, but it is not absolutely necessary. If institutional arrangements no longer preclude parties other than the ruling one from achieving a parliamentary majority (or electing a president, if the system provides for one), we can with some caution assert that a threshold to democratic rule has been crossed. Such might be said to be the case with Japan. Although the LDP's long-standing rule is indeed assisted by institutional arrangements such as the gerrymander in favor of rural areas, there is little doubt that opposition parties would be allowed to form a government if they garnered sufficient seats in the Diet. By contrast, a system may be structured so that the dominant party is *guaranteed* a majority in the legislature regardless of opposition strength or unity. Such, for example, was the system implemented by the Leninist regime in Poland for its parliamentary elections in 1989. In Taiwan, guaranteed party dominance of the Legislative Yuan and the National Assembly, which elects the president and approves constitutional revisions, has been produced by the

KMT's claim to represent all of China and, under the Temporary Provisions, by the resultant freezing in office of the aged parliamentarians elected from mainland districts.

The KMT has acknowledged that the situation must be rectified and agreed in principle that all representatives should be elected from Taiwan. Implementing such a change was another matter, however, as it not only would remove the barrrier to a rival party defeating the KMT at the polls at some future date but also would raise the issue of the island's identification with the mainland. In January 1989 the legislature passed a bill providing for voluntary retirement for the old mainland representatives, eased by a retirement package equivalent to US $143,000 for each member. The DPP opposed this bill strenuously, calling for immediate, mandatory retirement and no compensation.[29] The KMT CSC then announced a gradualist plan whereby the "supplementary" (i.e., Taiwan-elected) seats would be increased in stages and total membership in the parliamentary bodies reduced. The Legislative Yuan, which as of mid-1989 had a little more than 300 members, would shrink to 150 seats, and the National Assembly, which had 1,000 members, to 375. This plan would have left about 50 old mainlanders in the legislature by 1992, while the National Assembly would have retained a contigent until 1998. Few retired, however. In March 1990 the oldster-dominated National Assembly attempted to extend its term of office, to assume the right to initiate and veto resolutions in the legislature, and to meet yearly instead of every six years.[30] This move was foiled and the retirement timetable subsequently shortened when Taiwan's High Court ruled that all the old mainlanders must retire by the end of 1991. Lee Teng-hui indicated that this order would be carried out. KMT ranks split over what should replace the old system of representation. Reformers within the party joined with the opposition to favor election of all members from Taiwan constituencies, while KMT conservatives wanted some formula for retaining "national" (representing mainland districts) as well as overseas Chinese seats in the legislature and national assembly.[31]

Limits to electoral democratization in Taiwan. As of early 1991, the KMT had yet to become truly competitive. It still could not be voted out of office in the national-level parliamentary bodies. In addition, there was the matter of the indirect election of the president by the National Assembly as provided for in the present system. It is generally assumed that it would be easier for the KMT to preclude the election of an opposition presidential candidate in this kind of body than in a general election. A constitutional change providing for direct election of the president was under discussion; neither Lee nor other party notables had given any decisive indication of this as a part of the plans for democratization.[32]

Two more items deserve brief mention here. First, the KMT repeatedly announced its intention to make the mayors of Taipei and Kaohsiung elective by 1989 but ultimately failed to make this change, apparently because it feared that either a DPP candidate or one of its own recalcitrant younger legislators would run and win. This sort of move raises some doubt about whether the party will stick to its plans for electoral reform if it appears that they might actually result in an opposition victory. At the July 1990 National Affairs Conference (NAC), most delegates favored election of these posts but some conservatives proposed that more city mayors, not fewer, should be appointed.[33] Second, a revised election and recall bill passed at the same session as the retirement bill in January 1989 was a move forward in that it finally permitted the DPP and other opposition parties to operate legally. However, the bill retained provisions prohibiting individuals convicted in the past on sedition charges from running for office. This had the effect of excluding from the electoral arena a few principal DPP leaders convicted in 1979, and DPP legislators were unable to prevail upon the KMT to change this provision.

In sum, the KMT thus far has succeeded quite well in opening up an arena for party competition without alienating its control over outcomes.

The Legislative Arena

Contested elections of course mean little if the parliamentary bodies elected are no more than rubber stamps. Taiwan's Legislative Yuan has moved away from the rubber-stamp role to become a significant arena of democratization. There are two dimensions to this shift: (1) increased legislative activism and (2) closer relations between legislators and society. The atmosphere in the legislative arena provides some counterbalance to the picture of tutelary democracy that emerges if one only considers the electoral system.

Legislative activism. Within the Legislative Yuan, the more activist trend is associated with the Taiwan-elected members of both parties. There were 74 Taiwan-elected members, 200 old mainlanders, and 27 appointed overseas Chinese representatives as of 1989.[34] The younger, more constituency-oriented members have divergent ideas from the old mainlanders about the proper role and procedures of the Legislative Yuan. The former enjoy more clout than their numbers might suggest, partly because of the KMT's desire to maintain an image of harmony and consensus. Taiwan-elected members who are actively critical of government policies and the status quo and those who engage in highly confrontational tactics with government ministers include both KMT and DPP members.

The Legislative Yuan has emerged as a forum for debate and lobbying the government for policy change, as well as aggressive questioning of government officials. In 1987–1988, both the opposition DPP and Young-Turk KMT legislators criticized the government and demanded action on a range of issues, including nuclear plant safety violations, the handling by the

Central Bank of foreign exchange reserves, and farm import policy, as well as the policy toward mainland China. The government began to relax its restrictions on contact with the mainland in response to pressure from legislators, businessmen, and the public in general. The KMT's Policy Coordination Committee holds meetings with KMT legislators to seek their support but often is not successful. The legislative body's eightieth session (winter 1988) was extended twice because of delays caused by filibusters, boycotts of deliberations by DPP legislators, and the shelving of bills for further consideration by younger KMT members. Both opposition legislators and KMT Young Turks have opposed cabinet-initiated bills. The KMT has also engaged in bargaining and compromise with DPP legislators in efforts to stave off DPP boycotts of controversial bills (also with less than complete success).[35]

By the late 1980s, legislative activism had become evident in the areas of interpellation of officials from the executive branch, budget revision, and the initiation of legislation. With respect to the questioning of government officials, in 1987 legislators made 3,744 interpellations on cabinet policies and measures—1,523 more than in 1986. However, it was also true that the cabinet failed to reply to a substantial portion of interpellations from the seventy-third through the eightieth sessions. To strengthen the interpellation function, Taiwan-elected members adopted a follow-up question method, taking turns in questioning to prevent evasion by officials.[36] Younger KMT legislators formed three "interpellation groups" as well as two intraparty clubs with oppositionists and independents.[37]

In the area of budgetary powers, the legislature cut NT $12.6 billion from the government's budget for fiscal year 1988. About NT $4.7 billion of the cut was in funding for national defense and foreign affairs. The Legislative Yuan had only reduced the defense and foreign affairs portions once before, in 1981.[38] In the same session, the legislature took an active role in altering the government's tariff reduction schedule. DPP legislators also succeeded in cutting NT $2.5 million in government payments to China Airlines.[39] An increase in legislative activism also was evident with respect to the initiation of legislation. In 1987, legislators initiated ten bills, two of which became laws; in the past, the Legislative Yuan had only reviewed cabinet bills.[40]

Legislators, popular pressure, and lobbying. Alongside these kinds of legislative activism, democratizing trends were also evident in the relations between legislators and society. One trend was an increased role for representatives as channels for citizen demands and grievance. In the past, if petitions from citizens were received, legislators transferred them to the cabinet for response. Reportedly, the number of petitions increased sharply in the late 1980s. Legislators began holding discussions with petitioning constituents and pressuring administrative departments to respond.[41] The

Legislative Yuan became the focus of citizen demonstrations calling for redress of grievances. After the lifting of martial law, numerous demonstrations began to be held by a range of groups, notably farmers, to put pressure on the Legislative Yuan to act.[42]

The Legislative Yuan also has played an increased role as an arena for interest pursuit in the form of lobbying. Lobbying and the formation of lobbying organizations were relatively new developments and are not uncontroversial, inside and outside of the legislative body. Although Taiwan-elected legislators reportedly thought it "perfectly normal" that interest groups would form, the older members tended to view it as "an abnormal thing."[43] Tariff-lowering negotiations held in 1987–1988 provide a good example of lobbying trends and the changing role of the Legislative Yuan. To further open the ROC economy, tariffs were cut on a total of 3,575 imported items, including automobiles, petrochemicals, garments, and machinery, for an average cut of 50 percent. A revised tariff law, passed in February 1988, was the spark for heated debate in the legislative body, which undertook revisions in the reduction schedule sent to it by the cabinet.[44]

A particularly instructive case involves the tariffs on automobiles. The auto industry in Taiwan has been highly protected, and there is a widespread belief that the industry is inefficient and has had undue influence in high places over the years. A government plan to make the auto industry more competitive, drafted within the bureaucracy in 1985, called for a schedule of tariff reductions for imported automobiles from a level of 65 percent to 30 percent in six years. According to this schedule, the rate would have been reduced to 50 percent by 1988. In December 1987, KMT and DPP legislators urged the cabinet to cut the auto tariff by 10 percent, rather than only 5 percent, to 45 percent. They chastised the government for protecting the "privileges" of the auto industry at the expense of the agricultural sector and consumers.[45] The accelerated reduction was vigorously opposed by the domestic auto industry and workers who feared the competition from cheaper imports.[46] Despite the opposition, in early 1988 the legislature reduced the tariff on autos even further to 42.5 percent, a 12.5 percent reduction.

The automakers' failure to block the additional reduction was partly a result of their failure to realize in time the increasing independence of the legislature vis-à-vis the cabinet and bureaucracy. According to a source within the auto industry, the industry did not realize it had a serious problem with the Legislative Yuan until early January 1988, after the tariff reduction debate in the legislature had been in progress for some time. Before that, automakers felt complacent because they had "good relationships" with friends in government. Their connections, however, were not in the legislative branch. The automakers belatedly began to cultivate friendships with legislators in January, but by then it was too late. According to a source in the auto industry, "The industry was too naive, they neglected what was going on politically. They didn't realize the Legislative Yuan's increasing power.

Everything has been changing fast here . . . the auto people didn't adjust themselves."[47]

Not all industry lobbying against tariff reductions was unsuccessful. Reportedly, some legislators quietly readjusted upward the duties on certain imported raw materials, including lead and zinc alloys, cellophane, sodium sulfate, and coke, under pressure from upstream industries. This occurred when the tariff bill went to the Legislative Yuan's joint finance and economic committee for deliberation. The cabinet's tariff reduction plan called for the tariff on these items to drop to 2.5 percent, but the lawmakers changed it to drop only to 5 percent.[48]

There are qualifications to the picture of democratic activity in the legislature. The solicitude of legislative support by the KMT's Policy Coordination Committee cuts two ways. KMT young-turk legislator Jaw Shao-kang has complained that the legislature's status in the ROC remains low in the political structure because "the executive branch of the government dictates to the Legislative Yuan through the party."[49] In addition to the failure of the government to respond to a significant portion of interpellations, younger legislators who favor more initiation of bills are hindered by an absence of legislative assistants. Older members reportedly think that a relatively small number of assistants is enough and, moreover, they should be distributed to committees rather than work for individual legislators.[50] Because the legislative committees are large—about thirty or forty people meet at a time and the memberships are not fixed or limited—such an arrangement is not conducive toward an activist legislature. Retirement of the older members should promote the trend toward legislative initiative.[51]

It is also worth noting that opposition to government bills in the legislature is not entirely new. In the 1950s and 1960s, before there were any Taiwan-elected legislators, the mainlander KMT members divided into two factions, one of which assumed the role of an "opposition," while the other always supported the cabinet's bills.[52] This previous behavior points to the fact that opposition to an authoritarian government's proposals within a legislative chamber can be a product of intra-elite factionalism rather than an indicator of systemic democratization.

In addition, some aspects of the Legislative Yuan's increased prominence are probably better indicators of liberalization within an authoritarian, noncompetitive party system than signals of democratization. For example, there is the question of physically aggressive or demonstrative actions (or "antics," as they are frequently characterized in the press) in the Legislative Yuan. To relate only a few of numerous examples, opposition legislator Chu Kao-cheng "jumped on the speaker's table, tore the cords off microphones, grabbed the gavel and pounded the podium with it in a fruitless effort to prevent passage [of] a controversial part of [a] bill governing demonstrations."[53] The passing of the KMT's retirement bill in 1989, which cleared with 108 of 139 present voting yes, occasioned a major uproar in the

Legislative Yuan. DPP legislators stormed the speaker's podium, after which "yelling and chaos" continued for about an hour. DPP members then stood on the podium waving a white banner in protest.[54] In December 1990 opposition legislators "hurled orange peel and smashed furniture" in the legislature when the KMT pushed through a clemency bill that did not include DPP leader Huang Hua and others.[55]

Tolerance of confrontational behavior in the legislature suggests a softening of the regime's authoritarian posture. However, a need to engage in "antics" and even violence within a legislative chamber is likely to be a product of long-standing exclusion. It would be more an indicator of liberalization within an authoritarian system—of "opening up spaces for individual and group action . . . without altering the structure of authority"— than of democratization. The same might be said for demonstrations outside the Legislative Yuan or elsewhere. These actions are significant as a sign of liberalization, but they also may indicate the relatively undeveloped nature of institutionalized channels for participation and political parties as effective vehicles for interest articulation.

Notwithstanding, trends in the legislative arena, taken together, are indicators of a shift toward increased influence for elected officials. There was movement away from a monocentric, nonaccountable system, albeit within a period in which the ruling party still cannot be voted out of power. It became more difficult for state bureaucrats to count on automatic approval of programs, as was the case in the past. A cleavage grew between the elected and nonelected parts of the KMT, helping to dilute its character as an elite cadre party.

How does rule by a single party relate to this democratizing trend? One-party states in general are more likely than military regimes to maintain parliamentary institutions to endorse the party leadership's policies and lend an air of popular legitimacy. The existence of these institutions can provide an arena in which democratic politics can grow, once liberalizing cues have been given by the regime. In this sense a single-party regime may facilitate democratization. At the same time, however, a well-organized ruling party is better situated than a military junta to manipulate these institutions from within, giving an appearance of democracy without the substance, namely alienation of control over outcomes. This situation sustains a mode of liberalization without democratization, which may eventually evolve into a stable democracy but also runs the risk of increasing public cynicism about political institutions and a conviction that backstage manipulators control everything.

Veto Groups and the Political Process

The most obvious form of veto over outcomes is direct military intervention in civilian politics, as in Latin America. In Leninist or quasi-Leninist systems, the party controls the military and security agencies; however, these organizations by their nature may become instruments through which a party leader dominates, or attempts to dominate, the party. Edwin A. Winckler's analysis of the KMT's "leaderist" character (see Chapter 10 of this volume) suggests this would hold doubly for Taiwan. A security-related agency responsible directly to the leader that regularly intervenes in domestic political processes would be one kind of counterindicator to full democratization. Another counterindicator would be occupancy of high positions in party and government by military figures.

Regularization of "leaderist" institutions. An agency worthy of attention in Taiwan's case is the National Security Council (NSC). The NSC is an extraconstitutional agency set up in 1967 by President Chiang Kai-shek under the Temporary Provisions to make policy decisions concerning suppression of the Communist rebellion. It is directly under the president. Members include the ROC vice-president, the military chief of staff, the premier and vice-premier, and the ministers of defense, foreign affairs, finance, and economic affairs. Although the NSC became less active after Chiang Ching-kuo became president in 1978, it continued to play an important and constitutionally undefined role in the political process. According to a recent study, the NSC has its own bureaucratic network and supervises the National Security Bureau, which plans intelligence and control work.[56] As of 1990, the NSC's secretary-general remained Chiang Wego, half-brother of late President Chiang Ching-kuo, who was appointed in 1986. General Chiang's predecessor was Chiang Hsiao-wu, the late president's son. During Chiang Kai-shek's presidency, the NSC played key roles such as drafting national election regulations in 1969 through 1975, thus bypassing the legislature (see Chapter 4). It retained a significant political role even as liberalization proceeded in the late 1980s. As of 1988, the NSC reportedly retained the power to approve central government policies and annual budgets.[57] In 1989, it was still involved in electoral matters. It was the NSC that proposed the schedule for rejuvenating the parliamentary bodies, which was then approved by the KMT CSC and then officially approved by the NSC.

An indicator of democratization would be an end to the NSC's autonomous role in domestic politics and lawmaking. Not surprisingly, the NSC's relations with the president are less close under Lee Teng-hui, with the familial tie no longer a factor.[58] In 1990 Lee promised to abolish the Temporary Provisions, under which the NSC was set up, within a year. Speculation was that this would result in the NSC being given a more regular status and made accountable to the legislature, which if realized would represent a good indicator of democratizing trends.[59]

Military figures in civilian politics. The appointment to the premiership of recently retired General Hau Pei-ts'un by Lee Teng-hui in the spring of 1990 raised questions about military influence in civilian politics and its implications for liberalization and democratization. Civil libertarians were distressed by the general's appointment, while massive protests by students and DPP supporters were the occasion for violent clashes between police and demonstrators. Adding to general misgivings about a military figure assuming the post of premier was the fact that the army under General Hau had appeared to swim against the liberalizing tide by bringing libel actions against opposition journalists, restricting DPP campaigners in garrisoned zones, and prosecuting DPP sympathizers in the military. However, there was the possibility that Hau's civilian appointment would separate the general from his military power base and ultimately contribute to democratization by "domesticating" its most powerful figure.[60] In any event, this rather ambiguous turn of events points to the possibility that liberalization of a party dictatorship without full democratization may open the door to increased military influence in domestic politics just as well as it can lead to a full transition from authoritarian rule.

Disengagement of Party and State

The organization of a Leninist-type party-state is complex and subtle; by nature it consists of a second tier of consultative and decisional mechanisms. The party typically controls or guides the state at the top not only in the sense that its leading bodies parallel and oversee state organs, but also through concurrent membership of officials in party and state bodies and the fact that responsible officals are virtually all party members. These relationships may be manifest in the practice of the same person occupying the posts of party chairman and head of government. The intricacy of the party-state nexus in Taiwan cannot be adequately presented within the confines of this chapter. It is worth noting that mainland China's version of Leninism is more informal and dependent on one individual wearing two (or more) hats than the Soviet version. This particular tendency is evident in Taiwan as well. Two indicators of democratization in the system would be (1) incorporation of party or quasi-party, suprastate decisionmaking or consultative agencies into the regular state bureaucracy and accountability of such agencies to the legislature and (2) elimination of practices whereby key officials wear both state and party hats.[61]

Party and state: The KMT CSC and the economic planners. As a case in point let us consider relations between the Central Standing Committee (CSC) of the KMT, the key economic planning agency, and the legislature. Here we will see (1) overlapping of party and state personnel and lack of a clear boundary between the two spheres, (2) the autonomy of a small, elite party-state nexus from elected officials' oversight (and to a considerable extent from the rest of the bureacracy as well), and (3) legislative efforts to end these arrangements.

Politburo-like, the thirty-one-member KMT CSC includes the top state officials. According to Ping-ling Jiang and Wen-cheng Wu in Chapter 4 of this volume, it is the highest and most important decisionmaking body in the ROC. It forms an inner circle that has vast power in screening and approving all important government and party policies and the power of nomenclature—naming political appointees to important government and party posts.

Despite its high status, the CSC as a body cannot be said to represent the real locus of decisionmaking. An example of this can be seen its its relations over the years with a core of influential economic bureaucrats. The CSC has been "captured" by economic bureaucrats since the mid-1970s: "Technocrats who . . . climbed up through the governmental bureaucratic ladder began to emerge in the late 1960s. They became a mainstream in the CSC in the mid-1970s and have dominated it ever since . . . the technocrats first captured the cabinet and then the CSC" (see Chapter 4).[62]

A Taiwan scholar with access to the CSC's meeting notes for the late 1950s and 1960s maintains that in the realm of economic policy, "the main task of formulating policy is left to elites in the state," leaving the CSC to play a passive role. The CSC has been something of a rubber stamp for the party-state's top leadership (i.e., the president or his second-in-command) and for top economic bureaucrats, who were the core members of the CSC.[63] In the KMT party-state, "the economic bureaucracy acted as a superministerial shadow cabinet" that submitted proposals to the cabinet that were "rarely dropped or significantly revised."[64]

The "economic bureaucracy," however, refers here not to departments under the Ministry of Economic Affairs but rather to an extraministerial body, the Council for Economic Planning and Development (CEPD).[65] For most of its history, the economic planning agency (that is, the CEPD and a series of predecessors bearing different titles) was technically an ad hoc organization that operated outside the state budget and normal civil service recruitment procedures.[66] It recruited its own staff, who were paid at a much higher rate than counterparts in the regular bureaucracy. There was a major overlap between the chairman of the agency and other state organs. For most of the time before 1977, the state premier and the chairman of the CEPD were the same person, as was true for Chen Cheng, O. K. Yui, C. K. Yen, and Chiang Ching-kuo.[67] The influence of the CEPD fluctuated according to the power of the individual serving as its head, which in turn was a product of his relationship to the top leader. Between 1978 and 1984, the chairman of the CEPD was long-time Chiang associate Yu Kuo-hwa, who concurrently served as governor of the Central Bank. Moreover, Yu served as chairman of the KMT's finance committee during this same period.[68]

A democratizing trend? Because of its independent budget and the high pay of its staff, the CEPD was long a target of complaints from within the government. The Legislative Yuan in particular pressed for oversight of the agency. Legislators criticized the autonomy of the CEPD and angrily confronted its chairman when he appeared in the legislative chamber.[69] In 1984, regulations were passed making the CEPD a regular part of the government. Its budget must be approved by the Legislative Yuan; prospective personnel must take the civil service examination and hiring must be approved by the legislature.[70]

Another change was that the CEPD chairman from 1984 to 1988 (Chao Yao-t'ung) did not serve in concurrent posts in the manner of his predecessors. During his tenure the CEPD's influence was somewhat diminished, as his appointment was seen as a kind of exile for a troublesome official. The higher status in party ranks of Frederick Chien, the CEPD's chairman appointed by Lee Teng-hui in August 1988 (and elevated to the CSC immediately before that) was seen by some to imply renewed influence for the agency. In 1990 Finance Minister Shirley Kuo replaced Chien, a move that again was seen as a kind of exile for a former minister. In any event, none of the newer chairpersons have worn the multiple hats of their predecessors.

The CEPD remains a target of criticism for being more an agency of the KMT than of the government. In the words of one Taiwan economist, the emergence of bipartisan politics implies that the CEPD "should play the role as economic adviser to the Executive Yuan, while the political parties should establish their own economic planning organizations."[71] Nonetheless, the change in CEPD status and leadership provides two indicators of democratization on a modest scale: increased accountability to the legislature and less wearing of multiple hats.

Limits to disaggregation of party and state. Moving from the level of bureaucratic agencies to the country's top leadership level, we see the long-standing practice of one person serving simultaneously as president of the ROC and as chairman of the KMT. In 1990 there was a move within the KMT to separate the two posts, a reform that proponents cited as consistent with the worldwide democracy wave, as indeed it would appear to be at first glance. The reform, however, was not implemented, and the affair suggests the subtleties that can be involved in apparent democratizing processes. The issue of separating the two posts emerged as the product of inner-party maneuvering between President Lee and conservative opponents, the arena for which was the KMT CSC. It was the latter who cited the worldwide democracy wave and who, fearing Lee's reformist, nonmainlander tendencies, wanted to "clip his wings" by separating the presidency and party chairmanship, thereby separating Lee from the chairmanship.[72] A similar issue involved a discussion within the KMT of linking the party chairmanship with the post of premier, thus moving toward a cabinet system of government. This proposal also was enmeshed with a move by Lee's opponents to reduce his powers, which Lee allegedly foiled by appointing General Hau as premier, thus pleasing conservatives while discouraging reformers from making the premier more powerful.[73]

Party-state amalgamation is much evident in discussions of constitutional reform. Lee has put reform on the agenda, but the body studying constitutional change is a KMT commission. After the March 1990 demonstrations opposing the old National Assembly members' "power-grab," the president promised to call a "nonpartisan" National Affairs Conference (NAC) to discuss fundamental issues raised by student and DPP demonstrators, including separation of party and government.[74] The NAC met in July 1990 and was a new phenomenon in bringing together a broad range of KMT and non-KMT people, but its role is not institutionalized and its recommendations are not binding.[75]

In addition to inner-party, but relatively visible, manifestations of party-state interpenetration, there is the even more sensitive area of KMT-government financial links. Opposition politicians have raised this issue vociferously and attempted investigations of such business links; some younger KMT legislators have been critical as well. Opposition figures charged that economic benefits accrue to KMT business enterprises as a result of government monopolies or favoritism. Moreover, they claim undue political influence in that the KMT enjoys an unfair advantage in elections because it is able to transfer virtually unlimited amounts of funds from its government-favored enterprises to its candidates' campaign coffers.[76]

All of this suggests that disengagement of ruling party and state in Taiwan is a complicated affair, politically and analytically. It requires subtle analyses to discern whether a threshold that amounts to alienation of control over outcomes by the KMT has been crossed.

Assessment of Taiwan's Liberalization and Democratization

Let me begin by simply listing the "nonindicators," indicators, and counterindicators of liberalization and democratization in Taiwan based on the foregoing discussion.

"Nonindicators" of systemic change
1. Changes in composition of a ruling party in the direction of Taiwanization, technocratization, or "youthification."
2. More democratic procedures within the ruling party.

Indicators of liberalization but not democratization
1. "Glasnost"-type relaxation on censorship.
2. Demonstrations, and regulations permitting them.

3. "Antics" in the legislature.
4. Elections that cannot result in defeat of the ruling party.
5. Formation and legalization of opposition parties, but under conditions that cannot result in oppostion majorities.

Indicators of democratization
1. More competitive elections, with legalized oppositition parties as of 1989.
2. Emergence of the legislative arena, including legislative activism and lobbying directed at the legislature.

With qualifications, we also will add
3. Regularization of extraministerial agencies (e.g., CEPD) and increased accountability to the legislature.
4. Some reduction in wearing of multiple state/party hats.
5. Plans to retire aged parliamentarians by the end of 1991, in compliance with the High Court's order.

Counterindicators of liberalization or democratization
1. Arrests and imprisonment for sedition.
2. Exclusion of individuals convicted in the past of sedition from running for office.
3. KMT domination of the media.
4. Career inconvenience of joining the DPP.
5. Retention of the mainlander parliamentarians and, to a lesser degree, various plans to avoid having all-Taiwan-elected bodies.
6. Decision not to elect mayors of Taipei and Kaohsiung.
7. Indirect election of president.
8. Continued interpenetration of party and state roles and functions, including
   • ROC presidency and KMT chairmanship held by same person.
   • KMT party organs or ad hoc commissions as the fora for discussing /deciding constitutional questions.
   • Party-government financial links.
9. Continued existence of a political role for the NSC.
10. Continuance of the Temporary Provisions, under which the NSC was founded.

And probably
11. Elevation of a military figure to premier.

An analysis of this kind by nature has a moving target for its subject. Some items most likely will have moved from the "counterindicators of liberalization or democratization" to "indicators of democratization" list in the near future, though there may also be reversion. Keeping this caveat in mind, let us return to our distinction between democratization and liberalization. Changes in the ROC as of early 1991 still add up to liberalization more than democratization. They create necessary but not sufficient conditions for a full transition from authoritarian rule to institutionalized democratic rule. It is not inevitable that liberalization will lead to full democratization, or that liberalizing changes granted by the regime will be maintained in the absence of full democratization. "Democratic rule" as defined here does not necessarily mean "Western-style democracy" with party alternation in power (indeed not all "Western-style democracies" exhibit this characteristic).[77] It does at least imply "Japanese-style democracy," in which opposition parties have the potential to form a government. This, and other changes that would represent the alienation of control over outcomes by the ruling KMT, remain future possibilities. The ambiguities of the KMT's position on democratization in the early 1990s was nicely captured (perhaps unintentionally) by a correspondent who reported that the KMT was trying to "engineer a transition to democracy which neither violates constitutional procedures nor endangers one-party rule."[78]

What does the discussion suggest about Taiwan as a case of transition from authoritarian rule, regardless of what happens to our list of indicators in the immediate future? Comparing the situation in Taiwan to the regimes studied in the literature on transitions, the potential for a halfway house of liberalization without full democratization appears high. The KMT sees itself as a natural political player and has no professional role into which it might retire, as would a military. Moreover, the party has experience in competing in elections, and it has financial resources unavailable to its rivals and hegemony if not monopoly over the media. It is intertwined with the state bureaucracy, in particular the powerful economic bureaucracy. It has motives to liberalize and up to a point democratize (in particular, a desire to project a progressive image to the world, and present an alternative to the mainland, and an ideology that sees eventual democratization as a goal) regardless of opposition pressure. But it is not clear that the KMT is in a crisis such that it will be pressed to extricate itself by trespassing into democracy as a solution, as Di Palma puts it.[79] Whether such a crisis is a necessary condition for a decisive abandonment of authoritarian rule remains to be seen.

Notes

1. See especially Guillermo O'Donnell, Philippe C. Schmitter, and Laurence Whitehead, eds., *Transitions from Authoritarian Rule*, 4 vols. (Baltimore: Johns Hopkins University Press, 1986).

2. An analysis of the Spanish case appears in Donald Share, "Transitions to Democracy and Transitions Through Transaction," *Comparative Political Studies* 19 (4) (January 1987), pp. 525–548.

3. See Hung-mao Tien, *The Great Transition: Political and Social Change in the Republic of China* (Stanford, Calif.: Hoover Institution Press, 1989), p. 89.

4. Ibid., pp. 250–251.

5. See Edwin Winckler's comments in Chapter 10.

6. An exhaustive treatment of this democratization in Taiwan and changes in the role of the KMT would require attention to local-level politics and the KMT's grass-roots-level organization. Here the focus will be on developments at the national level.

7. Guillermo O'Donnell and Philippe C. Schmitter, "Defining Some Concepts (and Exposing Some Assumptions)," in *Transitions*, ed. O'Donnell et al., vol. 4, *Tentative Conclusions About Uncertain Democracies*, pp. 6–14, esp. pp. 10–11.

8. Ibid., p. 6.

9. See discussion in Adam Przeworski, "Some Problems in the Study of Transition to Democracy," in *Transitions*, ed. O'Donnell et al., vol. 1, pp. 47–63, esp. p. 56.

10. For example, see Share, "Transitions to Democracy," pp. 527–528.

11. O'Donnell and Schmitter, "Defining Some Concepts," p. 9.

12. Ibid.

13. Ibid.

14. Ibid.

15. Giuseppe Di Palma, *To Craft Democracies: An Essay on Democratic Transitions* (Berkeley: University of California Press, 1990), pp. 154–155.

16. Przeworski, "Some Problems," p. 58. Compare Schmitter and O'Donnell's formulation of a "procedural minimum" of elements including "secret balloting, universal suffrage, regular elections, partisan competition, associational recognition and access, and executive accountability." "Defining Some Concepts," p. 8. A problem with this is that all of these procedures could be present without a regime truly "alienating its control over outcomes."

17. Przeworski, "Some Problems," p. 58.

18. See *Taipei International Service* (April 9, 1989) in *FBIS* (Foreign Broadcast Information System) (April 19, 1989), p. 70; *Asiaweek* (April 21, 1989), p. 23; *New York Times* (May 20, 1989); and the *Far Eastern Economic Review* (*FEER*) (June 1, 1989), p. 20.

19. *FEER* (January 10, 1991), p. 12.

20. *Asian Wall Street Journal* (*AWSJ*) (July 11, 1988), p. 1.

21. See Tien, *Great Transition*, pp. 197–198.

22. Interview with DPP politician, March 1989.

23. Lu Ya-li, Chapter 6; and Tien, *Great Transition*, p. 16. The military denied that the case involved anything other than a routine transfer.

24. By 1990 the populace had taken to calling the old parliamentarians "old thieves" and the student protest directed at them received considerable sympathy. *FEER* (March 29, 1990), p. 34. On the other hand, a year later, General Hau's popularity with the public reportedly had soared as a result of his law-and-order stance. *FEER* (January 10, 1991), p. 12.

25. *AWSJ* (July 18, 1988), p. 1.

26. Native Taiwanese representation on the KMT Central Committee went from 17 percent to about 40 percent. Three-fifths of the committee members were new, and the average age went from seventy to fifty-nine. *AWSJ* (July 11, 18, and 25, 1988).

27. Conversely, competitive parties in a democratic system can be internally undemocratic (for instance, both major parties in Britain).

28. *FEER* (December 14, 1989).

29. The KMT predicted that about half of the old mainlander representatives from its three parliamentary bodies would retire before the end of 1989. *China*

News Agency, Taipei, in *FBIS* (January 30, 1989), p. 76. When a mainlander representative retires or dies, the seat is eliminated.

30. *FEER* (March 29, 1990).

31. *FEER* (July 19, 1990).

32. *FEER* (January 10, 1991).

33. *FEER* (July 19, 1990).

34. Tien, *Great Transition*, p. 146 (chart).

35. See *China Post*, Taipei (*CP*) (December 2, 1987, and January 4 and 22, 1988).

36. *CP* (January 4, 1988). The most unanswered questions concerned agriculture and fishery followed by the military and defense, foreign policy and economics, and trade. *CP* (March 29, 1988).

37. *CP* (March 31, 1988). The three interpellation groups were the "Twelve-Person Interpellation Club," the "Five-Person Joint Interpellation Club," and the "Fourteen-Person Joint Interpellation Club." The first two were all KMT. The third group had two KMT members and two independents. The two intraparty clubs were the "DC Club" and the "Sea Dragon Club" and included KMT, DPP, and Labor Party members. They were formed to "promote friendship between the rival parties." *CP* (February 29, 1988). A group of Taiwan-elected legislators also visited the United States and formed a club with US congressmen. *CP* (March 27, 1988). Tien (*Great Transition*, pp. 148–150) discusses the unsuccessful attempts of the Taiwan-elected members prior to 1988 to form factionlike groups to counter those of the old mainlander legislators.

38. About two-thirds of the total cut resulted from exchange rate differences but it was still much larger than the NT $1.19 billion cut from the 1987 budget. *CP* (January 4, 1988).

39. *AWSJ* (July 11, 1988), p. 1. The ownership of China Airlines is a source of speculation; it is consistently rumored to be connected with the Chiang family.

40. *CP* (January 4, 1988).

41. Ibid.

42. Interview with Taiwan-elected (1969) KMT legislator.

43. Ibid.

44. *CP* (December 13, 1987).

45. Ibid.

46. Two thousand workers from Taiwan's six major auto manufacturers also petitioned the Legislative Yuan against the reduction. *CP* (January 9, 1988).

47. Interview with auto industry source, March 1988.

48. *CP* (February 2, 1988).

49. *CP* (February 9, 1988). See discussion of the role of party branches in the legislature in Tien, *Great Transition*, p. 89, which supports this view.

50. Interview with auto industry source, March 1988.

51. In the winter of 1988 the Legislative Yuan planned to request an NT $41 million budget for fiscal 1989 to enable them to draft laws on their own. Unnamed sources said at the time that the Cabinet would probably agree but might trim the amount. *CP* (February 2, 1988).

52. Pang Chien-kuo, "The State and Economic Transformation: The Taiwan Case," (Ph.D. diss., Brown University, 1988), p. 49.

53. *CP* (January 9, 1988).

54. *China News Agency*, Taipei in *FBIS* (January 30, 1989), p. 76.

55. *FEER* (January 10, 1991).

56. See Tien, *Great Transition*, pp. 109–111. See also Winckler, "Taiwan

Politics in the 1990's," pp. 25–26; and Thomas Gold, *State and Society in the Taiwan Miracle* (Armonk, N.Y.: M. E. Sharpe, 1986), p. 62.

57. *Economic Daily News*, Taipei (reprinted in *CP*, January 21, 1988).

58. Chiang Wego was not nominated for the party CC by Lee Teng-hui in June 1988, which observers saw as a sign of decreased influence for the general. *AWSJ* (July 18, 1988). See also Tien, *Great Transition*, p. 110. See also Chiang's role during 1990 inner-party presidential manuevering: *FEER* (March 1, 1990).

59. See *FEER* (February 22, 1990).

60. *FEER* (May 17, 1991).

61. Reformist Leninist regimes (Deng, Gorbachev) typically set themselves the task of separating party and state. The goal is to make the system more efficient and to restrict the party's role to broad policy formulation and supervision. One must be careful not to equate rationalization with liberalization or democratization in the absence of other conditions (such as legislative accountability).

62. Pang, "The State," p. 39. In the past, the CSC has also been on the verge of "capture" by military-security types: between 1981 and 1983 a group headed by General Wang Sheng became the "de facto center of power" in the CSC. See Tien, *Great Transition*, p. 81. Since the succession of Lee Teng-hui, people who attend its meetings reportedly say that the Cabinet (which meets on Thursdays) rubber-stamps decisions already made in the CSC (which meets on Wednesdays). *AWSJ* (July 18 and 25, 1988). This may indicate that the CSC has become more coherent as a policymaking body under Lee's presidency but could also be the product of continuing concentration of power in the hands of the top leader and his closest advisers, who sit both in the Cabinet and the CSC.

63. Pang, "The State," pp. 36–39 and 46–48.

64. Ibid., p. 41.

65. The planning agency is sometimes viewed as the ROC's closest counterpart to Japan's MITI in its influence on economic policy functioning—a kind of "economic general staff." It formulates long-term economic plans and coordinates, follows up, and evaluates plan implementation. Ibid., pp. 36–39, 41, 46–48.

66. In the 1950s, the KMT created a number of ad hoc, supraministerial organizations to utilize US aid and develop the economy, of which one was the economic planning agency. Originally, it was financed by US aid. When aid ended in the 1960s, the planning agency retained its special status and was financed partly by a "Sino-American Fund for Economic and Social Development," which kept it out of the government budget. The present CEPD was formed in 1977. Interviews wih CEPD officials and Pang, pp. 32–40.

67. Pang, in *CP* (January 9, 1988), pp. 192–195.

68. *AWSJ* (July 11, 1988), p. 1.

69. For example, one legislator confronted then-CEPD chairman Yu Kuo-hwa and shouted that he was just from an "underground organization" and "could be arrested." Interview with CEPD official.

70. Pang, "The State," p. 41.

71. Dr. Liu Tai-ying, Chairman of the Taiwan Economics Research Institute, quoted in *CP* (January 21, 1988).

72. *FEER* (March 8 and 15, and May 31, 1990).

73. *FEER* (March 22, 1990).

74. *FEER* (March 29, 1990).

75. Legislators were not invited to the NAC. After it met, they voted that a legislative committee rather than a panel of presidential appointees should be empowered to implement the NAC recommendations for political/constitutional reform. *FEER* (July 19, 1990).

76. "KMT Business Empire Assailed as Democracy Takes Hold on Taiwan," *AWSJ* (July 11, 1988), p. 1.

77. For example, see Joseph LaPalombara's discussion of single-party hegemony in Italy in *Democracy Italian Style* (New Haven, Conn.: Yale University Press, 1987).

78. *FEER* (January 10, 1991).

79. Di Palma, *To Craft Democracies.*

CHAPTER 6

Political Opposition in Taiwan: The Development of the Democratic Progressive Party

ALEXANDER YA-LI LU

The establishment of the Democratic Progressive Party (hereafter DPP) on September 28, 1986, is one of the most significant events in Taiwan's political evolution.[1] Despite the fact that organized political opposition had been active since the mid-1970s, when a number of non-Kuomintang politicians formed the Tangwai to coordinate campaigns, the founding of the DPP is still important, primarily for two reasons. First, it marks the end of the ban on new political parties imposed in 1949 and the end of martial law, and second, it means the formation of a more cohesive and effective opposition to challenge the ruling Kuomintang's (KMT's) monopoly on power.

The emergence of the DPP as the outcome of the gradual democratization of the polity and modernization of the economy and society of Taiwan has received much scholarly and journalistic attention, but the role of the party (and prior to 1986 that of the Tangwai) as a force for democratization has not attracted as much interest.[2] The main issue addressed in this chapter is the role of the opposition in Taiwan's political development and democratization. Additionally, an attempt will be made to analyze the DPP in terms of its social base, ideology, and organizational structure as well as the problems that the new party faces. The chapter is divided into four parts. The first part is devoted to a brief account and analysis of the emergence and evolution of the DPP. The second part discusses the role of the DPP in Taiwan's democratization. In the third part, the ideology, organizational structure, social base, and problems of the new party are analyzed. The conclusion assesses the future prospects of Taiwan's party system.

Emergence and Evolution of the DPP

Prior to the early 1970s, organized political opposition with genuine mass support did not exist in Taiwan. Oppression by means of martial law made

121

the formation of political opposition a risky venture for those who made the attempt. The absence of a participatory political culture in a predominantly agrarian society further reduced the possibility of liberalization, because there was very little popular demand or pressure for enlarging the scope of political participation.[3] The fact that national parliamentary elections were suspended from 1949 until 1969 further hampered the evolution of an opposition party, as there was little incentive for non-KMT politicians to launch a movement to reach such a goal.

Lei Chen's attempt to form an opposition party in 1960 might suffice to illustrate the difficulties of such an endeavor. Lei, the founder and editor of the influential liberal journal the *Free China Fortnightly*, attempted to rally the handful of liberal intellectuals of mainlander origin associated with his journal and the dissident local politicians of Taiwanese origin to form a new party in early 1960. For this purpose, he formed an informal association whose ostensible objective was to study ways and means to improve the electoral system and to work for the correction of the many abuses of the election administration; its real aim was to serve as the core for the new party. The China Democratic Party was scheduled to be announced in mid-September. On September 4, 1960, Lei was arrested, charged with giving aid to a Communist agent and sentenced to ten years of imprisonment by a military tribunal. The arrest of Lei caused some prominent intellectuals to criticize the authorities, but otherwise it did not produce any ripple upon the surface of Taiwan's political life. Thus ended the only serious attempt to form an opposition party before the emergence of the DPP.

Observers are in general agreement that the Tangwai movement has been able to survive and prosper, and eventually become a political party, because of the economic and social modernization of Taiwan (see Chapter 2). As a result of rapid economic development and social change during the previous two decades, Taiwan already had a sizable "new" middle class by the 1970s and a literate urban working class. The new middle class is important to the opposition for three reasons. First, the leadership of the opposition are without exception members of the new middle class. The educational and occupational background of the DPP leadership is shown in Table 6.1.

The second reason that the new middle class is important to the opposition is that the Tangwai (and the DPP) draw many of their activists and supporters from the new middle class. Until now, the opposition has been mainly an urban phenomenon. Of the 20,000 members of the DPP, over 2,000 reside in the city of Taipei. The influence of the opposition in the rural area is still insignificant. In the cities, the public employees are staunch supporters of the KMT; the majority of the business community also tend to side with the ruling party, though the opposition draw some activists from young businesspeople of Taiwanese origin. Among intellectuals and professionals, the opposition is more popular, particularly its more moderate wing.

Table 6.1 Educational and Professional Background of the DPP Leadership

Education		Profession	
high school	3	legal	9
college	20	teaching	3
graduate	8	editing and	
		writing	2
		medical	2
		business	4
		politician	6
		minister	1
		other	4

Source: Democratic Progressive Party Weekly [Min-ch'ing Pao Chou-k'an] (October 15, 1987). Figures are derived from data about the members of the executive committee elected by the Second DPP Congress.

Third, the very nature of the new middle class gives an advantage to the opposition. The new middle class is composed mainly of intellectuals, professionals, and businesspeople who are different from the "old" middle class in three respects. First, they are much younger, better educated, and more Westernized in their values and attitudes. Second, the old middle class is mainly composed of public employees and shopkeepers who are either politically passive or are unconditional supporters of the ruling regime; the new middle class comprises a more diverse group that is generally more critical of the status quo. Finally, the majority of the new middle class are of Taiwanese origin, whereas among the public employees there are many mainlanders. Many members of the new middle class may not support the opposition, but they do believe that it has a useful role to play and at least has the right to exist. The moral support rendered by the new middle class is indispensable for the opposition. Apart from the new middle class, the literate urban working class is also very important to the opposition. This class, composed mainly of factory workers and service personnel such as cab drivers, salespeople, as well as other categories of the urban poor such as peddlers, are among the most loyal voters of opposition candidates and are enthusiastic participants in the activities sponsored by the opposition.

The opposition movement, which started in the early 1970s, has adopted three main strategies: (1) the formation of an organization to coordinate electoral campaigns of the dissident politicians, to serve as the core of an opposition party, (2) the magazine movement, and (3) the mass movement. Throughout the 1970s, the first two strategies were employed. The third strategy was used only by the end of the decade, and then with disastrous consequences. Recently, the mass strategy has again been employed more frequently.

In 1969, the authorities, with a view to filling the seats vacated by deceased members of the national parliament, instituted the system of supplementary elections.[4] Although only a small number of seats were contested then, the intense campaign convinced some non-KMT politicians that some sort of organization was essential in order to compete effectively with the well-organized KMT candidates. In the 1977 local election, the term "Tangwai" was used by the media to refer to the handful of non-KMT candidates who then made the attempt to coordinate their campaigns.[5] In that election, the Tangwai won twenty-two seats in the seventy-seven-member Taiwan Provincial Assembly and four out of twenty mayor or country magistrate posts. Such impressive results convinced them that time was ripe for organizing an opposition party. In 1978, they formed the Tangwai Campaign Corps (Tang-wai chu hsuan t'uan) to coordinate the campaigns of all non-KMT candidates in the supplementary election of that year.

After 1977 and 1978, the Tangwai movement gathered momentum, and some Tangwai politicians, such as Huang Hsin-chieh, Shih Ming-teh, and Yao Chia-wen, decided to launch a new party in defiance of the party ban. To achieve this objective, they founded the *Formosa (Mei-li Tao)*, both as an instrument to propagate their political ideas and as an organizational core for a new party. This attempt to form a new party was temporarily thwarted by the occurrence of the Kaohsiung Incident.

The Kaohsiung Incident of December 10, 1979, is probably the most important event in Taiwan's political development before the founding of the DPP. We will explore its implications, but before that, let us discuss briefly the magazine movement.

Because of the newspaper ban and the KMT control of the electronic media, the opposition was forced to rely upon magazines and the spoken word to propagate their political ideas throughout the 1970s and the first part of the 1980s until the lifting of the ban on newspapers in 1987. The importance of the magazine to the opposition was not merely as an instrument for propaganda, but also as an organizational network and a tool to be used for recruitment. In other words, a large and well-financed magazine might be a substitute for the core of a political party. Such being the case, Tangwai figures attached great significance to having their own magazines.

The founding of the magazine *Taiwan Political Review (T'ai-wan Chen-lun)* by Huang Hsin-chieh and Chang Chun-hong in 1975 is of special significance in an account of the evolution of the opposition. Some observers tend to regard this event as the start of the Tangwai movement. Although the magazine was banned by authorities within one year of its publication, its impact is very great. The quality of articles in the *Taiwan Political Review* is usually high; therefore the appearance of such a vehicle not only gave the opposition an effective tool to influence the new middle class, but it also convinced the general society that it was a responsible group deserving respect from the authorities. Moreover, the magazine subjected the political system and policies of the authorities to searching scrutiny and criticism in terms of democratic values, and thus it undermined somewhat the moral authority of the ruling group.

In addition to the *Taiwan Political Review*, several other Tangwai magazines appeared in the 1970s. These magazines were usually founded and owned by different Tangwai figures and reflected the owners' personal views on issues.[6] Until the appearance of the *Formosa*, there was no periodical to serve as the organ of the entire opposition. Most of these magazines had a small readership and thus were in a rather precarious financial position. In order to maintain themselves in the market, they had to carry many articles whose purpose was solely to discredit the authorities. To expose the seamy side of the private lives of high officials thus became a major preoccupation of these magazines; to express and propagate the political views of the Tangwai figures assumed a secondary position. The KMT authorities attempted to contain the damage inflicted upon their prestige by these magazines by means of two methods: censorship by the Taiwan Garrison Command and trial of certain more daring writers and publishers in courts for libel. Both these methods proved not only ineffective, but costly in terms of the public image of the regime.[7]

The motivation for the founding of the *Formosa* has already been mentioned. Unlike other Tangwai magazines, the *Formosa* attempted to represent the entire opposition. In fact, with the exception of Kang Ning-hsiang, almost all important Tangwai figures were included in its editorial board. In addition to its main office in Taipei, the *Formosa* set up various branch offices in many cities and small towns. All these offices were used as meeting places for the readers. Throughout the entire year of 1979, mass protest activities organized by the *Formosa* were carried out all over Taiwan.

To a large extent, the Kaohsiung Incident was the culmination of a long period of dissent. As a consequence of feverish activities of the Tangwai movement sponsored by the *Formosa*, clashes and skirmishes between the police and the Tangwai were frequent. On December 10, 1979, a large demonstration sponsored by the *Formosa* was held in Kaohsiung, the second largest city in Taiwan, to celebrate International Human Rights Day and protest against the authorities' alleged abuse of human rights. Violence broke out during the demonstration and 183 policemen were injured. Few demonstrators were hurt because the police were under instructions to not react with force. Some argued that the authorities simply employed the police to set up a trap for the Tangwai leaders to fall into in order to find an excuse to crush the opposition movement; some argued that certain hooligan elements infiltrated into the Tangwai movement and caused the riot, and the Tangwai leaders were not experienced enough to handle the situation. No matter what the truth is, the upshot is that more than 100 Tangwai leaders were arrested and sentenced from several years to life imprisonment for sedition or inciting the crowd to riot.

The Kaohsiung Incident was only a temporary setback for the

opposition. In the long run, the event and its aftermath proved beneficial to the cause of the opposition, for the harsh treatment meted out to the Tangwai leaders by the authorities generated much sympathy for the opposition, of which they made very good use in the supplementary election held in 1980. In the 1980 supplementary election, Tangwai candidates made a strong showing. Several opposition candidates defeated their KMT opponents simply because they were wives of imprisoned leaders, and as such they obtained many sympathy votes. Several defense lawyers who performed brilliantly during the trials of the Tangwai leaders were also elected.

In the 1981 local election, the Tangwai decided to present a common list of candidates recommended by Tangwai members of the national legislature. The fact that successful candidates were mostly from the list and that some veteran non-KMT politicians did not win simply because they were not on the list seems to indicate that Tangwai supporters had developed some sense of party identity. In 1982, Tangwai leaders formed the Tangwai Campaign Assistance Association (Tang-wai hsuen-chu huo-yuen Hui), whose mission was not just to coordinate campaigns, but also to provide assistance to Tangwai candidates. On September 28, 1982, Fei Hsi-p'ing, a prominent Tangwai figure, presented to the public a document entitled "Statement of Common Political Views" on behalf of the Tangwai. Among the six items listed in the statement, two deserve mention: (1) "The future of Taiwan should be determined jointly by the 18 million inhabitants on Taiwan" and (2) "Formulate the Basic Law in accordance with the spirit of the Constitution and political realities of Taiwan, nullify the Temporary Provisions, lift martial law, reorganize the national legislature, and end bans on new political parties and newspapers."[8] The issuance of this statement marks the first attempt of the Tangwai to present their common demands to the authorities and to inform the public of their viewpoints on key political issues.

In mid-1982, the Tangwai movement was engulfed in serious factional disputes. The two factions involved were the so-called Tangwai officeholders' faction, composed of the Tangwai legislators, and the so-called Tangwai writers' faction, whose members were the Young Turks associated with the newly formed Tangwai Association of Magazine Editors and Writers. The two groups differed on three issues. Concerning the main strategy that the Tangwai should adopt, the officeholders believed that to win as many seats as possible in the supplementary and local elections was the only way for the opposition to grow and to influence the political process. A mass strategy should be used only for the limited purpose of supplementing the electoral and parliamentary strategy. According to the officeholders, the national legislature, despite all its shortcomings, might still serve a useful purpose, and the Tangwai's participation in that body might give the opposition some leverage to pressure the authorities.

The Young Turks had only contempt for this electoral parliamentary strategy. According to them, in the KMT-dominated party-state, the national legislature could play only a marginal role vis-à-vis the executive branch. Even if the Tangwai won all the seats in the national legislature, its real influence in the political system would still be very limited. Moreover, given the fact that the majority of the seats were held by senior legislators of mainlander origin who did not have to run for reelection and who were almost all KMT loyalists, the representative function of the national legislature was quite questionable. Unlike the officeholders, the Young Turks were not convinced that in a system where the opposition won almost 25 percent of the votes, yet obtained only 4 percent of the legislative seats, they could really exert political influence through normal participation. To them, the main strategy for the opposition should be a mass protest movement. The parliament should be used by the opposition only as a place to expose the injustice and inequities of the system.

Concerning the relationship of the opposition to the KMT, the officeholders wanted to maintain normal channels of communication. Although they favored a confrontational attitude for tactical reasons, they did not believe that a state of confrontation between the two parties under any circumstance was in the interest of the Tangwai. The Young Turks believed that the Tangwai had to maintain a confrontational stance toward the Kuomintang as a matter of principle, as long as the basic structure of the political system remained unchanged. They attacked the officeholders' willingness to compromise with the Kuomintang in the Legislative Yuan as unprincipled capitulation. The veteran legislator Kang Ning-hsiang was singled out as the target of vituperative attacks that lasted for several months. He was denounced as soft toward the Kuomintang, unprincipled, and a secret collaborator.

Concerning the Tangwai movement itself, the officeholders believed that in order to grow into a more influential political force, the Tangwai had to win the support of certain local clientele groups that, though they did not share the political views of the Tangwai, were willing to give it some help. To do so, the Tangwai should not attempt to maintain its moral image at any cost, as some young members demanded. Moreover, the Tangwai should not impose a strict moral code upon its members, because to do so would make it difficult for them to win elections. In contrast, the Young Turks insisted that the Tangwai should maintain its moral image, because only by doing so would they be able to get the support of the common people. To get this support, they should refuse to accept the support or endorsement of local factions. Moreover, the Tangwai should enforce a strict moral code upon its members. Those who failed to live up to the high standard should be expelled. Among the virtues that they believed the members of the movement should have included self-sacrifice, devotion to the cause, and personal integrity.

The disputes between the two factions eventually evolved into a theoretical battle of two lines: the officeholders and their followers favored reform within the existing political structure and the other faction, known as the new tide faction after founding their own theoretical organ, the *New Tide Magazine* (*Hsin Cho-liu*), advocated reforming the structure. The fierce factional disputes in mid-1982 weakened the Tangwai, so in the 1983 supplementary election the Tangwai did not perform as well as they had in previous elections. Although the total share of votes they received did not decrease significantly, because of poor coordination and inadequate mobilization the parliamentary seats they obtained were reduced by half, and some experienced leaders such as Kang Ning-hsiang lost their seats.

After the 1983 election, some Tangwai leaders felt that unless a permanent organization were formed to replace the campaign assistance organization, which could only operate during the election time, it would be difficult for the Tangwai to avoid the troublesome situation in which they found themselves before the election. So the Tangwai Public Policy Study Association (Tang-wai Kung-kung Cheng-ts'e Yen-chiu Hui) was duly formed. The new organization not only maintained a small staff in Taipei, but it also established several branch organizations across the island.

Around mid-1986, after the third plenum of the Twelfth Central Committee of the KMT, the media carried unconfirmed reports that top leaders of the ruling party and the government were seriously considering the manner and timing for launching significant political reforms. The lifting of martial law and an end to the party ban were regarded by informed public as imminent. In this atmosphere of high expectancy and uncertainty, Tangwai leaders were actively engaged in the business of forming a new party. Having made careful preparations, they probably calculated that the party ban would end by mid-1986; therefore the new party would still have time to participate in the supplementary election scheduled to be held by the end of the year. But as the authorities remained indecisive on political reforms, the Tangwai leaders decided to announce the founding of the new party in order to improve their electoral chances. Thus the Democratic Progressive Party was "illegally" founded on September 28, 1986.

The Role of the DPP in Taiwan's Political Development

Some scholars feel that the role of the DPP in Taiwan's political development is more symbolic than substantive.[9] This view, however, fails to take into account Taiwan's unique political situation. In a well-established democracy, a party like the DPP might not exert much influence. With a rather small parliamentary contingent, rife with factional disputes and ill prepared for formulating concrete policy alternatives, the party seems doomed to play a marginal role.

But because the political realities in Taiwan are not yet those of a well-established constitutional democracy, the role of an opposition party is not exactly the same as that of a typical opposition party in a developed democratic state.[10] The DPP is essentially a party movement. On the one hand, it functions as a normal party by participating in elections, engaging in legislative work, and even running a few county and city governments.[11] On the other hand, it considers itself a mass movement, the principal mission of which is to mobilize the people to exert pressure upon the ruling KMT and government to democratize the political structure as well as to carry out other reforms.

As a mass movement, the DPP resorts mainly to two tactics: (1) political agitation and education of the masses and (2) mobilization of activists and supporters to participate in various party-organized or party-sponsored street demonstrations, mass rallies, and grand parades.

The Tangwai attached prime importance to agitating and educating the masses. It is a truism in Taiwan that the KMT won elections mainly through their better organization whereas the Tangwai won by conducting effective propaganda. The DPP has maintained this tradition of the Tangwai. The DPP mainly uses two tools for agitating and educating the masses: (1) small-circulation magazines and videotapes and (2) the spoken word. For the duration of the ban on newspapers, they had to rely on their highly politicized magazines to influence the people. The writers of these magazine articles regarded their articles mainly as weapons to attack the enemy, namely the KMT party-state system and government officials as well as KMT leaders. With plain and straightforward language, they depicted the undesirable features of the enemy in bold strokes. Objectivity and truth were usually not their primary consideration, as they were often carried away by their own sense of justice and moral indignation. But despite the inadequacies of these magazines as either serious journalism or truthful reporting, their impact upon Taiwan's political development is very significant, because they made a large number of people aware of the need for political and social change at a time critical for the island's political evolution and thus have made a positive contribution to Taiwan's democratization.

The other tool is even more significant. In the numerous political rallies organized by the opposition, dissident figures made passionate speeches, in Taiwan dialect, that attacked the KMT party-state. Because several opposition leaders are very effective public speakers, the rallies organized by the opposition usually draw large crowds, particularly during the election campaigns. Such oral agitation and education is carried out mostly during election time or when the opposition feels that they have been treated unfairly by the authorities on a particular occasion and the media did not give a fair report. With the lifting of the ban on newspapers in January 1987, the DPP was allowed to run its own daily newspaper. It does not yet operate a daily, probably because of lack of adequate funds. Individual figures made attempts to establish their own newspapers. Kang Ning-hsiang's *Capital*

Morning News (*Shou-tou Cho-pao*) began publication in mid-May 1989 but was terminated in 1990. The *Democratic Progressive News*, the official party organ of the DPP, is a weekly that started as a one-page newspaper, grew to a booklet of thirty-odd pages, and then became a two-page newspaper. Because the DPP spends only a relatively modest amount of money annually for propaganda, it has to rely heavily on less expensive means to spread its messages.[12] Recently, the DPP applied for licenses to operate its own broadcasting stations. The government, abandoning its previous excuse of "technical difficulties," is considering granting such applications.

Although the opposition was originally organized mainly for the purpose of coordinating and conducting election campaigns, it later shifted its main attention to leading mass protest movements. Concerning the role of mass protest movements, DPP leaders are in disagreement. Some believe that mass protest movements should be used only as a strategy to supplement the main strategy, namely the electoral and parliamentary strategy; others reject this view on grounds that given the unrepresentative character of Taiwan's national legislature and the small size of the DPP contingents in the three bodies of the legislature, electoral and parliamentary strategy is not effective in achieving its political objectives. These people believe that the main purpose of DPP participation in the national legislature should be to expose its weaknesses as both a representative body and as a lawmaking organization; the DPP members of the legislature should have no illusion that constructive work can be accomplished by the legislature.

Mass protest movements are very important to the DPP as a means to pressure the authorities. For the past year, the DPP has launched a series of mass protest movements on such issues as reorganization of the national legislature, popular election of the Taiwan provincial governor, judicial inequity, and political persecution of advocates of Taiwan independence.[13] Street demonstrations were held to commemorate the February 28, 1947, Incident and to petition the authorities to make that date the National Peace Day, and to render moral support to farmers arrested for their role in the May 20 Incident. On each occasion, several hundred people participated. For the near future, the DPP is going to organize a series of protest movements for the purpose of pressuring the government to force all senior legislators to retire and making the public aware of the desirability of founding a "new and independent state" and the political persecution of the advocates of this idea.

Despite the fact that some DPP figures tend to question the legitimacy of the political system, the DPP is very much concerned with winning elections. Since the early 1970s, the opposition received about 20–30 percent of popular votes in almost all elections, local and national; the legislative seats it obtained varied considerably from one election to the next, however. The opposition's ability to prevent the personal and factional disputes of their candidates from damaging their image and to mobilize the votes of their lower-class supporters might account for the difference. The performance of the DPP in the 1986 election is impressive. Throughout the 1987–1989 period, the party entertained high expectations for the election scheduled to be held by the end of 1989. Immediately prior to the election, media reported that some DPP leaders believed that they might obtain ten to fourteen posts of mayor and county magistrate.[14] The results of the election show that the DPP won a significant victory.

Of the twenty-one seats of county magistrates (city mayors), the DPP obtained six (and another seat was won by a pro-DPP independent). To compare with the preceding election, the KMT lost three seats. In the election for the Legislative Yuan members, the DPP won twenty-two seats, a net gain of ten seats. The party's performance in the election for the city councilmen of Taipei and Kaohsiung is equally impressive. Even more important than the additional seats that the party won is that for the first time the DPP candidates got significant votes in every constituency in Taiwan, and the party obtained 38.3 percent of the votes cast in the election for county magistrates (city mayors). Depending on one's political stance, the fact that candidates affiliating with the Alliance for the Formation of a New State (Hsin Kuo-chia Lien-hsien) won twenty seats (seven in the Legislative Yuan and thirteen in the municipal councils of Taipei and Kaohsiung) is a matter of either elation or concern.

Despite the fact that the DPP has a rather small contingent in the national legislature (for example, only eleven party members and two supporters out of 297 members in the Legislative Yuan in the late 1980s), its role is quite out of proportion to its numerical strength. Part of the reason for this is that the majority of the KMT legislators are senior members elected in 1947 on the mainland. These people, because of their age and vulnerable position, can no longer participate actively in the legislative process.

In recent years, some DPP legislators have resorted frequently to disruptive tactics in legislative proceedings, and the use of invective and other forms of coarse and crude language in parliamentary debates. Public opinion is divided about the propriety of such behavior. DPP supporters hold that it is justifiable, given the unrepresentative character of the national legislature, whereas supporters of the ruling party contend that even in the present situation, such behavior should not be exonerated.

Social Base, Ideology, Organizational Structure, and Factionalism of the DPP

The Social Base of the DPP

The pattern of party division in a society often reflects underlying social cleavages. The main social cleavage in Taiwan is of subethnic or provincial origin.[15] Income disparity, needless to say, is also a factor, but definitely a far less important one (see Chapter 8).

The KMT has often been accused by opposition radicals of being a mainlanders' party, or the party of "Chinese overlords" who colonized Taiwan.[16] This accusation is not entirely justifiable, given the fact that the current leader of the KMT is a Taiwanese and over 70 percent of its 2.5 million members are Taiwanese, but, however, even with its "Taiwanization" affirmative action program, the leadership of the KMT still contains more mainlanders than Taiwanese.[17]

To some extent, the political opposition in Taiwan is caused by the resentment of some Taiwanese for the mainlanders' domination in political and administrative fields. The DPP, at least their moderate leaders, do not want to be labeled a Taiwanese party. To counter the public impression that the DPP is the party of a special provincial group, the DPP often goes out of its way to emphasize that it is a party for all citizens residing in Taiwan. The DPP also tries to explain that when the term "Taiwanese" is used in the party's publications (it is often used by the DPP to refer to a group of people distinct from the Chinese) it refers to all people currently residing in Taiwan. But in spite of all these efforts, the DPP has not yet won the allegiance of mainlanders. Out of its 20,000-odd members, the percentage of mainlanders is negligible. In the leadership of the DPP, there are only two or three mainlanders.[18]

Two events might have a far-reaching impact upon the relationship between the DPP and the mainlanders. One of these, which occurred in September 1988, involved the only mainlander in the DPP Central Executive Committee, Lin Chin-chieh (who quit the party in mid-1991), and the former party chairman, Yao Chia-wen. In early September 1988, Lin issued an open letter to Yao in which he attacked, inter alia, the attitude of discrimination of some DPP members against mainlanders.[19] The other event involved the veteran Fei Hsi-p'ing. Fei, a senior member of the Legislative Yuan of mainlander origin, has made important contributions to the Tangwai and the DPP. But in recent years he has become increasingly less popular among the young activists in the DPP, partly because his position as a senior legislator has become an embarrassment to a party whose declared mission is to get all senior legislators dismissed, and partly because of his espousal of the unification of China. In early December 1988, the new DPP leader Huang Hsin-chieh made a deal with Fei; Fei promised to retire from the Legislative Yuan voluntarily if the DPP would accept three conditions, the most important of which was that the DPP accept a system of reserved quota for mainlanders in the reorganized legislature. Huang basically accepted Fei's conditions, but in a meeting of the DPP Central Executive Committee, Huang was overruled. Fei became so enraged that he issued a statement in which he declared that because some DPP members held strong parochial views and employed high-handed methods against those who disagree with them, he had decided to leave the DPP.[20]

With only about 20,000 card-carrying members (the activists), the DPP is certainly a small party. But because the party cannot provide any material incentive to those who join it, and because for people in some professions the act of joining might cause some personal inconvenience, the number does not reflect the real strength of the party.[21] Although it is difficult to know exactly the real strength of the DPP, available voting data can be used to make a rough estimate. In all elections held during the past decade, the KMT usually received about 65 to 70 percent of the votes, and non-KMT candidates obtained about 30 percent. But because not all non-KMT candidates were affiliated with the Tangwai, nor all Tangwai figures joined the DPP, some deductions have to be made to assess the extent of DPP grass-root support. After examining the data, I estimate that the DPP share of the vote is 20 to 25 percent, which, translated into numerical figures, is around 3 million adults. These people may be regarded as DPP supporters or sympathizers.

Who are these people? What are their common characteristics? No systematic empirical study has been made. From scattered data, casual interviews with DPP leaders, and a comparative study of regional voting patterns for opposition candidates in the past two elections, I have come to the tentative conclusion that DPP supporters share several common characteristics. First, the overwhelming majority are Taiwanese, particularly of Fukien extraction. The Hakka's support is substantial, but less than that of the Fukien-dialect speakers, and also less firm. Second, the typical DPP supporter is probably younger than a typical supporter of the KMT. To some people, the KMT is a party for the status quo and people with privileges whereas the DPP represents a new approach. This view may not be entirely correct, but the DPP benefits by this stereotype among the younger generation. Third, the DPP contains a higher percentage than the KMT of people who are either poor or have an uncertain economic future. In other words, despite the fact that neither the KMT nor the DPP is a class party, the KMT has more millionaires and successful business leaders in its ranks. Apart from these common characteristics, the DPP also contains two categories of people who are widely apart in terms of education and political outlook.

One group contains young intellectuals and professionals. Some of them support the DPP out of their commitment to a competitive party system. These people may not approve some features of the DPP ideology, but they are willing to support the party because they believe that an opposition party is needed to maintain a genuine democratic system. The other group is of varied social and educational backgrounds, mostly of low social status and little education, who share a common animosity toward the KMT for various ideological and personal reasons. Some of these people tend to identify the mainlanders as supporters of the KMT. Most support the DPP mainly because they believe that it is a political movement of the Taiwanese. In addition, the influential Presbyterian church in southern Taiwan is a strong supporter of the DPP: it supports Taiwan independence and is very critical of the policies of the government. Among the approximately 100,000 members of the church are some respected community leaders and intellectuals in southern Taiwan. Although not all members of the church support the DPP, a significant number do give the party very firm support. The church's international connections are also very useful to the opposition movement.

Regional voting patterns for opposition candidates seem to indicate that the main strength of the DPP still lies in urban areas. For example, of the three constituencies where the party won more than 30 percent of the votes in 1986, two are the large cities Taipei and Kaohsiung; in the least urbanized constituency of east Taiwan, the party's share of votes was zero. Apart from the factor of urbanization, a particular region's political tradition is also important in explaining the strength of the opposition. In Taiwan, there are three areas where the opposition has been strong: (1) the area including the Chi-shan township and adjacent rural villages in the Kaohsiung county, where the Yu family has maintained firm control and great popularity,[22] (2) Ilan County in the northeastern part of Taiwan, where a strong anti-estab-lishment popular sentiment has existed for many decades, and (3) the area including Chia-yi City and adjacent villages, where the late Hsu Shih-hsien was very popular as an opposition mayor and where the current mayor is one of her daughters. Regional voting data show clearly that traditional loyalty to a particular political personality is relevant to the maintenance of support for the opposition, just as it is relevant to the maintenance of KMT strength.

Ideology and DPP Positions on Particular Issues

In the 1977 election campaign, the Tangwai candidates adopted a common platform emphasizing two themes: liberal democracy and self-determination. These themes have since become the two major components of DPP ideology. In the DPP platform adopted in 1986, there were more than two dozen articles concerning social welfare. But with some exceptions, DPP politicians pay only lip service to social welfare issues.

Political liberalism and the realization of full-fledged democracy is the theme upon which the DPP has based its moral claim; this theme is also the glue that holds the party together. Both the KMT and the DPP claim that their ultimate aim is to realize liberal democracy. In the past, however, the KMT maintained that because the Chinese Communists refused to renounce the use of force against Taiwan, the government could not declare the termination of the state of emergency. Therefore, Taiwan should take a cautious approach toward broadening the scope of political participation. Although in his inauguration address delivered in May 1990 President Lee Teng-hui promised to terminate the state of emergency in one or two years, the restrictions on political participation would remain in effect as long as the Communist threat lasted. Most of these restrictions would probably be gradually removed, however. For example, it is widely believed that popular election of the mayors of Taipei and Kaohsiung and the governor of Taiwan Province will be held in the early 1990s.

Moreover, the KMT argues that because Taiwan is only part of China, its political system and practices cannot be made to fit every detail of the Constitution, which is designed for all of China. The KMT further refuses to thoroughly amend the Constitution on the ground that such an action might weaken the consensus of the political community and erode the base of legitimacy of the political system. The KMT rejects the demand of some people to declare the Temporary Provisions to the Constitution null and void by saying that they are an integral part of the Constitution and their usefulness still exists.

The DPP criticizes the reasons of the KMT as mere excuses to preserve its monopoly of power and special privileges. The DPP believes that if Taiwan is willing to renounce its claim of representing the entirety of China, peaceful relations can be maintained indefinitely between the two sides of the Taiwan Strait and therefore the state of emergency should end and all restrictions on political participation should be removed. In order to realize full democracy, the political system and practices should be made to conform entirely to the Constitution. If this cannot be done, the Constitution should be amended to reflect the political realities or it should be replaced by a Basic Law.

In the DPP platform, three particular political issues are of main concern. The first issue is the monopoly of power of the KMT and its role in society. The DPP demands that a clear separation between the state and the party should be maintained (Article 28 of the party platform). The KMT should cease to control or supervise the military, the police, and the intelligence agencies (Article 29). Second are the emergency structure and regulations. The DPP maintains that the National Security Law should not be enacted, because it is a substitute for martial law (Article 30). They demand that the Temporary Provisions and all administrative decrees that are in violation of the Constitution be declared null and void immediately (Article 31). All members of the national legislature should be elected by the people, and the quotas for overseas Chinese communities and women's and professional associations should be eliminated (Article 34). The provincial governor of Taiwan Province and the mayors of Taipei and Kaohsiung should be elected by the people (Article 35). The third issue is human rights. The DPP platform lists the conventional human rights of a typical bill of rights. Two of the thirteen articles are of particular interest. One is a request to the authorities to make public and declare void the blacklist used to regulate entry and exit applications to ensure the right of citizens to go abroad and to reenter Taiwan (Article 17). The other is the demand for the establishment of the jury system: "For the prosecution and trial of cases on sedition, a jury consisting of representatives of all political parties, members of parliament and respected social leaders with a reputation of probity should be formed and the trial should be publicly conducted" (Article 24).

The DPP tends to underestimate the importance of recent political reforms in Taiwan. Some DPP leaders maintain that these reforms are cosmetic and have no real effect upon the distribution of power in the society, whereas others believe that, though these reforms are not insignificant, they still leave much to be desired. Moreover, the DPP rejects the prevailing view that these reforms were initiated by the KMT leadership themselves. To them, they are the authorities' reaction to popular pressures, especially those from the Tangwai and the DPP.

The other theme—self-determination—is more controversial (see Chapter 9). In the DPP Basic Political Platform, two articles specifically deal with self-determination. Article 3 of the section on national defense and foreign policy states that "the future of Taiwan should be determined by all inhabitants in Taiwan. According to the principle contained in the U.N. Covenant on Social and Cultural Rights, all people possess the inherent right of self-determination. . . . The future of Taiwan should be determined jointly by all inhabitants in Taiwan in a free, uncoerced, universal, fair and equal way. No government or coalition of governments have the right to determine the political affiliation of Taiwan." Article 4 in the same section further states, "Problems concerning the two parties along the Taiwan Strait should be settled by all inhabitants through the free exercise of their will. . . . We oppose any settlement reached by the KMT and CCP governments through negotiation, in violation of the principle of people's self-determination."

The principle of self-determination, which is the most important political principle of the DPP, is, however, rather ambiguous and subject to different interpretations. Several DPP leaders affiliated with the radical New Tide faction have, on various occasions, admitted openly that "self-determination" is simply a code word for "Taiwan independence." But some others, motivated either by tactical considerations or because of personal conviction, have rejected such an interpretation.

According to the less radical version, self-determination is merely a general principle to be observed in settling the so-called Taiwan issue. Because the people in Taiwan have maintained their de facto independence for a half century and because they absolutely refuse to accept Communist rule, no one should force them to live in a unified China under communism; the international community should assume a moral responsibility to assist the people of Taiwan to avoid such a fate. Despite the KMT's staunch anticommunism, some DPP figures are highly suspicious of the KMT. They believe that this "mainlanders' party or regime" (or, in their language, "the regime of outsiders") might negotiate with the CCP and betray Taiwan when and if faced with the prospect of losing power. These people believe that to advocate self-determination serves two useful purposes: One is to alert the people of Taiwan to the "danger" they are facing, so that they may take more positive action to eradicate the root of this danger. The second purpose is to internationalize the Taiwan issue so that when the danger of Communist rule, either through military conquest or negotiated settlement, becomes imminent, international public opinion may be mobilized to deter the threat.[23]

According to this version, self-determination is simply a method or a process; it is not an end state of affairs. People may decide to make Taiwan an independent state, to maintain the status quo, or to seek unification of China. As long as the choice is freely made by the people, the principle is maintained.

The majority of DPP leaders and activists are probably in favor of independence.[24] But most leaders in the less radical Pan-Formosan faction and a few in the New Tide faction prefer a cautious and gradual approach to reach the goal. In contrast, most leaders in the New Tide faction and the majority of party activists desire an approach involving more risk taking and that is more direct and confrontational.[25] Disagreement on this matter has reached a critical level, which leads some observers to believe that the DPP might split if this issue is not properly handled.[26]

Because of a lack of consensus in the party and the leadership's concern with the reaction of the KMT, no concrete demand was made in the DPP Platform concerning self-determination. Only a few articles manifest Formosan nationalism: For example, "school instruction should be conducted bilingually in principle. This should first be carried out in primary schools and kindergartens" (Article 133). "To affirm the historical and cultural status and value of Taiwan, it is necessary to compile local color instruction materials, promote local color education; to inspire the students' affection for their homeland, it is necessary to include the history of Taiwan in the curriculum of educational institutions of all levels" (Article 137). "We oppose the imposition of restriction of Taiwanese language TV programs to a limited amount of time" (Article 139).

Some DPP theorists are busy developing a theory, still in an inchoate stage, justifying Taiwan's independence. In general, they rest their case on three propositions. First, Taiwan was not part of China for most of its history: it was a colony of the Netherlands, China, and Japan. Although most Taiwanese are descendants of Chinese migrants, they do not feel that they are culturally Chinese because of the separate development of the island. Moreover, because Chinese culture is continental oriented and Taiwanese culture is oceanic, the Chinese and the Taiwanese do not share cultural affinity.[27] Additionally, the Chinese rule of Taiwan has never been a happy one for the Taiwanese, and can never be so, because the Chinese are used to a centralized authoritarian system and have to impose this oppressive pattern of government upon any other people under their rule.[28] Moreover, China does not own Taiwan; in other words, the sovereignty of Taiwan is uncertain.

Second, according to contemporary principles of international law and human rights, every people should have the right to determine their own political future. An independent Taiwan will not only be in the best interest of the Taiwanese people, but it will also contribute to the maintenance of peace in East Asia because it will renounce any intention of recovering the Chinese mainland and will live in peace with mainland China.[29]

Finally, Taiwan is now an independent state de facto. The refusal of the KMT government to make it independent de jure and the KMT government's maintenance of the "myth" that it is the legitimate government of the entire China have cost Taiwan dearly. On the one hand, because of the KMT government's "unrealistic" stand, the process of liberalization and democratization has been considerably delayed and political difficulties have been multiplied domestically. On the other hand, international isolation has been deepened and more difficult to handle because of it.

Some staunch advocates of Taiwan independence in the DPP hold the view that an independent Taiwan would be able to rejoin the international community as a respected member. It might be admitted to the UN, and it might be able to establish diplomatic relations with the major powers. To the charge leveled by critics that the declaration of Taiwan independence would provoke Communist China and probably result in a military assault launched by Beijing, the standard reply of the advocates is the following: (1) The fact that Beijing has not yet launched an armed attack upon Taiwan is because of its own political, economic, and military weaknesses rather than Taiwan's domestic development, (2) In the event of an armed attack on an independent Taiwan, international public opinion will rally on the side of Taiwan, and the United States will assist Taiwan by fulfilling its commitment in the Taiwan Relations Act, and (3) Taiwanese people have to take some risks in order to have a better future.

DPP leaders favoring a more cautious approach argue that independence is a distant goal. In the present context, the issue should not occupy a prominent position in the agenda and deliberations of the DPP. To spend too much time and energy on this issue is risky and counterproductive, and such a course of action might split the party, provoke the KMT unnecessarily, and deviate the DPP from its main task at the present stage of its development— to pressure the authorities to completely reorganize the national legislature.

Social welfare demands constitute the third major component of the DPP Platform. Most of the proposals contained in the platform are rather commonplace and do not offer clear alternatives to the KMT policies. The only demand of major importance that is different from the current practice is to establish as quickly as possible a system to provide free medical care and health insurance for all people. For this purpose the DPP has attempted to trim defense expenditures. The DPP also demands that no new nuclear power stations be established and that all existing facilities be closed within ten years.

Despite the fact that there are twenty-three articles in the DPP Platform concerning social welfare and the interests of labor, most DPP leaders merely pay lip service to these issues. This lack of interest naturally led some supporters to become disappointed and disillusioned with the party. A small group of DPP members left the party to form the new Worker's Party in 1987. But at the present these issues do interfere with party unity.

Organizational Structure

In appearance, the organizational structure of the DPP is similar to that of the KMT. The pattern of structure emphasizes centralization of power and the authority of the party apparatus. But in reality the DPP simply cannot operate in the way its organizational chart indicates. The party suffers from a lack of authoritative direction.

The organizational structure of the DPP is diagramed in Figure 6.1. The DPP Congress is theoretically the policymaking body of the party. It elects the party chairman, members of the Central Executive Committee, and the Central Advisory Commission. Because of its size (in the Third Congress, held on October 29–30, 1988, the number of members was 228) and the fact that it meets only once annually, its decisionmaking power is minimal.

The decisionmaking power is shared by the chairman and the thirty-one-person Central Executive Committee, especially the eleven-person standing committee of the CEC. Unlike the chairman of the KMT, who is very powerful, the chairman of the DPP suffers from a lack of adequate authority. Prior to the recent party congress, the role of the chairman was mainly symbolic and ceremonial. In order to make the chairman more powerful, several revisions were made in the party charter: the tenure of the chairman was extended from one year to two years, the limit on the number of terms that the chairman can serve was changed from one to two, and the election of the chairman by the Central Executive Committee from its own members was changed into election by the Congress from the Central Executive Committee. Whether these revisions will strengthen the position of the party chairman and terminate the "undesirable state of dual leadership of the chairman and the Central Executive Committee" remains to be seen.[30]

Factionalism

The main weakness of the DPP, however, does not lie in its formal structure, but rather in its rampant factionalism. There are two major and two minor factions in the DPP. The Pan-Formosan faction, led by Huang Hsin-chieh, and the New Tide faction are the main rivals. The Kang faction of Kang Ning-hsiang is a minor faction.

Figure 6.1 Organizational Structure of the DPP

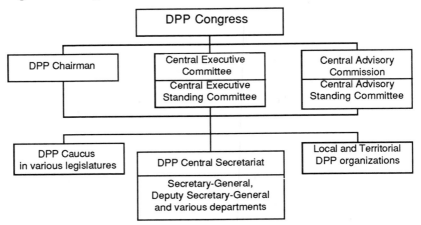

Factional disputes are mainly about two themes: (1) whether the DPP should take an explicit stand in favor of Taiwan independence and (2) which strategy, election-parliamentary struggle strategy, or mass movement strategy should be employed as the main strategy. The New Tide faction, composed mainly of young intellectuals (party staff workers and editors and writers of various anti-KMT magazines) take the position that the DPP should no longer delay announcing publicly that it is for Taiwan independence and should work more actively for the cause. They also maintain that the party should use mass protest movements as the main strategy. The Pan-Formosan faction, composed mainly of officeholders or former officeholders, believe that the DPP should regard the issue of parliamentary reform as its main concern for the time being. Although they do not neglect the mass movement strategy, they believe that electoral-parliamentary strategy should be the main strategy. The two minor factions basically side with the Pan-Formosan faction.

Immediately before the Third DPP Congress, factional disputes became rather intense. Huang Hsin-chieh, leader of the Pan-Formosan faction, and Yao Chia-wen, the chairman elected in the Second Congress and supported by the New Tide faction, were engaged in a close race for the chairmanship. In September 1988, Lin Chin-chieh, who supported Huang, published an open letter to Yao in his *Progress Weekly*.[31] In this letter, Lin severely criticized

Yao's leadership and what he called the "line of the party." Lin singled out three aspects to criticize. These are worth reviewing in some detail, because they are indicative of current (early 1991) splits in the DPP.

The first was the frequent and unnecessary use of the mass movement strategy. According to Lin:

> Since the founding of our party, we have virtually used the streets as our home. A series of street demonstrations have made all of us exhausted, the treasury of our party empty, many of our comrades in prison or facing prosecution. At such cost, nearly all of the objectives which we sought to achieve have not been attained. . . . As all of our mass movements have not achieved any concrete results at considerable cost, it is time that we should evaluate our whole approach. Have we given our party members solid training to conduct street demonstrations? Are our cadres competent in leading the demostrations? Or is it that we have too many people whose only concern is how to show off, instead of leading effective mass movements?

He suggested that mass movement strategy should be used less frequently but more effectively.

The second dispute concerned unification versus independence. "From this dispute, we have suffered severe losses, but gained no advantage." He noted that the issue of the future of Taiwan was very serious. "But, nowadays the issue has been treated in an emotional way, and reduced into a couple of slogans. Moreover, it is highly divisive." Under these circumstances, Lin argued, people do not enter into serious discussions on the implications of Taiwanese independence, such as its feasibility and the possibility of a third option apart from either independence or unification. "In our party, on the serious issue of Taiwan's future, there are only two groups of people, those who shout slogans and those who refuse to shout slogans, yet are so intimidated as to be silent."

Third, Lin criticized the "unhealthy" relationship that the DPP maintains with various overseas Taiwanese associations and groups. According to Yao, the DPP should maintain very close ties with various Taiwanese associations and groups abroad because the party should develop its theory abroad while developing its organization in Taiwan. Lin believes that "only the island of Taiwan provides the proper soil for our movement." The difference in their attitudes toward the Taiwanese groups abroad is rather significant in the factional disputes. Because several large groups are strong advocates of Taiwan independence and some leaders of these groups are suspected by the government as being involved in revolutionary conspiracies, the moderates in the DPP prefer to keep some distance from them, even if they are not totally opposed to accepting their help. The radical leaders are of the opinion that the connections with the overseas Taiwanese groups are an asset to the party and must be cultivated.

More generally, Lin severely criticized Yao's leadership. According to

Lin, Yao's elitism and support of the radical advocates of Taiwan independence have brought about a serious crisis for the DPP. According to Lin, self-determination should not be reached in the way that Yao has in mind: "A few leaders of the DPP frame a couple of slogans and through propaganda make people 'understand' and accept. . . . This procedure is the typical way of elitism and we might run the risk of developing into a fascist party by following such a procedure." Lin believes that virtual independence of Taiwan can be attained by peaceful means: "Taiwan inhabitants of all provincial origin should be included in our movement. The discriminatory attitude toward mainlanders and the anti-Chinese sentiment on the part of some of our party members are bound to bring disaster to the Taiwanese society."

On October 30, 1988, Huang Hsin-chieh was elected by a small margin. In the new Central Executive Committee, the two major factions reached a delicate balance: the Pan-Formosan faction and their allies won sixteen seats, while the New Tide faction and their allies got fifteen. The elevation of the popular and experienced Huang Hsin-cheih and his conciliatory attitude after the election have produced salutary effects. Factionalism has been temporarily submerged. But as the issues that produce the fundamental disagreement remain, factional disputes may break out again.

Since Huang Hsin-cheih's assumption of the DPP chairmanship, several events have produced renewed tension between the two major factions.[32] The most serious dispute between the two factions occurred in early 1990 and concerned whether the party should participate in the National Affairs Conference scheduled for late June. The conference was initiated by President Lee to resolve the deepening constitutional crisis engulfing the country in July 1990. The Pan-Formosan faction believed that the party should participate, but the New Tide faction held that unless the KMT made more concessions regarding the DPP's number of seats in the conference and agenda setting, the party should not participate. After prolonged negotiations between the KMT and the DPP, and after the interfaction negotiations, the DPP eventually participated.

Future Prospects for Taiwan's Party System

The founding of the DPP has caused much speculation about the future prospects for Taiwan's party system. One theory is that Taiwan is going to develop a party system similar to that of Japan. People holding this view argue that given the prestige, popularity, enormous resources, and organizational expertise of the KMT, it is very difficult for the small, faction-ridden DPP to develop into an equal rival in the foreseeable future, even if all the conditions of equal competition are established. So it is unrealistic for the DPP to aim at becoming a governing party in the coming decade.[33] The role most suitable to the DPP is to provide some check upon the ruling party and the government, and to pressure the authorities to carry out policies beneficial to the people.

Pro-DPP observers dismiss this view as pro-KMT propaganda. According to these people, the outwardly strong position of the KMT is based on a rather shaky foundation. With the departure of powerful leaders, the ruling party is afflicted with factionalism, the apathy of grass-roots party members, and the antagonism between a reform-minded elite, which rose up the political ladder through winning a series of elections, and the conservative party bureaucrats. Because of the weakened position of the KMT and the objective circumstances of Taiwan, the DPP's chances of rapid growth are good. Therefore, it is reasonable to expect it to become a serious rival of the KMT, and it is reasonable even to assume the responsibility of governing in the next decade. All in all, these people seem to think that Taiwan will have a two-party system in ten to fifteen years.

I am inclined to accept the first view, except that I do not think the role of the opposition should be limited to that of a critic of the government. Given the enormous resource at its command and its popularity among several influential segments of society, the KMT's position as the dominant party will remain unchallenged for the foreseeable future. The DPP, in contrast, will enjoy a slow but steady growth and expansion. Unless a serious dispute causes an irreparable split, it will most likely become a significant contender of the ruling party in all elections in the future.

In April 1989, the DPP formally registered with the Ministry of Interior, in accordance with the newly passed Civic Organizations Law, and thus acquired the status of a legal party. The legal equality of the political parties, however, does not ensure actual equality in all respects. At the present time, the KMT still enjoys two kinds of special privileges. On the one hand, it still maintains special party branches in all administrative agencies, military units, and various semigovernmental organizations; on the other hand, the treasury of the ruling party still is filled by the government through a variety of contracts and subsidies. Although these special privileges are being reduced, they still exist. Their total elimination seems to be a necessary condition for equal competition of the parties. But in such a competitive situation, Taiwan may have a party system that in its rough outline is similar to that of Japan.

Notes

1. For an analysis of the implications of the event, see Y. Chou and A. J. Nathan, "Democratizing Transition in Taiwan," *Asian Survey* 27 (3) (March 1987), pp. 277–299.

2. See J. F. Copper, "Political Development in Taiwan," in *China and Taiwan Issue*, ed. H. Chiu (New York: Praeger, 1979), pp. 37–76, and his "Taiwan

in 1986: Back on Top Again," *Asian Survey* 27, pp. 81–91; and N. Kristof, "Opposition Party Strong in Taiwan Vote," *New York Times* (December 7, 1986), p. 3.

3. Elections for local offices such as members of county assemblies and the Taiwan Provincial Assembly were held as early as 1949. The political aspirations of the rural elite were to a certain extent satisfied.

4. For an account and analysis of the development that led to the adoption of the system of supplementary election, see R. Clough, *Island China* (Cambridge, Mass.: Harvard University Press, 1978).

5. The literal meaning of the term "tangwai" is "outside of the party." Those who form the opposition desired to rally all those who did not belong to the Kuomintang to their fold. In addition, because to form a party was not legal, it was regarded a good tactic to form a "nonparty"; thus the term was adopted by them.

6. The more notable ones include *Pa-shih Nien-tai* [The eighties], published by Kang Nien-hsiang; *Sheng Ken* [The deep plough], by Hsu Yung-hsiu; *Chien-chin Chou-ken* [Progress weekly], by Lin Chin-chieh; and *Kuan-huai* [Care], by Chou Chin-yu.

7. The censorship encouraged the magazines to publish more insulting material, and because the Garrison Command could not confiscate all copies of the banned publication, the censorship gave the publication free publicity and promoted its sale. The court cases usually served to make the defendant a martyr in the minds of the Tangwai supporters and obtained votes for him when he decided to run for public offices.

8. See Kang Ning-hsiang, *Wei-chi yu Hsi-wing* [Crisis and hope] (Taipei: 1983), pp. 54–55 for the full text.

9. For example, L. Pye is of the opinion that the emergence of the Tangwai is "interesting" but not highly significant. See L. Pye, "Taiwan's Development and Its Implications for Beijing and Washington," *Asian Survey* 26, pp. 611–626.

10. For the nature of political opposition in the West, see R. Dahl, ed., *Political Oppositions in Western Democracies* (New Haven, Conn.: Yale University Press, 1966).

11. Of the four mayors and county magistrates elected on the Tangwai ticket, only one joined the DPP. The reason for this is probably that to serve as the administrative head of a local government and to be an opposition leader simultaneously in today's Taiwan still involves serious role conflict, which very few are prepared to accept.

12. In 1987, the DPP spent only NT $2 million for propaganda. See *Min-chin Pao Chou-k'an* [Democrative progressive news], no. 34 (November 4–10, 1988), p. 16.

13. See ibid., p. 17.

14. Many observers, however, are of the opinion that it is overoptimistic on the part of DPP leaders to think that they might capture so many posts. See *China Times* (January 2, 1989), p. 3, for an analysis of the DPP's grounds for such optimism.

15. See Lu Ya-li, "Future Domestic Developments in the Republic of China on Taiwan," *Asian Survey* 25 (11) (November 1985), pp. 1075–1095, for an analysis of this issue.

16. See Lin Chou-shui, "The Establishment of Consciousness of Being Taiwanese: The Erosion of Consciousness of Being Chinese on Taiwan and the Movement of the Building of a New Nation-State of Taiwan," in *Democratic Progressive News*, no. 24 (August 27–September 1, 1988), pp. 32–37; *DPN*, no.

25 (September 2–8, 1988), pp. 36–37; *DPN*, no. 26 (September 9–15, 1988), pp. 28–32; and especially *DPN*, no. 26, pp. 29–30.

17. For example, in the current KMT Central Committee, the percentage of mainlanders is 65.6 percent, while that of Taiwanese is 34.4 percent. For the previous CC, the respective figures are 80.7 percent and 19.3 percent.

18. In the thirty-one-person Central Executive Committee, only one person is a mainlander, and in the eleven-person Central Advisory Commission, there were two mainlanders, before Fei Hsi-p'ing's recent departure from the DPP.

19. Lin Chin-chieh, "An Open Letter to Chairman Yao," in *Progress Weekly*, no. 154 (September 3–9, 1988), pp. 4–17.

20. See *China Times* (December 20, 1988), p. 2.

21. The case of a military officer, Captain Chen Shen-ching, is illustrative. Captain Chen was transferred to Quemoy after he had been discovered to be a member of the DPP. The DPP charged the military with discrimination, but the military defended its action as a routine personnel transfer. See *Democratic Progressive News*, no. 30 (October 7–13, 1988), p. 10.

22. The founder of this political family is Yu Teng-fa, who started his career as a real estate agent and later became a landowner and philanthropist. After Taiwan was reverted to China, Yu entered into politics as a KMT member of the National Assembly. The corruption of many KMT politicians and officials caused him to leave the party. As an independent, he was elected as a county magistrate of the Kaohsiung County. As a capable administrator and a courageous critic of the KMT, he became highly popular and was able to found his political dynasty. Now three of his family members hold three of the most important elective positions in the Kaohsiung County: his daughter-in-law is the county magistrate, his granddaughter is the delegate to the Provincial Assembly from that county, and his grandson is a member of the Legislative Yuan. In addition, his son-in-law served once as the county magistrate, and his daughter was once a member of the Legislative Yuan.

23. See Lin Shih-wen, "The DPP's Diplomacy Aims at Improving Taiwan's Future Prospects," *Democratic Progressive News*, no. 30 (October 10–13, 1988), pp. 6–9.

24. In accordance with a resolution passed at the Second DPP Congress, the DPP held ten meetings in various cities in Taiwan from January 31, 1988, to April 3, 1988. After each meeting, a poll was taken to assess the attitudes of the activists attending the meeting about whether they approved of adding the statement of "People should have the freedom of advocating Taiwan independence" in the Action Program of the DPP. In these ten meetings, 61.85 percent of the activists approved, while 35.1 percent of the activists did not. See *Democratic Progressive News*, nos. 28–29 (September 23–October 6, 1988), pp. 77.

25. The New Tide faction consists of the activists who were associated with the Association of Tangwai magazine editors and writers. These people are usually younger, somewhat better educated, and more radical in their political attitudes. Many of them are committed to Taiwan independence and want to realize it quickly. Some of them also believe that the DPP should pay more attention to the interests of the lower classes. Their mouthpiece was once the magazine *Hsin Cho Liu* [New Tide]. The core of the Pan-Formosan faction is the small group of followers of Huang Hsin-chieh, who founded the *Formosan Magazine*. But many of the more moderate elements are also affiliated with this faction. They believe that a less radical and confrontational strategy should be employed. Although many of them are not opposed to the goal of Taiwan independence, they believe

that to treat it as a concrete objective to be reached within a definite time period is unrealistic.

26. See *China Times* (October 31, 1988), p. 3.

27. See Kuo Chun, "Can Chinese Culture Be a Unifying Force to Unify Taiwan and China?" *Democratic Progressive News*, nos. 28 and 29 (September 23–October 6, 1988), pp. 92–95. The author of this article states that "the so-called Chinese culture refers to the way of life and value system commonly shared by the Chinese [or the people on mainland China]. This culture is entirely different from Taiwanese culture. The Taiwanese cannot accept the way of life and value system of the Chinese. Any attempt to force Taiwan to 'unify' with China is presumptuous, and those who hold such a notion show a total ignorance of their own cultural level and content. Communist China should devote more attention to improve Chinese culture" (p. 95).

28. See Lin Chou-shui, "The Establishment of Consciousness," pp. 32–37.

29. See Tsai Yu-chung, "There Is Only One Way to Live: Establishing a New and Independent State," *Democratic Progressive News*, nos. 28, 29 (September 23–October 6, 1988), pp. 103–111, 108. Tsai states that "the two states, China and Taiwan, may become allies. The relationship between them will be based on mutual interests and mutual benefits. They will jointly develop and promote economy, science and technology, trade, culture and education . . . and cooperate in all these areas of human endeavor . . . to improve the livelihood and welfare of both states" (p. 109).

30. Chang Chun-hong, "On the Organization and Functions of the Opposition Party" [Fan-tuai-tang ti Tsu-chai yu Kun-lun] (Paper presented at the Conference on Political Development of the Republic of China, December 20–21, 1988, sponsored by the Department of Political Science, National Taiwan University).

31. See Lin Chin-chieh, "An Open Letter to Chairman Yao" [ke Yao-chu-hsi ti Kun-kai Hsin] *Progress Weekly* [Chien-chin Chou-ken], no. 154 (September 3–9, 1988), pp. 4–17.

32. One incident is the publication of Chang Chun-hong's book, *The Road to Power* [Tao Chih-cheng-chih-lu] in mid-1989. In the book, Chang and his associates mounted a severe criticism of the political strategy of the New Tide faction. Given Chang's position as the general secretary of the DPP, this has caused some ill feelings. But this incident was solved amiably. The other event was the massacre of students and workers in Beijing by the Communist Chinese troops in 1989. In the wake of the event, leaders of the New Tide faction, such as Yao Chia-wen, demanded that the DPP leadership take a more unequivocal stand for Taiwan independence and criticized Huang Hsin-chieh for his lack of concern for this position. See *Independence Evening Post* (June 6, 1989).

33. See "Can the DPP Become a Governing Party in the Foreseeable Future?" *Independence Evening Post* (December 24, 1988), p. 2. This is an interview with Chen Shui-pien, a member of the Standing Committee of the Central Executive Committee of the DPP. Chen believes that by 1995 the DPP will probably become the governing party. According to Chen there are two ways by which the DPP might reach its goal of replacing the KMT as the ruling party: (1) by securing more than 50 percent of the seats in a new national legislature, and/or (2) by amending the constitutional provision on the election of the president to replace the current practice of election by the National Assembly with direct election by the people.

PART 3

The Electoral System and Electoral Behavior

CHAPTER 7

The Electoral System and Voting Behavior in Taiwan

FEI-LUNG LUI

Elections are an essential part of a democratic system. For most citizens in a democracy, elections may be their only form of political participation. Through elections, they directly or indirectly choose their government leaders. Elections provide the foundation of governmental legitimacy and the means by which citizens influence public policy.

After the adoption of the Constitutional Law of the Republic of China in 1946, elections for the members of the National Assembly and the Legislative Yuan were held in 1947. In Taiwan, local self-government was initiated in 1950. Elections for local government executives and representative body members were held every three or four years. As of 1989, voters in Taiwan had participated in nearly eighty elections for various public officials and representatives. Elections now lie at the heart of political life in Taiwan. The aim of this chapter is to outline the institutional and operational characteristics of the electoral system of the Republic of China on Taiwan and to illustrate their effects on the voting behavior of the Chinese people.

The electoral system operating in Taiwan was and still is very complex and somewhat controversial. It is complex because it consists not only of geographical and occupational representation, but also of special representation of national minorities within the country and of Chinese living abroad. It is controversial because these elections could not be conducted fairly and smoothly under the conditions existing several decades ago or even at the present time.

In order to describe the determining characteristics of voting behavior, political scientists distinguish among a candidate orientation, party orientation, issue orientation, and personal relationship orientation.[1] In Taiwan, voting behavior is still mainly oriented around personal relationships. Candidate orientation comes next in importance, followed by issue and party orientation. In order to understand how this state of affairs came about, we need to know something of the relevant historical and social background.

149

Historical and Social Background

The political system as prescribed in the Constitution of the Republic of China was designed for a country of vast territory and population. When the Constitution was adopted in 1947, the Republic of China had thirty-five provinces, twelve special municipalities, one special administrative district (Hainan), and two special regions (Mongolia and Tibet). The population was estimated around 500 million people, most of whom were illiterate and knew nothing about constitutional democracy.

As declared in the Preamble, the Constitution of the Republic of China was written more or less in accordance with the teachings of Sun Yat-sen, the founding father of the republic. Dr. Sun was a man of idealism who envisaged that China should be not only a democracy, but also a direct democracy. He argued that direct democracy should be practiced at the county as well as the national level. So the citizen of a county and its equivalent should have powers to elect and recall its magistrates and county councillors and powers of initiative and referendum on legislative matters. At the national level, a National Assembly should be elected directly by the people.

Sun combined the three Western democratic powers of legislature, executive, and judiciary with the two traditional Chinese powers of examination and control in the central government. Thus there are five separate branches (Yuan) of the central government with a president at the apex. Formally, the president was to function similarly to the president of the German Weimar Republic at first; after the adoption of the Temporary Provisions Effective During the Period of Communist Rebellion in 1966,[2] the system resembled the French Fifth Republic.

There are three representative bodies at the national level: the National Assembly, the Legislative Yuan, and the Control Yuan. The first of these—the National Assembly—is composed of more than 3,000 delegates directly elected by the people every six years. At least one delegate comes from each county and its equivalent, with powers to elect and recall the president and vice-president of the republic and to revise the Constitution. The Legislative Yuan, composed of more than 700 legislators directly elected by the people every three years, has the power to make laws, review the budget, and give consent to the nomination of the premier of the Executive Yuan. The Control Yuan, composed of about 250 members elected by the Provincial Assemblies and their equivalent, has the power to impeach, censure, consent, and audit.

Members of the National Assembly and the Legislative Yuan are elected to represent geographic regions, occupations, minorities living in the country, and Chinese citizens residing abroad. The quota of each type of constituency is roughly in proportion to its percentage of national population. For conducting elections, election commissions are established from the national and provincial level on down to the county and its equivalents. The county election commissions are in charge of compiling an electoral register for constituencies based on geography and national minority status. For occupational and women's groups, the electoral registers are compiled by their respective national or provincial associations. For overseas Chinese representation, the electoral register is compiled by Chinese diplomatic officers. Each eligible elector has only one franchise of their choice if they are eligible for inclusion in two or more constituencies.

Election for members of the Control Yuan is on the basis of geography, with five members elected by each Provincial Assembly and two by Special Municipal Assemblies without regard to their relative population. The Mongolian and Tibetan Regional Assemblies may, however, elect eight members each. Overseas Chinese associations worldwide are grouped into eight districts from which one member of the Control Yuan is elected collectively. Table 7.1 shows the legally allotted seats and actually elected seats of the three central representative bodies by constituency in 1947. (Tables 7.1 through 7.11 appear in the appendix at the end of this chapter.)

The elections for the three central representative bodies in 1947 after the promulgation of the Constitution were seriously obstructed by the Chinese civil war and the Communists' occupation of several provinces. The election of overseas Chinese representatives in some foreign countries prompted protests from the host countries' governments. Even more serious problems arose from the fact that there was no genuine census in 1947 and the electoral registers were not available in many provinces and regions. Therefore, the elections for the central representative bodies were not fair and proper.

Although these elections were challengeable, they provided the government some basis of legitimacy. When the national government was moved to Taiwan in 1949, more than half of the members of these representative bodies came to Taiwan. However, because they were unable to subject themselves to reelection, the legitimacy of the regime has become a subject of debate.

Taiwan, the only province remaining under the actual jurisdiction of the government of the Republic of China after 1949, is different from the provinces of mainland China in a variety of ways. Under Japanese occupation for fifty years, the Taiwanese people enjoyed an era of relative peace and, therefore, a more prosperous economy and better education than the average Chinese across the Taiwan Strait. However, the Japanese ruled Taiwan as a colony with all the influential positions reserved to themselves. They also kept cultural relations between the people on both sides of the strait to the minimum possible. When Taiwan was returned to China in 1946, the people of both sides actually knew very little about each other.

In addition, unemployment and soaring food prices, combined with a controlled economy and government mismanagement, resulted in the unfortunate incident of February 28, 1947. Many mainlanders and local people alike lost their lives. The trauma of this incident is still felt and is sometimes exacerbated by its use to incite hatred toward the ruling party so as to mobilize local people in elections.

Taiwanese society can be considered fairly modern in view of its level of economic development, education, and urbanization. However, Taiwan's culture is still deeply rooted in Chinese tradition. Economic development, education, and other modernizing forces cannot possibly erase all the traits associated with traditional society in a few years. In addition, because of Taiwan's small size and good transportation network, it is not easy to be physically separated from one's parents and other relatives. Filial piety, respect for lineage, mutual assistance, and all other primary "duties" are not to be abandoned without inviting serious criticism. A customary saying, "to be an official is temporary, to be a man is permanent," sums up the belief that one cannot perform government duties without taking care of personal duties to friends and relatives at the same time. Therefore, to elect one of their own into an executive or legislative office is very important to voters. This is why primary social relations usually come first in measuring the relative importance of factors determining one's voting behavior. This topic is discussed at greater length further in the chapter.

Electoral Systems

In the Republic of China on Taiwan, ten kinds of public offices are elected directly or indirectly by the people:

1. The president and the vice-president of the republic
2. Delegates to the National Assembly
3. Members of the Legislative Yuan
4. Members of the Control Yuan
5. Provincial and Special Municipal Assemblymen
6. County magistrates and city mayors
7. County and city councillors
8. Chiefs of townships and their equivalent (Hsiang)
9. Representatives of townships and their equivalent
10. Village chiefs and their equivalent

Figure 7.1 shows the relationships among the various elected offices listed here.

Among those offices elected directly by the people, the members of the Legislative Yuan, Provincial and Special Municipal Assemblymen, county magistrates, and city mayors may be regarded as the most important; county and city councillors and township chiefs come next; and representatives of townships and village chiefs are the least important. In this chapter I will

Figure 7.1   Chart of Relationships of Various Elected Offices

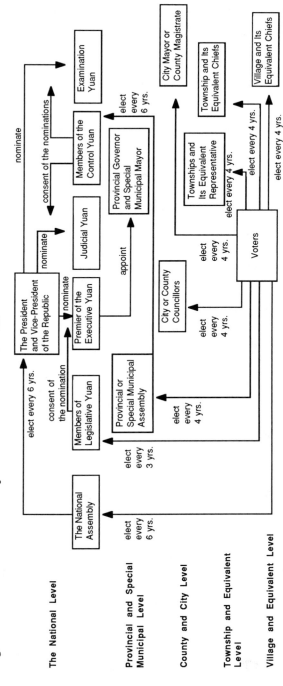

hereafter discuss mainly elections of the most important and the next important offices.

Elections in Taiwan were introduced in 1946—the second year after Taiwan's return to China—when representative bodies were established from the provincial level down to the county (city) and the township level with their representatives indirectly elected by the next lower representative bodies. In 1950, local self-rule was begun in Taiwan: all the chief executives and representative bodies under the provincial level were elected directly by the people. Provincial Assembly members have been elected directly since 1954. In 1969, elections were held for supplementary members to the National Assembly and the Legislative Yuan and indirectly for the members of the Control Yuan. Although the old members elected in 1947 continue to hold the majority of seats in the three national representative bodies, the newly elected supplementary members are more energetic and have gradually become the main actors on the stages of the national representative bodies. Local self-government at the county and lower levels has achieved a great deal. The thousands of candidates and millions of voters who have participated in the campaigns and elections have learned the democratic way of life. Some local government officials have achieved prominence at the national level. For instance, Chu Lien-fei rose from township chief to county magistrate and then became a member of the Taiwan Provincial Government Committee and is finally, at present, a member of the Legislative Yuan.

The Constitution of the Republic of China adopts the principles of universal suffrage and equal, direct, and secret voting. Guided by these principles, the Election Law provides the following stipulations on the eligibility of both electors and candidates. The requirements can be categorized as positive and negative:

Positive Requirements
1. Nationality: Voters must be either native or naturalized Chinese; candidates must have been naturalized for over ten years; in cases of restored citizenship, they must have been naturalized over three years.
2. Age: Twenty for voters; twenty-three for candidates; twenty-five for township chiefs; thirty for county magistrates and city mayors; and thirty-five for members of the Control Yuan.
3. Domicile: Must have lived continuously for at least six months either in their domicile of origin or of choice.
4. Scholastic Background and Experience: A junior high school graduate or its equivalent for village chiefs, township representatives, and county or city councillors; a senior high school graduate or its equivalent for township chiefs, provincial and special municipal assemblymen, delegates of the National Assembly, and members of the Legislative Yuan and the Control Yuan; a junior college graduate or its equivalent for the county magistrates and city mayors. In

addition, for candidates for township chiefs and county magistrates and city mayors, some kind of administrative experience is also required.

Negative Requirements

1. For voters and candidates:
   - Having been deprived of civil rights and not yet been reinstated.
   - Having been declared incompetent and not yet been reinstated.
2. For the candidates:
   - Commitment of crimes, ranging from heavy offenses against national internal or external security, corruption, offenses to the social order during an election period by assembling a crowd and using violence, offering to make or accept a bribe or other improper benefits in order to get others' commitments to withdraw from an election or to engage in a certain kind of voting in an election.
   - Having been placed on probation that has not yet been completed.[3]
   - Having been proclaimed bankrupt and not yet been rehabilitated.
   - Having been suspended from official appointment or from official duty for a certain period that has not yet expired.
   - Special Status: Those who are in active service in the military or police forces, full-time students still in school, or those who are handling election business, are temporarily prohibited from being candidates for office.

The Election Law also places a number of restrictions on campaign activity, such as:

1. The duration of the campaign is limited to a few days ranged from three to fifteen days for candidates of different offices.
2. The candidate may use a certain amount of money in campaigning, as prescribed by the Election Commission, based on the kind of election, population and district size, and price index. The candidate may not accept contributions from foreign individuals or associations of any kind, nor can they accept contributions from other candidates in the same election. The candidate should establish an account book recording all transactions of money received and spent in the campaign and report it to the Election Commission within thirty days after the polling day.
3. The candidate may assemble crowds and present his political views only in two kinds of meetings: candidate-sponsored and Election Commission–sponsored meetings, with the former held before the latter.
4. For candidate-sponsored meetings, the sponsor should report to the Election Commission when and where the meeting will be held two

Can't advertise on TV or radio

days ahead. No more than six meetings may be held in a single day and no meeting may last more than two hours.
5. Only the candidate and his registered assistants may make public speeches in the political view presentation meetings.
6. A candidate may establish a few campaign offices and employ a few assistants as prescribed by the Election Commission.
7. No candidate, his assistants, or other person shall assemble a crowd for a parade for campaigning purpose.
8. No candidate, his assistants, or other person shall mobilize voters signing their names or advertise on mass media for campaigning purpose.
9. No candidate or his assistants may let off firecrackers; no other person may do the same for them.

These are the main prescriptions set by the Election Law for candidate qualifications and restrictions on campaign activities. In the past forty years, these prescriptions have been modified several times. A great deal of speculation arose regarding the intentions of the ruling party in instituting these changes. A key consideration is whether or not these changes have constituted a barrier to entry for opposition candidates. Another is whether these restrictions on campaign activities are stacked against opposition candidates.

In addressing these questions, it is important to note that over the past forty years Taiwanese elections were held under a variety of different electoral regulations. At first, elections for members of the National Assembly, the Legislative Yuan, and the Control Yuan were held in accordance with their respective Election and Recall Acts. These were all enacted in 1947 and set few restrictions on candidate eligibility and on campaign activities. When elections for local governments were instituted in 1950, the Taiwan Provincial Government promulgated its own electoral regulations with the central government's approval.

Because the Taiwanese people take elections seriously, regulations had to make more detailed prescriptions on the eligibility of candidates and place more restrictions on campaign activities. When elections for supplementary members to the three national representative bodies were held from 1969 to 1975, they were conducted under a presidential decree in accordance with the Provisional Amendments for the Period of Mobilization Against the Communist Rebellion. This decree adopted most of the prescriptions of the Taiwan provincial electoral regulations. So did its substitute—the Act of Election and Recall of Public Officers During the Period of Communist Rebellion of 1980—which replaced the Taiwan provincial regulations and is still in effect. This act was amended in 1983 and 1989.

Among the numerous amendments, five changes may be considered more important. First, adding academic and administrative experience requirements for candidates, especially candidates for township chief, county magistrate, and city mayor seems to be proper and to constitute no barrier to entry for any serious potential candidate. Carrying out the duties of a representative or an administrative chief requires some minimum knowledge and administrative experience. Given Taiwan's educational development and the fact that serving a term (four years) as a township representative or a county councillor is interpreted as administrative experience, this requirement has not been taken seriously by any candidate.

Second, those who have committed heavy offenses against national internal or external security, or who have been found guilty of corruption, have been disqualified as candidates by the Act of Election and Recall of the Members of the National Assembly (Legislative Yuan and Control Yuan). In the 1983 amendment, those who assembled crowds and used violence during the election period or offered or accepted bribes to get others' commitments to withdraw from election or to engage in a certain kind of voting were also disqualified from the candidacy for any public office. Because ticket buying and threats of violence are pervasive in Taiwan during elections, one can hardly say that such restrictions are improper or are stacked against any ordinary candidate.

Third, it has been argued that there are too many restrictions on campaign activities. These restrictions may be grouped into two kinds: restrictions on meetings for the presentation of political views; and restrictions on other types of campaign activities. The government party is strong in organization and numerous party bureaucrats can be used to campaign for KMT candidates, whereas the opposition is weak in organization and the manpower needed to engage in canvassing the voters. Opposition candidates usually have to resort to stirring up public sentiment by protesting government maladministration and unfair election regulations. As a result, when the election competition gets fierce, meetings can lead to social conflict and violence. This is why candidate-sponsored meetings to express political views should take place previous to the Election Commission–sponsored meetings. It is hoped that a balanced presentation of views in the Election Commission–sponsored meetings may have a cooling effect on public sentiments. That is also why there are so many restrictions on assembling crowds and parades during the election period.

Fourth, when the thirty-seven-year-old martial law was lifted in 1986 and several parties nominated candidates to participate in the 1989 election, the Election Law had to adapt to the new situation. The most important change was the inclusion of many articles prescribing the role of political parties in the election. For the first time, the Election Law prescribes that members of the Central Election Commission who have the same party affiliation should not be over one-half of its total membership. And the supervisors of a polling station should not belong to only one political party in order to assure the impartiality of its work. Political parties may sponsor meetings for the presentation of political views in the campaigning period and party workers who have been registered with the Election Commission may give public speeches in meetings and disseminate publications for campaigns.

Fifth, the 1989 amendments to the Election Law have several financial assistance clauses that might produce important effects in future elections. One is that candidates who use their own money for campaigning within the amount prescribed by the Election Commission may list it as an income tax deduction item. Another is that a candidate may receive contributions of up to NT $20,000 from individuals and up to NT $300,000 from profit-making corporations. The contributor may list that money as a tax deduction or as an operational cost. Finally, any candidate who polls up to three-fourths of the votes received by the last one on the winners list in an electoral district may receive a subsidy from the government according to the votes he polled at NT $10 per vote.

In view of the above, one can hardly make an assertion that the Election Law stacks the odds against the opposition, especially when one examines the electoral district system that Taiwan has adopted. When elections for members of the three central representative bodies were held in 1947, all were elected in single nontransferable votes (see Table 7.1 at the end of this chapter). National Assemblymen were basically elected in single-member districts (at the level of the county or its equivalent). Members of the Legislative Yuan and the Control Yuan were basically elected in multimember districts that ranged from two to nine members, with the former elected directly by the people and the latter indirectly by the Provincial and Municipal Assemblies. When elections for members of local representative bodies and supplementary members of the three central representative bodies were held in Taiwan, the system of single nontransferable votes in multimember districts was also adopted. Considering the usual impact of district magnitude on electoral outcomes, this system should help smaller parties a great deal. Tables 7.2 and 7.3 show the relationship between district magnitude and election results in the election for supplementary members of the Legislative Yuan and of the Taiwan Provincial Assembly and for Taipei and Kaohsiung municipal councillors in 1989.

From these tables we notice that the opposition candidates did rather poorly in the single-member districts but better in the multimember districts. In elections for supplementary members of the Legislative Yuan in 1989, DPP candidates polled 41.76 percent of the votes in the three-member districts. In elections for members of the Taiwan Provincial Assembly and the Taipei and Kaohsiung municipal councils in 1989, the DPP candidates polled 30.22 percent of the votes. Although no generalization on the relationship between district magnitude and election results can be made at present, it is safe to say that the district apportionment has not been used against the opposition party intentionally.

However, the most controversial problem is that the members of the three national representative bodies elected in 1947 on mainland China are not subject to elections to renew their mandates. Meanwhile, as the population of Taiwan has grown a great deal since 1947, people eligible to vote have not had the chance to send their representatives to the national representative organs. The government did not know how to deal with the first of these two problems until recently, but it decided to let people in Taiwan elect some supplementary members to the national representative bodies after 1969. The number of these supplementary members was small at the beginning but grew larger later. Table 7.4 shows the ratio between the supplementary members (including those elected in Taiwan and selected from overseas Chinese) and their senior colleagues since 1969.

Because the number of senior members contracted very fast because of death and retirement, and because the supplementary members are more active and energetic, they gradually took the leadership in these representative bodies. This trend first appeared in the Control Yuan and then in the Legislative Yuan. Because the role of the National Assembly is mainly confined to the election of the president and vice-president of the republic and meets only once every six years, the transition of its leadership progresses at a slower pace. Despite the Taiwanese people's lack of democratic experience before the first election of members to the National Assembly in 1947, they like very much to participate in elections—either as candidates or as voters. The average number of candidates is usually twice the number of seats contested, sometimes much higher when the contested office is deemed very important. The polling rate is usually around 60 percent to 70 percent, and sometimes as high as 80 percent. It is usually higher than that of a Western democratic country. It also means that elections are rather competitive in Taiwan, though sometimes county magistrates and city mayors are elected without contest. (See tables 7.5–7.10 at chapter's end.)

From the foregoing statistics, several features of the electoral system became apparent. First, the Kuomintang—the ruling party—has not monopolized the elections, as one might assume. They have often failed in important elections. For example, in five contests for the mayor of Taipei, KMT candidates failed three times. In elections for county magistrates and other city mayors, non-KMT candidates often capture three or four seats, about one-fifth of them. In the most recent election, in 1989, non-KMT candidates captured seven seats—about one-third of local executives. Elections for members of the Taiwan Provincial Assembly are deemed very important by local people because the Provincial Assembly is powerful in budget making and other areas. Non-KMT candidates usually poll about 30 percent of the votes and win one-fifth or one-fourth of the Provincial Assembly's seats. In the most recent election, in 1989, non-KMT candidates captured 37.8 percent of the votes and almost 30 percent of the seats. However, they did not do so well in elections for county and city councillors and township chiefs, where KMT candidates won 77.2 percent of the seats in local representative bodies and 91.58 percent of township executive offices in the 1990 elections. It seems that the KMT has a better rank-and-file organization and the non-KMT—especially the Democratic Progressive Party—can capture more votes by appealing to high-level issues of national identification. This problem has recently been high profile in Taiwan and deserves more care and attention.

Voting Behavior

Studies of voting behavior in various countries have posited four different voting orientations: party, candidate, issue, and primary relationship. In party orientation, the voter identifies with a political party and supports its nominated candidate. By party orientation, we mean the voters support candidates mainly for their personality and characteristics deemed better than other candidates. In issue orientation, voters support candidates mainly for their position on certain issues. In primary relationship orientation, the voter supports a candidate mainly because of a personal link such as those based on friendship (including schoolmates, colleagues, and game companions), kinship, or a common neighborhood. In Taiwan, scholars disagree on the number and weighting of voter orientations. This is because the determining factors of human behavior are very complex. It is difficult to weight which factor is more important than the other. When we studied the voting behavior in the 1986 elections for supplementary members of the Legislative Yuan and the National Assembly in northern Taiwan (including Taipei County, Keelung City, and Ilan County), we found the behavior patterns as shown in Table 7.11, though the findings are still tentative.

Although political parties play a very important role in modern government, in traditional China as well as in present-day Taiwan the party is still associated with factions and tricks. Despite party leaders' constant exhortation that party workers are at the service of the people, the servants often turn out to be the bosses. Therefore, the image of political parties is usually negative, and people who support a party's nominee often do so for reasons other than party orientation. Only those who have strong identification with a party will vote for nominees based on party affiliation.

The question then arises why the KMT has garnered between 60 and 70 percent of the votes despite the small percentage of party-oriented voters. The answer may be twofold: First, KMT members are mostly leaders in their respective fields or groups and thus are in a better position to transmit their preferences through their primary relationship networks. Second, the KMT has a better organizational strategy, assigning each KMT candidate a "responsibility zone" that includes several villages or their equivalent where the candidate has better personal connections.

As we shall deal with the "primary relationship" in greater depth later, let us discuss the so-called responsibility zone here. In Taiwan, elections for members of representative bodies are in multimember districts where a candidate not only competes with candidates from other parties but also with candidates from his own party. The responsibility zone is basically a campaign structure using personal primary relationships of the assigned candidate and local leaders and other prominent people to mobilize votes for him. The major actors in the responsibility zone are local leaders, including village chiefs, neighborhood chiefs, village administrators, and local KMT party workers. They have influence because they keep in close contact with people in a given neighborhood. KMT candidates are prohibited from openly competing for votes in another's responsibility zone. The relative importance of the candidates' own primary relationships and those of the local KMT leaders varies in rural and urban areas. In rural areas where a candidate has many primary relationship networks, and even the local KMT leaders are his own men, his primary relationships are dominant. In an urban area where a candidate has fewer primary relationships, local KMT leaders play a more important role. Because the urban area is more complex socially and urban people are usually more educated and better informed, they are more vulnerable to different political appeals, so the influence of local KMT leaders is decreasing. The zone system does not guarantee a victory for KMT candidates in the future.

According to our survey, issue orientation also counts for little in Taiwan's voting behavior. For voters to be issue oriented, they have to know where the candidates stand on issues. And to be informed, they have to read the leaflets distributed by the candidates, scan the electoral bulletins issued by the government, attend the candidate- or government-sponsored political view presentation meetings, or obtain information on the candidates' views through mass media or other channels. Yet, in our survey of a hotly contested Tannan County election, only half of those interviewed read the electoral bulletin, and less than one-tenth of those who did retained anything significant from reading it. Roughly one out of five voters had attended the political view presentation meetings in person. But few went off knowing what the candidates were in favor of rather than what they were against. In other words, only a few truly voted on issues.

However, if there are not too many voters who are truly or positively issue oriented in Taiwan, there are quite a few who are negatively issue oriented, who vote to protest. If we look closely enough, we will find that on many policy issues such as economic policy and environmental policy, KMT and non-KMT candidates are not really far apart. It is on the levels above and below public policy where the differences arise. Above the policy level, the two sides clash over state identification, system legitimacy, the composition of the central representative bodies, and a host of other high political issues. Below the policy level, what is most controversial is the claim that the administrative branches of government at various levels are unfair, impotent, or unresponsive to public needs.

It is our belief that high political issues concern those few who are well educated and those with a family member who happened to be a victim of the unfortunate February 28, 1947, Incident. A greater number of people demand only greater democracy and wider participation. Even more are discontented only because they have suffered at the hands of lower-level administrators, and the opposition provides a ready outlet for their grievances. Because most city dwellers are either well educated and free from the influence of primary relationships or victims of maladministration of lower-level bureaucrats, the non-KMT candidates can usually mobilize a large protest vote in urban areas. Supported by the multimember single-ballot voting system, anyone who can collect one-fifth or even one-tenth of the total votes in a district from the issue-oriented people "above the policy level" or "below the policy level" has a good chance to win a seat in the representative bodies. This is why there are a few extremists in the Legislative Yuan and the National Assembly who have taken striking gestures, such as attacking high-ranking government officers with a water gun on the floor of the Legislative Yuan. It is also for this reason why some students of the electoral system in Taiwan propose to change the multimember single-ballot voting system to a single-member plurality voting system so as to encourage the moderates and to eliminate the extremists.[4]

In our survey we found that candidate orientation is highly influential in determining voter behavior in Taiwan. A voter is candidate oriented if he or she pays considerable attention to the candidates' personal qualities such as education, moral character, management skills, initiative, and enthusiasm. In our study we have specifically requested the respondents to give their assessment of candidates' moral character, knowledge, management skills, and willingness and ability to promote public well-being. We find that the higher the candidate scores on these five important personal qualities, the more likely he is to win. The image of a candidate is thus crucial. Those with an eye on public office often strive to achieve a favorable image for themselves while treading gently to avoid scandals. In a way, the emphasis on personal qualities blends public and private interests nicely.

Primary social relations, as we pointed out earlier, are the most important link and communication channel in social, economic, and political life in Taiwan as well as the main determinant of voting behavior. In human relations, in Taiwan as elsewhere, personal connections are closer and therefore more influential than impersonal relations. Morris Janowitz and Dwaine Marvick's concept of "primary group pressures"[5] and Heinz Eulau's concept of the "primary zone"[6] are something similar to our concept of "primary relationship." In actual politics, the old US political machines, the Koenkai of Japanese Diet members,[7] and the patron-client relations in many developing countries represent similar structures linking political actors with constituents.

In Taiwan, one who intends to run for a public office first has to use his primary relations to build up campaign networks in each village and its equivalent. The longer and the more extensive this buildup, the more certain his campaign success. The former Taoyuan magistrate, Hsu Sin-liang, built an extensive primary relationship network when he was a member of the Taiwan Provincial Assembly by associating with several young leaders in each village in the form of pledging each other to a sworn brotherhood. This network was so strong that Hsu was able to defeat a wholehearted campaign by the KMT in the election for Taoyuan County magistrate in 1977. The responsibility zone system, which the KMT has effectively used as a mobilizing mechanism in elections for many years, is basically a tool pulling the strings of the primary social relations of the candidate, his assistants, and the KMT leaders. It would be totally useless if there were no primary relations in the "zone" to be mobilized. However, although this strategy has proven successful in winning elections, it has also fostered a tendency in candidates toward self-reliance. By self-reliance, we mean that if a candidate has to use his own primary relationships to build up a campaign network strong enough to win the election with or without the help of local KMT leaders in the responsibility zone, he will be more independent in his political behavior afterward. This is why KMT members in the representative bodies tend to be more independent and party influence seems to be diminishing.

Concluding Remarks   *but only recently*
                                a party elections

After four decades of elections in Taiwan, the electoral law is becoming less restrictive. The current rules are not biased against small opposition parties. In fact, the opposite is probably the case, and as the data presented in this chapter show, the Kuomintang has not monopolized electoral support to the extent that is often thought. The administration of elections has also become more fair. The organization of both the central and local Election Commissions and the polling stations is now bipartisan. Most restrictions on campaigning have been lifted, and those that remain do not systemmatically discriminate against the opposition.

When we turn from the electoral rules to campaign strategy and the basis of voting behavior, traditional patterns become visible. KMT and opposition DPP candidates both still use primary relationships and networks in order to succeed electorally. These primary relationships are also the most important determinant of electoral behavior.

The DPP has also restored to antigovernment, and even antiregime, arguments in order to garner protest votes, however. The fiercer the attack, the more emotional the words, the more cheers will echo from a sympathetic audience. As a result, more reasoned debate has all but disappeared, and during election campaigns, society tends to be split by extreme, and even violent, expressions of opinion.

In facing this danger, President Lee Teng-hui convened a National Affairs Conference in 1990, inviting delegates from different parties, especially those with strong dissident origins. He sought to reach a broad consensus on the Republic of China's international status, but the conference failed to reach broad agreement. Given the level of disagreement on the status of the country, popular elections for significant offices such as governor of Taiwan Province and president of the Republic could severely intensify both political and social divisions.

Appendix

Table 7.1 Seats Allotted and Elected for the Three Central Representative Bodies in 1947

Representative Methods	Members of the National Assembly		Members of the Legislative Yuan		Members of the Control Yuan	
	Allotted Seats	Elected Seats	Allotted Seats	Elected Seats	Allotted Seats	Elected Seats
Geographical:						
Counties and their equivalent	2,177	2,141	622	622	199	165
Mongolia	57	57	22	22	8	8
Tibet	40	39	15	14	8	6
National minorities						
Borderlands	34	34	6	6	0	0
Inner provinces	17	17	0	0	0	0
Overseas Chinese	65	22	19	8	8	1
Occupational associations						
National	271	268	89	8	0	0
Provincial and its equivalent	216	216	0	0	0	0
Women's associations						
National	20	20	0	0	0	0
Provincial and its equivalent	148	147	0	0	0	0
Total	3,045	2,961	773	760	223	180
Actually reported participation in first meeting in 1948	2,878		648		N.A.	

Source: Chung-Yang Hsuan-Chu Wei-Yuan-Hui, *Chung-Hua-Min-Kuo Hsuan-Chu Kai-K'uang* (Central Election Commission, *Summary of Elections in the Republic of China*, Book 1, pp. 109–110.

Table 7.2 District Magnitude and Election Results in Elections of the Supplementary Members of the Legislative Yuan in 1989

District Magnitude	No. of District	Total Seats	Candidates KMT	Candidates DPP	Candidates Other	Votes Polled (%) KMT	Votes Polled (%) DPP	Votes Polled (%) Other	Seats Won (No.) (%) KMT	Seats Won (No.) (%) DPP	Seats Won (No.) (%) Other	Deviation from Proportionality KMT	Deviation from Proportionality DPP	Deviation from Proportionality Other
1	8	8	15	6	9	70.92	16.97	12.11	7 / 87.50%	0 / 0.00%	1 / 12.50%	+ 16.58%	− 10.97%	+ 0.39%
2	11	22	32	13	22	65.30	15.98	18.72	17 / 77.27	2 / 9.90	3 / 13.64	+ 11.97	− 6.88	− 5.09
3	3	9	11	6	8	52.24	41.76	6.00	6 / 66.67	3 / 33.33	0 / 0.00	+ 14.43	− 8.43	− 6.00
4	6	24	28	13	26	54.95	23.40	15.65	15 / 62.50	6 / 25.00	3 / 12.50	+ 7.55	− 4.40	− 3.15
5	3	15	26	7	14	66.43	26.04	7.52	11 / 73.33	4 / 26.67	0 / 0.00	+ 6.90	+ 0.43	− 7.52
6	2	12	18	6	13	63.68	34.49	1.83	8 / 66.67	4 / 33.33	0 / 0.00	+ 2.99	− 1.16	− 1.83
11	1	11	16	6	7	61.70	25.09	13.21	8 / 72.73	2 / 18.18	1 / 9.09	+ 11.24	− 6.92	− 4.12
Total	34	101	146	57	99	63.54	23.10	13.36	72 / 75.03	21 / 15.14	8 / 9.83	+ 11.49	− 7.96	− 3.53

Source: Compiled by the author from reports of local election commissions.

Table 7.3 District Magnitude and Election Results in Elections of Members of the Taiwan Provincial Assembly and Taipei and Kaohsiung Municipal Councils in 1989

District Magnitude	No. of District	Total Seats	Candidates			Votes Polled (%)			Seats Won (No.) (%)			Deviation from Proportionality		
			KMT	DPP	Other	KMT	DPP	Other	KMT	DPP	Other	KMT	DPP	Other
1	7	7	8	5	3	75.13	18.87	6.00	7 / 100%	0 / 0.00%	0 / 0.00%	+24.87	−18.87	−6.58
2	4	8	10	3	6	72.16	21.26	6.58	6 / 75.00	2 / 25.00	0 / 0.00	+2.84	+3.74	−6.58
3	5	15	17	11	4	68.04	27.68	3.68	11 / 75.00	3 / 20.00	1 / 6.67	+4.09	+7.68	+2.99
4	3	12	12	7	7	64.77	30.22	5.01	8 / 73.33	4 / 33.73	0 / 0.00	+1.90	+3.11	−5.01
5	2	10	10	3	2	57.70	28.38	13.92	5 / 66.67	3 / 30.00	2 / 20.20	−7.70	+1.62	+6.08
6	4	24	28	14	13	64.85	18.32	16.82	17 / 50.00	3 / 12.50	4 / 16.67	+5.98	+5.82	+0.15
7	3	21	22	10	11	66.43	22.65	10.92	14 / 70.83	6 / 28.57	1 / 4.76	+0.24	+5.92	−6.16
8	1	8	10	4	5	69.05	22.29	8.67	7 / 66.67	1 / 12.50	0 / 0.00	+18.45	−9.79	−8.67
10	4	40	41	21	13	64.07	23.66	12.27	29 / 87.50	8 / 20.00	3 / 7.50	+8.43	+3.66	+4.77
12	1	12	10	4	5	87.68	7.44	4.88	7 / 72.50	4 / 33.33	1 / 8.33	−29.35	+25.89	+3.45
14	1	14	17	6	7	74.45	22.23	3.32	10 / 58.33	4 / 28.57	0 / 0.00	−3.02	+6.34	−3.32
Total	35	171	185	88	76	68.95	22.60	8.44	121 / 71.43	38 / 28.57	12 / 0.00	+6.96	+4.02	+2.94

Source: Compiled by the author from reports of local election commissions.

Table 7.4 Ratio Between the Supplementary Members and Their Senior Colleagues in the National Representative Bodies

Years	National Assembly				Legislative Yuan				Control Yuan			
	Senior Members		Supplementary Members		Senior Members		Supplementary Members		Senior Members		Supplementary Members	
	No.	%	No.	%	No.	%	No.	%	No.	%	No.	%
1969	1399	98.94	15	1.06	468	97.70	11	2.30	69	97.18	2	2.82
1972	1344	96.20	53	3.79	419	92.09	36	7.91				
1973									63	80.77	10	12.82
											5[a]	6.41
1975					377	87.88	37	8.62				
							15[a]	3.50				
1980	1152	93.81	76	6.19	309	76.11	70	17.24	42	56.76	22	29.73
							27[a]	6.65			10[a]	13.51
1983					270	73.37	71	19.29				
							27[a]	7.34				
1986	880	91.28	84	8.71	224	69.14	73	22.53	37	53.02	22	31.88
							27[a]	8.33			10[a]	14.50
1989					150	53.57	101	36.07				
							29[a]	10.36				

Source: Ministry of the Interior, *Statistic Data Book of Interior*, 1970, 1973, 1976, 1981, 1984, 1987, and 1990.
[a] Supplementary members selected from the overseas Chinese.

Table 7.5 Elections of the Supplementary Members of the National Assembly, 1969–1986

Year	Seats Open	Candidates	Polling Rate (%)	KMT Won			Non-KMT[a] Won		
				Seats	Seats (%)	Votes (%)	Seats	Seats (%)	Votes (%)
1969	15	29	54.72	15	100	79.7	0	0	20.3
1972	53	78	68.61	43	81.13	72.0	10	18.87	28.0
1980	76	185	66.43	61	80.26	66.4	15	19.74	33.6
1986	84	169	65.43	68	80.95	68.3	16	19.05	31.7

Source: Chung-Yang Hsuan-Chu Wei-Yuan-Hui, Chung-Hua-Min-Kuo Hsuan-Chu Tong-Chi Ti-Yao (Central Election Commission, *Summary of Election Statistics of the Republic of China*: 1946–1987).

[a]Non-KMT includes the Young China Party, the Democratic Socialist Party, the Democratic Progressive Party, and its precedents—Tangwai and other independents.

Table 7.6 Elections of the Supplementary Members of the Legislative Yuan, 1969–1989

Year	Seats Open	Candidates	Polling Rate (%)	KMT Won			Non-KMT Won		
				Seats	Seats (%)	Votes (%)	Seats	Seats (%)	Votes (%)
1969	11	25	55.00	8	72.7	76.0	3	27.3	24.0
1972	30	55	68.18	30	83.3	70.2	6	16.7	29.8
1975	37	61	75.97	30	81.1	78.7	7	18.9	21.3
1980	70	218	66.36	56	80.0	72.1	14	20.0	27.9
1983	71	171	63.17	62	87.2	70.7	9	12.8	29.3
1986	73	302[a]	65.38	59	80.8	69.9	14 –	19.2	30.1
1989	101		75.17	72	71.3	60.1	29	28.7	39.9

Sources: Chung-Yang Hsuan-Chu Wei-Yuan-Hui, Chung-Hua-Min-Kuo Hsuan-Chu Tong-Chi Ti-Yao (Central Election Commission, *Summary of Election Statistics of the Republic of China*: 1969–86); 1989 data based on newspaper reports.

[a]Of the candidates: KMT 140, non-KMT 162.

Table 7.7 Elections of the Members of Taiwan Provincial Assembly, 1951–1989

Year	Seats Open	Candidates	Polling Rate	KMT Won			Non-KMT Won		
				Seats	Seats (%)	Votes (%)	Seats	Seats (%)	Votes (%)
1951	55	140		40	84.2	68.8	12		31.2
1954	57	110	74.4	48	80.3	67.8	9	15.8	32.2
1957	66	118	78.2	53	79.5	65.4	13	19.7	34.6
1960	73	126	72.52	58	82.4	68.0	15	20.5	32.0
1963–1964	74	137	69.26	61	84.5	75.5	13	17.6	24.5
1968	71	129	74.28	60	79.5	68.9	11	15.5	31.1
1972	73	121	70.33	58	72.7	64.1	15	20.5	35.9
1977	77	125	80.40	56	76.6	70.3	21	27.3	29.7
1981	77	189	71.94	59	76.6	69.8	18	23.4	30.2
1985	77	158	72.08	59	70.1	62.1	18	23.4	37.8
1989	77	157	75.89	54(76)			23(81)	29.9	

Sources: Chung-Yang Hsuan-Chu Wei-Yuan-Hui, Chung-Hua-Min-Kuo Hsuan-Chu Tong-Chi Ti-Yao (Central Election Commission, *Summary of Election Statistics of the Republic of China:* 1951–1981); 1985–1989 data based on newspaper reports.

Notes: In 1951, members of the Taiwan Provincial Assembly were elected indirectly by the county and city councillors; from 1954 they have been elected directly by the people. Of the candidates in 1989, seventy-six were from the KMT, eighty-one from the Democratic Progressive Party and independents.

Table 7.8 Elections of the County Magistrates and City Mayors in Taiwan, 1950–1989

Year	Seats Contested (candidates)	Seats Uncontested	Polling Rate	KMT Won Seats	KMT Won Seats (%)	KMT Won Votes (%)	Non-KMT Won Seats	Non-KMT Won Seats (%)	Non-KMT Won Votes (%)
1950–1951	21(90)	0	79.61	18	85.9	N.A.	3	14.1	N.A.
1954	13(38)	8	24.85	19	90.5	71.8	2	9.5	28.2
1957	18(40)	2	78.20	20	95.2	65.0	1	4.8	35.0
1960	13(35)	8	72.49	19	90.5	72.0	2	9.5	28.0
1964	15(47)	6	69.05	17(24)	81.0	73.1	4(22)	19.0	26.9
1968	15(43)	5	74.06	17(24)	85.0	72.4	3(19)	15.0	27.6
1972	11(39)	9	70.31	20	100.0	78.6	0	0	21.4
1977	13(36)	7	80.39	16(20)	80.0	70.4	4(16)	20.0	29.6
1981	17(56)	2	71.94	15(27)	78.9	59.4	4(29)	21.1	40.6
1985	18(54)	3	72.08	17	81.0	62.6	4	19.0	37.4
1989	19(69)	2	75.90	14(27)	66.6	52.7	7(42)	33.3	47.3

Sources: 1950–1980 data are based on Chung-Yang Hsuan-Chu Wei-Yuan-Hui, Chung-Hua-Min-Kuo Hsuan-Chu Kai-K'uang (Central Election Commission, Summary of Elections in the Republic of China, Book 1; 1985–1989 data are based on newspaper reports.
Note: Figures in parentheses show the candidates contesting the seats.

Table 7.9 Elections of County and City Councillors in Taiwan Province, 1950–1990

Year	Seats	Candidates	Polling Rate(%)	Seats Returned				
				KMT(%)	YCP(%)	DSP(%)	DPP(%)	Nonpartisan
1950–1951	814	1,827	80.73	513(63.02)	4(0.49)			297(36.48)
1952–1953	860	1,844	79.72	516(60.00)		2(0.23)		342(39.77)
1954–1955	928	1,579	78.88	657(70.8)				271(29.2)
1958	1,025	1,621	78.31	657(64.1)	1(0.10)			367(35.8)
1961	929	1,629	73.83	579(62.32)	2(0.21)	1(0.11)		347(37.35)
1964	907	1,563	76.76	670(73.87)	5(0.59)	2(0.22)		230(25.36)
1968	847	1,262	78.02	626(73.9)	5(0.59)	1(0.12)		215(25.38)
1973	850	1,480	73.30	625(73.53)	3(0.35)			222(26.12)
1977	857	1,271	80.47	717(83.66)	1(0.12)			139(16.22)
1982	799	1,683	75.38	640(80.10)	2(0.25)			157(19.65)
1986	837	1,472	71.16	659(78.73)				178(21.27)
1990	842	1,743	72.10	650(77.20)			47(5.58)	145(17.22)

Sources: 1950–1982 data are based on Chung-Yang Hsuan-Chu Wei-Yuan-Hui, Chung-Hua-Min-Kuo Hsuan-Chu Kai-K'uang (Central Election Commission, *Summary of Elections in the Republic of China*, Book 2; 1986–1990 data are based on newspaper reports.

Note: KMT = Kuomintang, Nationalist Party
YCP = Young China Party
DSP = Chinese Democratic Socialist Party
DPP = Democratic Progressive Party

Table 7.10 Elections of Township and Its Equivalent Chiefs in Taiwan Province, 1951–1990

Year	Seats	Candidates	Polling Rate(%)	Seats Returned			
				KMT(%)	YCP(%)	DDP(%)	Nonpartisan
1951	360	1,077	67.52	254(20.55)	1(0.28)		105(29.17)
1952–1954	360	804	62.13				
1955–1957	360	573	41.77				
1959–1960	313	563	58.48				
1964–1965	319	580	63.56	294(92.16)			25(7.84)
1968	313	525	77.58	268(88.62)			45(14.38)
1973	313	488	79.28	288(92.01)			25(7.99)
1977	313	438	73.88	292(93.29)			21(6.71)
1982	312	755	80.44	288(92.30)			24(7.70)
1986	309	594	76.08	289(93.52)		6(1.94)	20(6.47)
1990	309	757	72.02	283(91.58)			20(6.47)

Sources: 1950–1980 data are based on Chung-Yang Hsuan-Chu Wei-Yuan-Hui, Chung-Hua-Min-Kuo Hsuan-Chu Kai-K'uang (Central Election Commission, *Summary of Elections in the Republic of China,* Book 1; 1985–1989 data are based on newspaper reports.

Table 7.11 Voting Orientations in Northern Taiwan in 1986

Orientation		Issue	Candidate	Party	Traditional Relations	Personal Interest	At Random	Others	Don't Know	Total
Legislator	No.	57	171	49	86	16	22	1	21	423
	%	13.5	40.4	11.6	20.3	3.8	5.2	0.2	5.0	100%
National Assembly	No.	49	124	47	77	6	21	0	18	342
	%	14.3	36.3	13.7	22.5	1.8	6.1	0	5.3	100%

Source: Fei-lung Lui and Yih-yen Cheu, *Voting Behavior in a Transitional Society: The Case of Taiwan* (Unpublished report for the National Science Council, 1987), p. 161 (in Chinese).

Notes

1. Angus Campbell, Philip E. Converse, Warren E. Miller, and Donald Stokes, *The American Voter* (New York: John Wiley, 1960).

2. According to the Constitution, the president of the Republic of China plays a role almost similar to that of a cabinet government because his act of promulgation of laws and issuance of orders has to be countersigned by the premier of the Executive Yuan. Though he may coordinate and regulate whenever the five branches of the central government are at odds, he still may not take actions swiftly and independently—even when a special emergency occurs and the country needs him to do so. This is why the National Assembly had to adopt the Temporary Provisions of the Constitution in accordance with the procedure for constitutional amendments at the very beginning of its promulgation and effectiveness in 1948 when the Chinese Communists had rebelled openly nationwide. The Temporary Provisions consists of eleven articles, which were adopted by the National Assembly at five different times. The contents of these articles, if those of procedural and nonsubstantial significance can be ignored, may be grouped into the following three categories.

a. Those that augment the presidential power to cope with emergencies during the period of the Communist rebellion:

- Taking emergency measures to avert an imminent danger to the security of the state or of the people, or to cope with any serious financial or economic crisis, by resolution of the Executive Yuan Council, without being subject to the procedural restrictions prescribed in Article 39 or Article 43 of the Constitution. However, the Legislative Yuan may require that it be modified or abrogated in accordance with Paragraph 2 of Article 57 of the Constitution. Article 39 of the Constitution says that "the President may, in accordance with Law [i.e., Law Regarding to the Declaration of Martial Law], declare martial law with the approval of or subject to confirmation by the Legislative Yuan. When the Legislative Yuan deems it necessary, it may by resolution [of a plural majority] request the President to terminate the martial law." And Article 43 says, "In case of a national calamity, an epidemic, or a national financial or economic crisis that calls for emergency measures, the President, during the recess of the Legislative Yuan, may by resolution of the Executive Yuan Council, and in accordance with the Law on Emergency Orders, issue emergency orders, proclaiming such measures as may be necessary to cope with the situation. Such orders shall, within one month after issuance, be presented to the Legislative Yuan for confirmation. In case the Legislative Yuan withholds confirmation, the said orders shall forthwith cease to be valid." Therefore, the declaration of martial law and issuance of emergency orders by the president are subject to the approval or confirmation of the Legislative Yuan. If the Legislative Yuan withholds approval or confirmation, the president may not request the Legislative Yuan for reconsideration. But in cases of emergency measures taken by the president in accordance with the Temporary Provisions, they need not be approved or confirmed by the Legislative Yuan, and when the Legislative

Yuan requests that it be altered, the president still may request reconsideration by way of the Executive Yuan. If the Legislative Yuan fails to kill it by more than two-thirds of the members present, the emergency measures may not be further challenged. In other words, the emergency measures can be upheld with the support of one-third plus one member of the Legislative Yuan.

- During the period of Communist rebellion, the president and the vice-president may be reelected without being subject to the two-term restriction prescribed in Article 47 of the Constitution. This of course greatly strengthens the position of the president and the vice-president.
- During the period of Communist rebellion, the president is authorized to establish, in accordance with the constitutional system, an organ for making major policy decisions concerned with national mobilization and suppression of the Communist rebellion and for assuming administrative control in war zones. Thus, the National Security Council was established in 1967, through which the president's policymaking powers have been greatly augmented, so that his role in the political system is now almost similar to that of the president of the French Fifth Republic.

b. To strengthen the central representative bodies without their being subject to the restrictions prescribed in Articles 26, 64, or 91 of the Constitution. By this provision the president is authorized to promulgate decrees providing for supplementary elections of new members to the National Assembly, the Legislative Yuan, and the Control Yuan in order to improve the functioning of these representative bodies.

c. To meet the requirements of national mobilization and the suppression of the Communist rebellion, the president may make adjustments in the administrative and personnel organs of the central government as well as their organizations. Thus, the Central Personnel Administration was established under the Executive Yuan in 1967. Powers of the Ministry of Personnel of the Examination Yuan were partially transferred to the Central Personnel Administration.

3. In accordance with the Chinese criminal code, probational measures include the following:

a. Reformatory education: A person is not punished because they have not completed their fourteenth year of age, or their punishment is reduced because they have not completed their eighteenth year of age and after execution or remission of punishment may be ordered to enter a reformatory to receive reformatory education.

b. Custody: A person who is not punished because they are insane, or their punishment is reduced because they are feeble minded, deaf, and dumb, and their punishment has been executed or remissed, may be ordered to enter a suitable establishment for custody.

c. Compulsory cure: A person who commits the offense of taking opium, morphine, heroin, or drugs of this kind, or who repeatedly commits an offense because of intoxication, or any criminal who has an infectious disease, may be ordered to enter a suitable place for compulsory cure before or after the execution of punishment.

d. Compulsory labor: A person who makes the commission of crimes a habit or occupation may, after execution or remission of punishment, be ordered to enter a labor establishment to perform compulsory labor.

e. Protective control: A person who is conditionally released or whose punishment is suspended may be put under protective control by a police authority, a self-governing body, a charitable institution, the nearest relative, or other appropriate person.

f. Expulsion from the country: An alien who has been sentenced to imprisonment or a more severe punishment may be expelled from the country after execution or remission of punishment.

4. Professor Yang Tai-Shun and Professor Hsieh Fu-sen of the National Chengchi University have made this proposal.

5. Morris Janowitz and Dwaine Marvick, *Competitive Pressure and Democratic Consent* (Ann Arbor: University of Michigan, 1956).

6. Heinz Eulau, "Life Space and Social Networks as Political Context," in *Politics, Self, and Society: A Theme and Variations* (Cambridge, Mass.: Harvard University Press, 1986), pp. 300–324.

7. Gerald L. Curtis, *Election Campaigning Japanese Style* (New York: Columbia University Press, 1971), pp. 126–152.

CHAPTER 8

Electoral Competition and Political Democratization

FU HU AND
YUN-HAN CHU

The role of electoral competition in the democratic transition process is little understood and generally underappreciated in the now considerable literature on political democratization.[1] It is our contention that in a society with no previous experience of democracy, democratic legitimacy takes root mainly through competitive electoral processes. In newly industrializing societies, elections are the principal mechanism through which changes in the social structure that have been brought about by rapid industrialization are translated into a political force for weakening the entrenched authoritarian order and for pushing the democratization process forward.[2] The purpose of this chapter is to offer a coherent analysis of this important democratizing mechanism in the context of an East Asian NIC, the Republic of China on Taiwan.

For a long time, Taiwan has been known among students of comparative politics for its economic dynamism and political stasis. But over the past ten years, elections have given rise to an organized political opposition that has begun posing real challenges to the ruling party, mainly through electoral means. Increased electoral support has emboldened the opposition to break the legal limitations on their organizational growth, to express their dissatisfaction with the existing political system in ways never before tolerated, and to step up their push for democratic changes. The emerging challenge has compelled the ruling elite to adopt wide-ranging democratic reforms. These reforms, in turn, accentuated the political stake of elections to the ruling elite and fostered the ascendance of native politicians with electoral support within the Kuomintang (KMT). Thus the emerging partisan competition in the national elections is both a manifestation of, and a catalyst for, democratization in Taiwan.

In this chapter, we examine the relationship between electoral competition and political democratization from the vantage point of candidates and voters. We analyze the nature of electoral competition in terms of candidates' campaign issues and the social and ideological orientation of partisan voters. We proceed in three steps. In the first section, we give a brief historical account of how elections have evolved from a sideshow of an entrenched one-party authoritarian rule to an integral part of the legitimating institutional arrangements, despite the worrisome potential of the elections to weaken the authoritarian structure. We then present the contours of the emerging partisan competition between the KMT and the Democratic Progressive Party (DPP) based on both electoral turnout data and our survey data of the 1983 and 1986 elections for national legislators.[3] In the third section, the nature and systemic significance of the recent electoral competition is examined in terms of the social and political cleavages manifested in campaign issues and electoral choice at the level of candidates and voters. Important micro-level details are added to the broad profile of electoral competition. In the conclusion, we show how our empirical data might shed light on the future of the democratic transition in Taiwan.

Elections and the Democratic Opening of a One-Party Authoritarian Regime

In the contemporary era, few authoritarian regimes in the developing countries have done without some form of democratic facade.[4] For almost three decades since its initial consolidation on Taiwan, the KMT regime is one of the few regimes that relied very little on democratic forms for its legitimacy.

The KMT regime in Taiwan entered the 1970s with a proven formula for maintaining the political dominance of the mainlander elite at the national level and for controlling a limited popular electoral process implemented at the local level. Formally, the KMT state maintained a complicated five-branch (Yuan) national government, with a functioning legislature claiming to represent all the provinces of China with its life-term members elected in 1948 on the mainland. It also intentionally retained a cumbersome four-tier administrative system designed for the whole of China, starting with the national then down to provincial, county/city, and town/borough level. Limited home rule has been implemented since 1950. The natives were allowed to elect their representatives up to the provincial level and executive heads up to the county/city level.

Under the surface, the KMT maintained a stable political order through an elaborate ideology akin to socialism, a cohesive and highly penetrating party apparatus organized along Leninist democratic centralist lines (see Chapter 5), and a powerful, pervasive, but less visible, security apparatus reinforced by martial law. The official ideology, Sun Yat-sen's eclectic Three Principles of the People—nationalism, democracy, and people's livelihood—advocated the commensurability of the interests of the capitalist class and working class, the need for regulating private capital, and the advancement of state capital. Through its exclusive control over socialization in the schools and the mass media, the mainlander elite constructed an ideologically indoctrinated popular coalition.[5]

The party apparatus consisted of crosscutting functional units organized along both regional and corporatist (sectorial) lines (see Chapter 10).[6] At the grass-roots level, the KMT utilized existing patron-client networks to establish complex local political machines within the party structure throughout the island. Within each administrative district below the provincial level, the KMT nurtured and kept at least two competing local factions striving for electoral offices and, more important, for a share of region-based economic rents in the nontradable goods sector, distributed by the party-directed spoil system.[7] Above the local level, the KMT controlled and demobilized all modern social sectors through preemptive incorporation of business and professional associations, labor unions, state employees, journalists, intellectuals, students, and other targeted groups. The KMT also captured the rents created by natural monopoly and governmental procurement at the national level and used them to cushion the economic security of their loyalist mainlander followers.

Finally, wherever indoctrination or co-optation failed, the security apparatus stepped in. Under the rule of martial law, the security authority was prepared to suppress even a hint of political stirring. For almost three decades of its rule, the KMT faced a very unorganized and weak political opposition that consisted primarily of defiant local factions and has had no national political aims and posed little threat to the KMT's dominant position.

Thus, for an extended period of time, the ruling elite saw no pressing need for even a limited electoral opening at the national level. Initially, the electoral system was installed by the emigrant regime at the local level for co-opting native elites and for incorporating existing local patron-client networks into a superimposed party apparatus. A series of developments, however, gradually transformed both the nature and significance of the electoral process.

First, elections became the major institution to assimilate emerging economic and social forces into the political system. Facing recurring electoral challenges, the party-sanctioned local factional networks are more adaptive than the formal party apparatus to socioeconomic changes. When traditional clientelist networks could no longer deliver votes as effectively as they had previously, faction-centered or candidate-centered clientelism was expanded to incorporate more secondary associations and regional business concerns, especially in the rapidly urbanized areas. More and more new contenders, vying for political access and economic privilege, were drawn into the electoral process because electoral success could be readily translated into instant social prestige and handsome economic gain. With an ever-expanding economy, both the cost and stake of elections became even greater for the established factions.

Thus, as more social resources were mobilized into the electoral process, elections became more institutionalized. Elections became the institution in which local political elites found their self-identity and upon which the entire local power structure came to rest. Increasingly, the national ruling elite found out not only that they could not do without elections, but also that they had to deal with the rising pressure from both within and without the party for electoral opening at higher levels.

Another unavoidable political consequence of rapid socioeconomic change is the rise of a new breed of political opposition in the elections (see Chapter 6). With rapid urbanization, diffusion of education, and a general rise in material well-being, the opposition who dared to initiate ostensible challenge to the legitimacy of the KMT regime have found more and more ready ears among an increasingly articulate, self-assured, and economically secure electorate. This development culminated in the local election of 1977, in which a loosely coordinated opposition group, bearing the label of Tangwai, literally outside the (KMT) party, made considerable gains in contesting local and provincial electoral offices. The opposition has turned the campaign process into an effective medium of "resocialization" for fostering the growth in popular demand for democratic legitimacy.

Drastic changes in the external environment also compelled the ruling elite to become more responsive to the rising popular demand for political opening. During the 1970s, a series of diplomatic setbacks, the loss of the Security Council seat in the UN to the PRC, and derecognition by major allies severely undermined the KMT's claim to be the sole legitimate government of all of China. A series of peace overtures initiated by the PRC in the late 1970s and the emerging détente across the Taiwan Strait also began to melt down the siege mentality among the public. Thus the KMT elite felt the need to turn inward and to rely more on the legitimating function of electoral institutions. Limited electoral opening of national representative bodies was first instituted in 1972 but was expanded in 1980 and again in 1989.

The limited opening of national representative bodies for electoral contest provided a ground for the formation of an islandwide coalition among independent candidates with national political aims. As Lu outlines in Chapter 6, the Tangwai moved cautiously toward forming a quasi party. At the same time, it became increasingly costly for the ruling elite to use repressive measures against popularly elected opposition leaders, as was demonstrated in the Kaohsiung Incident, in which a number of prominent dissident leaders were prosecuted and jailed for treason. After a temporary setback, members of the Tangwai soon regrouped and regained their electoral momentum in the 1980 election. In the 1983 election, the national leadership of the Tangwai was united under the Tangwai Candidates Campaign Support Committee, and the committee established a formal procedure of endorsement. This ad hoc association was upgraded to a quasi-party organization called the Public Policy Research Association in 1984. Finally, on the eve of the 1986 election, a formal party, the Democratic Progressive Party (DPP), was declared. The new party was able to consolidate its electoral support in the subsequent election.[8]

Since 1983, encouraged by its electoral gains, the Tangwai/DPP has stepped up its confrontation with the regime on the sensitive issue of Taiwan's future. Many Tangwai/DPP leaders explicitly linked the goal of democratization directly to the issue of Taiwanese identity and the principle of self-determination. This linking amounted to a direct attack on the long-cherished official principle of one China, which has provided the ideological justification for the political monopoly of the KMT. DPP candidates could not resist exploiting this long-suppressed but potentially highly divisive issue, with its wide popular appeal among the nonmainlander electorate. Because this latent subethnic cleavage cuts across the socioeconomic cleavage, it is an effective counterstrategy to the KMT's all-class appeal; it is also an issue capable of uniting DPP members of different interests and ideals under a common cause.

The limited opening conceded to the DPP also greatly loosened the regime's authoritarian grip on the society. It ignited a broadly based popular demand for political decompression and started a reciprocal cycle between political liberalization and democratization in the early 1980s. Suddenly, the KMT regime found itself reigning over what Hsin-huang Michael Hsiao calls a demanding civil society and an upsurge of social protests and all kinds of contentious collective actions.[9] Eventually the KMT regime was compelled to respond to these developments with accelerated "Taiwanization" within the party's power structure and a general political decompression culminating in the lifting of the martial law and other longtime political bans in the first half of 1987.

The Rise of the DPP in Electoral Competition

To appreciate the meaning of the rise of the Tangwai/DPP in electoral competition, we need to understand the institutional arrangements that structure the campaign process and constrain the possibility of the emergence of an opposition party (see also Chapter 7). In addition to the legal ban on forming new parties and the restrictive campaign and electoral laws that prohibit candidates from forming coordinated campaign efforts across different electoral districts, there are other institutional barriers for a national opposition party to emerge. First, the election system is structured to discourage cooperation among candidates. Under a system of multiseat districts and the nontransferable vote rule, candidates of the same party have to divide up popular votes among themselves. The KMT, with its enormous resources and organizational endowment, can effectively play the balancing and coordinating role among party-endorsed candidates, but the opposition have to create such coordinating mechanism and authority among themselves and from scratch. For the same institutional reason, the campaign is necessarily candidate centered. Especially in elections at the local level, party label carries very limited additional votes for candidates.

Next, a Tangwai/DPP candidate cannot win a seat by resorting to national political issues alone. In the real campaign process, the Tangwai/DPP candidates face challenges not from the national KMT leadership but from the KMT-nominated local politicians, who typically amass abundant financial resources, extensive patron-client networks in a given community, and, most important, well-run vote-getting (as well as vote-buying) machines. A national party label in itself does not help an opposition candidate. Finally, Tangwai/DPP candidates had little choice but to compete under the partisan rules that were designed to contain the ability of DPP candidates to mobilize discontented voters and amplify the competitive advantage of most KMT candidates.

In Table 8.1 is a detailed tally of percentage shares of electoral turnout received by Kuomintang, Tangwai/DPP, and independent candidates respectively in the past four elections—those of 1980, 1983, 1986, and 1989.[10] Because of a system of dual representation, the overall electoral return can be decomposed into two categories:[11] (1) the percentage shares of total popular vote by regional districts and (2) the percentage shares by occupational/aboriginal districts. The table also shows the percentage shares of overall electoral return.

As shown by the data in Table 8.1, despite all the aforementioned obstacles, Tangwai/DPP candidates have gradually made inroads in the electoral competition since their meager start in the 1980 election. In that election, just one year after the Kaohsiung Incident, the opposition was in disarray. The hastily regrouped opposition camp had great difficulty enlisting enough candidates to run under the Tangwai banner. Nevertheless, they still managed to place contenders in fourteen cities and counties (out of a total of twenty-one) and secure 9.5 percent of the total return in the category of regional district votes and 8.28 percent overall. Encouraged by the unexpected electoral gains, Tangwai leaders stepped up their effort to recruit more independent political figures. In the 1983 election, under a new system of formal endorsement, Tangwai-endorsed candidates contested in all twenty-three cities and counties.[12] Together they won 18.9 percent of the popular votes in the category of regional district and 16.7 percent overall.

The total popular vote received by the KMT candidates steadily declined from 73.64 percent of total electoral turnout in 1980 to 60.6 percent in 1989, and in the critical category of regional districts from 72.1 percent to 59.7 percent. The Tangwai/DPP's total electoral gain rose from a mere 8.28 percent in 1980 to 28.2 percent in 1989. But the most marked changes took place in the total electoral return for the independent candidates, which dropped from 18.09 percent in 1980 to 8.72 percent in 1986. It is clear that

Table 8.1 Kuomintang, Tangwai/DPP, and Independent Candidates' Percentage Shares of Electoral Turnout in Regional District Votes and Occupational District Votes in the 1980, 1983, 1986, and 1989 Elections

	1980	1983	1986	1989
		Regional Districts		
Kuomintang	72.1	70.5	66.7	59.7
Tangwai/DPP	9.5	18.9	24.6	29.7
Independent	18.4	10.6	8.8	10.5
		Occupational and Aboriginal Districts		
Kuomintang	82.4	87.5	84.7	65.5
Tangwai/DPP	1.3	3.1	6.9	19.9
Independent	16.3	9.4	8.4	14.6
		Overall		
Kuomintang	73.64	72.86	69.06	60.6
Tangwai/DPP	8.28	16.68	22.22	28.2
Independent	18.09	10.46	8.72	11.2

Sources: The electoral turnout data of individual candidates were provided by the Central Election Commission of the Executive Yuan, and the data of candidates' party affiliation were based on Hsiao-fong Lee, *The Forty Year Democratic Movement in Taiwan*, Taipei: *Independent Evening News*, 1988.

the rise of the DPP was as much at the cost of independents as of KMT candidates. It also means that the rise of the DPP signifies a transformation of the electoral opposition from an unorganized amalgamate of independent candidates into a formal islandwide political alliance.

For the Tangwai/DPP, increased electoral support, however, did not automatically translate into comparable party strength in the national legislative body. For example, in 1983, Tangwai won 16.68 percent of total popular votes but only 8.6 percent of total elected seats in the Legislative Yuan. Table 8.2 shows the distribution of elected seats among Kuomintang, Tangwai/DPP, and independents in the 1980, 1983, 1986, and 1989 elections. Why such a discrepancy between the popular vote and the seats? First, under the nontransferable rule, the better-coordinated KMT enjoys considerable organizational advantage in maximizing the seat/vote ratio. For KMT candidates, the party coordinated the distribution of electoral gains to make sure that each party-endorsed candidate received roughly the same number of electoral votes. It usually does this with great precision, as each regional party headquarter has a substantial number of "iron votes" at its disposal. Table 8.2 shows that in the 1986 election the KMT translated 69.06 percent of popular vote into 80.6 percent of elected seats while the DPP received 22.22 percent of the popular votes but got only 16.7 percent of contested seats.

Table 8.2 Distribution of Elected Seats Among Kuomintang, Tangwei/DPP, and Independents in the 1980, 1983, 1986, and 1989 Elections

	1980	1983	1986	1989
Kuomintang				
Number of seats	56 (16)	61 (18)	58 (17)	72 (13)
Percentage	81.2	87.1	80.6	71.1
Tangwai/DPP				
Number of seats	6 (0)	6 (0)	12 (1)	21 (3)
Percentage	8.7	8.6	16.7	21.0
Independent				
Number of seats	7 (2)	3 (0)	2 (0)	8 (2)
Percentage	10.1	4.3	2.8	8.0
Total	69	70	72	101

Source: Central Election Commission, Executive Yuan.
Note: Parenthesized figures are the number of seats elected by the occupational/aboriginal district electorate.

The dual representation system presents a second roadblock for the opposition. In the category of occupational and aboriginal districts, non-KMT candidates were always handicapped by the entrenched presence of the ruling party in these organized social sectors. In Table 8.2, parenthesized figures are the number of seats elected by the occupational/aboriginal district electorate. In the 1986 election, out of the total fifty-eight seats won by the KMT candidates, seventeen seats fell in the category of occupational/aboriginal districts, while Tangwai/DPP candidates nailed down only one. However, the KMT's firm grip on the organized social sectors starts to wane in the 1989 election.

Table 8.3 shows how well the privileged political status of KMT national elite is protected by retaining the lifelong members in the Legislative Yuan and how slow the progress toward full democracy has been. So far, the number of seats directly elected by the island's electorate constitutes only a very limited portion of the entire chamber of the Legislative Yuan. In 1986, the seventy-two elected seats amounted to less than one-quarter of the total seats, and in 1989 the elected seats still constituted little more than one-third of the entire chamber.[13] These simple statistics explain why the DPP has placed so much emphasis on democratic reform, without which much of their hard-won electoral support has been sidetracked. This also explains why the ruling party has been willing to initiate the transition. With these archaic arrangements, there is little chance that the opposition that emerged in the election and the competition it brought about posed a real challenge to the KMT regime.

Another important development accompanying the rise of the DPP is that more voters have developed partisan attitudes toward one of the two parties. Apparently, intensified electoral competition, the growing national

Table 8.3 Proportion of Newly Elected Seats to the Total Seats in the Legislative Yuan

	1980	1983	1986	1989
Number of seats				
Elected members	69	70	72	101
Entire chamber[a]	406	368	324	287
Percentage	17.0	19.0	22.2	35.1

Source: Central Election Commission, Executive Yuan.
[a]The entire chamber consists of elected, appointed, and lifelong members.

significance that the elections have acquired, and the increased symbolic meaning accorded to party label have accelerated the growth of partisanship among the electorate.[14] There also emerged a strong tie between a voter's party preference and his or her vote decision. To a degree, the DPP has successfully turned this limited electoral process into a political contest between the two parties at the national level. The DPP exists not only as a party in name but is also increasingly being viewed by the electorate as an actual party.

In our postelection survey of the 1983 election, more than half of the partisan voters, voters who voted for either a KMT candidate or a Tangwai candidate, indicated that they did not have a clear preference for either camp (see Table 8.4).[15] But three years later, over 70 percent of the partisan voters had acquired party preference in one direction or the other.[16] The chi-square statistics indicate that the positive association between party preference and electoral choice is extremely strong for the 1983 data and even stronger in 1986.[17] This partisan structure among the electorate has become an important and predictable source of electoral support. Both parties drew more than half of their popular vote from their respective group of partisans.

In summary, the rise of the DPP in recent elections has been quite significant. Although the DPP candidates have carried less than a quarter of the popular vote so far—not any more than the combined popular votes of all non-KMT candidates in earlier elections—the systemic meaning of the electoral challenge is qualitatively different. First, the DPP is a formal party organization rather than just a statistical sum of non-KMT candidates. With its leadership and organization, the DPP can integrate its popular support from various constituent bases into a coherent national political program. Also, the DPP as a party has already established its identity among a substantial portion of the electorate, and it has bolstered the growth of partisanship among the electorate. More important, the DPP has built its electoral support largely from its demand for comprehensive democratic reform to realize majority rule. The rise of the DPP has elevated elections to a test of regime legitimacy as well as a true contest for the control of

Table 8.4 The Growth of Party Preference Among the Electorate and Its Relation to Electoral Choice

	Party Preference			Total
	Pro-KMT	None	Pro-DPP	
	1983			
Vote for KMT candidates	427 95.96%	443 78.27%	441 49.44%	914
Vote for DPP candidates	18 4.04%	123 21.73%	45 50.56%	186
Total	445	566	89	1,100

Chi-square statistic = 133.5 P = .000 D.F. = 2

	1986			
Vote for KMT candidates	474 94.80%	204 78.16%	22 19.47%	700
Vote for DPP candidates	26 5.20%	57 21.84%	91 80.53%	174
Total	500	261	113	874

Chi-square statistic = 328.9 P = .000 D.F. = 2

Source: Central Election Commission, Executive Yuan.

government. These observations can be substantiated empirically at the micro level, to which we now turn.

The Social and Political Cleavages Manifested in the Recent Electoral Competition

In this section we examine the nature of electoral competition at two levels—at the level of candidates and correspondingly at the level of the individual voter. First, we examine the campaign manifestos employed by candidates of the two camps to entice the voters, especially the issue voters. This examination helps us verify the kinds of socioeconomic or ideological interests that KMT and DPP candidates respectively represented, or the kind of social or political cleavages they intended to exploit. Next, we compare the social and political composition of the KMT supporters with that of the DPP supporters. This comparison reveals the kinds of social and political cleavages and the degree of their intensity manifested in electoral competition.

We apply content analysis to the platforms that the candidates prepared for dissemination in the official campaign bulletins of the election of 1986. For a systematic comparison of candidates' issue positions, we have compiled a list of thirty-four often-cited issue statements extracted from the candidates' platforms as expressed in their campaign pamphlets, posters, and the official campaign bulletins in the past two elections. In Table 8.5, we present a complete list of those issue statements. Furthermore, to evaluate the systemic significance of these issue statements, we grouped these thirty-four issue statements into three categories: national identity, political regime, and public policy. Within each category, items are broken up into their respective subcategories. In Table 8.5, the four items belonging to the level of national identity are divided into two subcategories—items underscoring a "Chinese complex" and items underscoring a "Taiwanese complex."[18] The twelve items belonging to the level of political regime are also divided into two subcategories—items underscoring regime maintenance and items underscoring democratic reform. The eighteen items belonging to the level of public policy are classified into five subcategories — items underscoring the concern for national development, social security, postmaterialist values, improvement in foreign relations, and administrative reform.[19] We went through the official bulletin to see which of the thirty-four statements or their equivalents were adopted by party-endorsed candidates, and then we aggregated the findings to yield a sum for each of the thirty-four items of the number of candidates in each party that have adopted a particular issue statement or its equivalent.[20] The results are reported in the right-hand columns of Table 8.5.

The analysis shows that the KMT and DPP candidates clearly diverged on issues in the political community and political regime categories but converged on most issues in the public policy category. A common feature of the platforms of the DPP candidates is that they all highlighted issues concerning alternative views about the political community. Statements underscoring self-determination and local identity were cited by all DPP candidates. DPP candidates also unanimously endorsed issue statements concerning democratic reform, such as "general reelection of the national representative bodies," "the freedom of forming new parties," and "protecting basic human rights." These views are in direct contrast with the concentration of KMT candidates on public policy issues. Many of the KMT candidates took a clear stand on the issue of national identity. Most of them, however, avoided taking a clear stand on the issues concerning the political regime.[21] Unlike the 1983 election, few KMT candidates during the 1986 election stood up to defend the necessity or legality of the existing authoritarian arrangements.[22] This points to the possibility that many KMT candidates were to some extent tacitly in favor of many issues concerning democratic reform. In terms of structural possibility, it is quite likely that many KMT candidates share some common ground with the DPP candidates not least

Table 8.5 The Difference in Emphasis on Various Issues Between KMT-Nominated as Well as KMT-Sanctioned Candidates and DPP-Nominated Candidates: A Content Analysis of Candidates' Campaign Platforms

	Number of KMT candidates taking a stand on (N = 51)	Number of DPP candidates taking a stand on (N = 17)
Issue Positions with Regard to National Identity		
Chinese Complex		
To adhere to the unification of Taiwan with mainland China on the basis of the Three Principles of the People, and to oppose separatism and localism	25	0
To love the national flag and protect the name of the country with a view to glorifying patriotism	1	0
Taiwanese Complex		
That Taiwan's political future should be determined by all the residents on the island of Taiwan	0	17
To recognize the history, language, and culture of Taiwan, with a view to deepening the identification with the land of Taiwan	0	13
Issue Positions with Regard to Political Regime		
Regime Maintenance		
To strengthen the leadership apex and oppose the defamation of the leader	2	0
To have sympathy for the country's present unusual situation and give firm support to the government policies	0	0
To oppose mass protest and street demonstration in order to maintain the order of society	2	0
To maintain the harmony of society and ban the expression of radical political ideas	0	0
To oppose too many political parties coming into being, with a view to enhance the nation's political stability	0	0
To centralize political power and curtail the external constraints in order to establish a government of high caliber	0	0
Democratic Reform		
To favor the general reelection of the national repesentative bodies with a view to expanding political participation	0	17
To oppose both the abuse of and the monopoly on political privileges	0	17
To realize the independence of justice and completely eradicate the interference of politics	1	17
To uphold the freedom of forming new parties, with all parties having equal opportunities to compete and to form the government	0	17
To immediately lift the ban on martial law with a view to protecting basic human rights	0	17
To lift the ban on establishing new newspapers and other mass media such as television stations, with a view to promoting freedom of speech	0	17

(continues)

Table 8.5 (continued)

	Number of KMT candidates taking a stand on (N = 51)	Number of DPP candidates taking a stand on (N = 17)
Issue Positions with Regard to Five Types of Public Policies		
National Development		
To make good use of foreign reserves to promote national development	8	13
To advance economic development and improve the environment for foreign trade	24	15
To upgrade the transportation system and improve the traffic condition	28	2
To promote researches on leading-edge technology and enhance our national defense	15	0
Social Security		
To protect the right to making a livelihood of farmers, workers, and fishermen	29	15
To take good care of veterans, reserve military personnel, and the families of military personnel	16	0
To increase the income of military personnel, civil servants, and teachers	31	0
To improve the income of the lower class and narrow the gap between the poor and rich	5	4
To install unemployment and health insurance for the entire population and to increase welfare benefits	42	17
Postmaterialist Values		
To legislate a comsumer protection law in order to protect comsumers' rights	16	10
To protect women's rights and eliminate discrimination against women	18	15
To protect the ecological environment and eliminate environmental pollution	42	17
To streamline the armed forces and shorten the time of military service	1	14
Improvement in Foreign Relations		
To break through the diplomatic predicament and return to the international community	16	16
To promote athletics as a national movement and take part in international competition in order to win honor for the country	5	1
Administrative Reform		
To reform the tax system in order to ease the burden of the people	30	6
To increase the police force and maintain law and order	21	0
To keep government officials cleared of corruption and to sweep away bribery	26	15

because democratic reform would certainly enhance their own standing within the KMT party power structure.

On the issues concerning economic growth, social security, postmaterialist values, improvement in foreign relations, and administrative reform, candidates of the two parties converged most of the time, with a major qualification that DPP candidates avoided all issue statements with the implication of enhancing state power. On the other hand, many KMT-endorsed candidates adopted the issue position for a strong defense, for improving the welfare of civil servants, the military, and veterans, and for expanding the police force.[23]

Our content analysis confirms the antisystem as well as antistate nature of the campaign waged by the DPP candidates. The DPP candidates and the KMT candidates are clearly differentiated on the issue of national identity. The DPP candidates have tried to set the tone of the election in terms of regime legitimacy, whereas the KMT candidates tried to direct the focus of the election to public policy issues.

Also clear from our content analysis is that neither the KMT candidates nor the DPP candidates have tried to project images in class or group terms. Candidates of both parties made appeal to (or avoided offending) voters of all social stripes, from business elites to the lower class, from consumers to environmentalists, and from taxpayers to crime victims. The only exception is that only KMT candidates claimed to present the interest of state employees.

Much of what we found about the nature of electoral competition based on the analysis of candidates' platforms is echoed by what we find at the level of the individual voter. To examine the social bases and value bases of party support, we include four independent variables—value orientation toward democracy,[24] attitude toward national identity,[25] subethnic origin, and socioeconomic class[26]—in a multivariate analysis. Only in a multivariate framework are we able to evaluate the relative influence of each of these variables on a voter's party choice when the effect of other variables and the complex interactive relationship among them are taken into account.[27] Because most of our variables are categorical in nature,[28] we conduct the analysis within the framework of log-linear analysis.[29]

Table 8.6 displays the gist of our log-linear analysis results.[30] In the first row, the effect of the variable party choice indicates the baseline multiplicative effect on the probability of voting for a KMT candidate or a DPP candidate because of the simple fact that there are more KMT voters than DPP voters to begin with.[31] The odds 3.07 is the ratio between the two multiplicative parameters.[32] An odds of 3.07 means that on average a voter is 3.07 times more likely to be a KMT voter than a DPP voter.[33] This is the baseline from which we evaluate the inflence of independent variables on party choice.

From the first row down, the first column reports the multiplicative

Table 8.6 Social and Ideological Correlates of Electoral Choice in 1986
Multidimensional Log-Linear Analysis (N = 953)

| Effects | Estimates of Multiplicative Parameters | | Odds |
	KMT	DPP	KMT/DPP
Main effect of party choice	1.752	0.571	3.07
The effect of origin on party choice			
Min-nan	1.146	0.873	1.31
Hakka	0.672	1.489	0.45
Mainlander	1.300	0.770	1.69
Effect of class on party choice			
Farmer	1.207	0.829	1.46
Labor	0.917	1.091	0.84
State employee	1.174	0.852	1.38
Middle class	0.766	1.305	0.59
Capitalist	0.882	1.134	0.78
Other	1.140	0.877	1.30
Effect of identity on party choice			
Positive	1.309	0.764	1.71
Negative	0.764	1.309	0.58
Effect of democratic legitimacy on party choice			
Positive	0.933	1.071	0.87
Negative	1.071	0.933	1.15
Interactive effect of origin and democratic legitimacy			
Min-nan			
Positive	0.745	1.343	0.55
Negative	1.343	0.745	1.80
Hakka			
Positive	1.141	0.876	1.30
Negative	0.876	1.141	0.77
Mainlander			
Positive	1.177	0.850	1.39
Negative	0.850	1.177	0.72

D.F.= 105 Likelihood ratio chi-square= 72.5 Prob. = .993

effect on the probability of voting for a KMT candidate as a result of one's sociological or predispositional attributes, and the second column the multiplicative effect on the probability of voting for a DPP candidate. A mutiplicative parameter greater than 1.0 means a positive effect and mutiplicative parameter less than 1.0 means a negative effect. For example, in the first column, fourth row, the parameter 1.300 means that the probability of voting for a KMT candidate changes by 1.3 times (or increases by 30 percent) given that one is of mainlander origin. The parameter 0.77 means that the probability of voting for a DPP candidate changes by 0.77 times (or decreases by 23 percent). The third column reports the multiplicative effect of mainlander origin on the relative probabilities, i.e., odds. In sum, the odds associated with different categories of the four explanatory variables—subethnic background, socioeconomic class, democratic values, and national identity—describe the departure from the baseline odds as a result of one's particular social or dispositional attribute. For example, in the fourth row, an odds of 1.69 means that a mainlander voter is *relatively* more likely by 1.69 times to vote for a KMT candidate than to vote for a DPP candidate, other things being equal.[34] In the third column of Table 8.6, an odds greater than 1.0 always means a positive association between that particular sociological or predispositional attribute with voting for a KMT candidate and an odds less than 1.0 means a negative association. Finally, at the bottom section of the table, the multiplicative effects associated with positive and negative democratic value in a given category of subethnic origin describe the departure from the average bivariate associations between subethnic origin and party choice on the one hand and between democratic value and party choice on the other given the combination (interaction) of one's particular attribute of subethnic origin with a particular stand on democratic value items. For example, for a voter with both a Min-nan origin and a positive democratic value, the odds of voting for a KMT candidate versus a DPP candidate change not only by 0.87 times because of the effect of a democratic value and by 1.31 times because of the effect of a Min-nan origin but also by additional 0.55 times because of the interaction effect of democratic value and subethnic origin. Therefore the combined effect of the two attributes is 0.63, which is the multiplicative product of 0.87, 1.31, and 0.55. This means a voter with both a Min-nan origin and a positive democratic value is 0.63 times (or 37 percent) less likely (as compared with the baseline odds) to vote for a KMT candidate than a DPP candidate.

We can now proceed to give the findings of the log-linear analysis a more substantive interpretation. The nature of electoral competition can now be gauged in terms of the sociopolitical cleavages revealed in the different sociopolitical compositions of the two voter groups. First, as expected, mainlander voters are the most dedicated supporters of KMT candidates, whereas Hakka voters are least supportive of the three major subethnic groups. Second, it is clear that KMT candidates drew relatively more votes from state employees, farmers, and housewives and retirees, the two largest groups in the category of "Others," whereas DPP candidates gained *relatively* more support among the middle class, the business class, and the working class, all three classes in the modern private sector. This is a very significant result. It suggests that in Taiwan, a state-dominated society, the more salient aspect of socioeconomic cleavage is not defined by capitalist production relations but by state power. Economically speaking, the middle class, business class, and working class are all relatively less dependent on the state, and, socially speaking, it is more difficult to incorporate members of the three groups in the modern (and mostly urban) sector into factional clientelist networks.

Somewhat less surprising is the finding that voters with a positive score on the democratic value scale are relatively less likely to vote for a KMT candidate than a DPP candidate by an odds of 0.87. Also, voters with a positive score on national identity, i.e., in the direction of upholding Chinese identity, are relatively more likely to vote for a KMT candidate than a DPP candidate by an odds of 1.71. It shows that value orientation to democracy and national identity attitude are significantly correlated with party choice even when the effect of a voter's subethnic origin and socioeconomic class and the complex interactive relationship among them are taken into account. The direction of association is fully consistent with the findings of our content analysis.

The relationships between subethnic background and party choice and between democratic value and party choice, however, are more complex than they first appear. Our model points to a complicated interactive effect of subethnic origin and democratic value: The relationship between one's belief in democratic values and electoral choice is conditioned on one's subethnic background. For a Min-nan voter, a positive orientation to democratic values is negatively associated with voting for KMT candidates. But for Hakka and in particular mainlander voters, the picture is entirely different. Those mainlander voters who score positive on the democratic value scale are actually relatively *less* likely to support a DPP candidate. It is possible that mainlander and Hakka voters did not perceive the KMT regime as undemocratic as the DPP alleged it to be. Also, the two groups might regard the antisystem strategy of the DPP candidates a bit too disruptive to a stable transition to democracy, while Min-nan voters found the demand for democratic reform quite congenial with the emphasis on Taiwanese identity, given their dominant position in the island's subethnic makeup.

Our log-linear analysis results allow us to ascertain that in Taiwan a substantial portion of voters are quite perceptive to the clear differences in political platforms between the KMT and DPP candidates. A high degree of cognitive congruence exists between voters' own political attitudes and their electoral choice. This suggests that the political strategy of the DPP candidates was, to a degree, effective, especially among the Min-nan voters. But only to a degree: in the final analysis, the cumulative odds between voting for a KMT candidate and voting for a DPP candidate, considering every possible combination of social and political attributes, is still far greater than 1.0 in most cases.[35] The DPP candidates have not yet secured the majority support of any major constituency defined in either social or political attributes.

This analysis also suggests that the underlying political cleavages over democratic legitimacy and national identity issues are just as significant as social cleavages along subethnic and socioeconomic class lines. Socioeconomic cleavage in Taiwan has been less salient in the past elections than in other developed countries because political and subethnic cleavages cut across the socioeconomic divisions. Our data also reveal a potential tension between issues of democratic legitimacy and Taiwanese identity, in particular for mainlander and Hakka voters. It is possible that Hakka and mainlander voters worry about the entanglement of the demand for democratic reform with the emphasis on Taiwanese identity.

However, we do not want to overstate the systemic significance accorded to the political cleavages manifest in electoral competition. It is important to point out that this multivariate model does not constitute a full-fledged model of the voting decision at the individual level. Typically, a candidate's stand on particular issues is not the foremost determinant of electoral choice, and even in cases where it is admittedly decisive it is usually not the *only* deciding factor.

In fact, the entire electoral system is designed to minimize the importance of issues. First, the election is only a supplemental election. It is far from a true political contest for control of the Legislative Yuan, much less the entire policy process. Second, as we explained earlier, under the system of multiple-seat districts and a nontransferable rule, the campaign is necessarily candidate centered rather than party centered despite the effort by many DPP candidates to cast elections in terms of two-party competition. Third, the campaign process is subjected to strict legal restrictions designed to amplify the advantage of KMT candidates in organizational and financial resources and to contain the reach of antisystem propaganda through printed materials, canvassing, and mass rallies. Mass media, especially the television networks, which are all under the state's direct control, are overwhelmingly partisan. As a result, for most candidates the key to electoral success is to assemble an extensive mobilization machine built around a multilayered interpersonal network and empowered by a sizable campaign fund. Mobilization and vote buying through interpersonal networks are the most effective campaign strategies, especially in the rural areas and in older communities of the urban area. All major local factions have had one such machine well in place and have established the necessary business operations to translate electoral success into economic gain.

Thus, just as propaganda is not the most effective strategy of vote getting for most candidates, concern for policy and political issues was not the decisive factor of vote choice for the majority of voters either. As our data from the 1986 election survey indicate, only about one-third of the DPP supporters indicated that their chosen candidates' campaign issues significantly affected their voting decision (see Table 8.7).[36] Predictably, the proportion of issue voters is even lower among the KMT supporters. Almost three-quarters (74.1 percent) of KMT supporters indicated that other non-issue factors, such as a candidate's own caliber or character, party affiliation, and social connections in the forms of lineage, communal affinity, and group association, were influential.[37]

Thus, to see how effective the two party candidates have been in enticing the support of voters with issues, we need to explore further what issues actually activated the issue voters and to examine the contrast in salient issues between KMT issue voters and DPP issue voters. In our survey, each respondent, who indicated that his or her chosen candidate's campaign issues significantly affected their voting decision, was provided with the same list of thirty-four often-cited issue statements and was asked to pick one or more items that they regarded as most appealing to them during the campaign. As in the earlier content analysis, the thirty-four items are grouped into three categories—political community, political regime, and public policy—and, within each category, items are further broken up into their respective subcategories (see Table 8.5 for the complete list and classification scheme).

In Tables 8.8 and 8.9, we report the differences in issue preference between KMT issue voters and DPP issue voters. The figures in the first column of Table 8.8 indicate that ninety-three KMT issue voters (or as much as 47.9 percent of all KMT issue voters in our sample) and only two DPP issue voters picked at least one of the issue statements underscoring a Chinese complex. In the second column, the figures indicate that sixty-four DPP issue voters (or as much as 97 percent of all DPP issue voters) did not pick any of the issue statements underscoring a Chinese complex. We also see that 43.9 percent of DPP issue voters found items underscoring a Taiwanese complex appealing, whereas only 5.6 percent of KMT issue voters did the same.

Our figures in Table 8.8 also show that more than half (51.8 percent) of KMT issue voters found items underscoring system maintenance appealing. Or, to put it somewhat differently, of the 105 issue voters who picked at least one item in the system maintenance subcategory, 101 are KMT supporters. And 83.3 percent of DPP issue voters picked at least one item in the democratic reform subcategory. Overall, all four subcategories—the Chinese complex, the Taiwanese complex, system maintenance, and democratic reform—are highly discriminant. Taken together, they can help us tell a KMT issue voter from a DPP issue voter with great predictive power.

In contrast, public policy issues do not discriminate at all. Table 8.9 displays the differences in issue preference between the two groups of issue voters over five subcategories of public policy issues. Only issues emphasizing improvement in international status help us tell a KMT issue voter from a DPP issue voter, and only barely. As the very high probability levels of the chi-square statistic suggest, issues in the other four

Table 8.7 Percentage of Issue Voters Among KMT and DPP Supporters in the 1986
Election

	Modes of Vote Decision		
	Issue Voting	Non-issue Voting	Total
KMT voters	195 25.9%	558 74.1%	753
DPP voters	65 33.5%	129 66.5%	194
Total	260	687	947

Chi-square statistic = 4.1 D.F.= 1 P-level = 0.043

Table 8.8 The Salience of National Identity Issues and Political Regime Issues to
KMT and DPP Issue Voters (N = 260) in the 1986 Election

	National Identity				Political Regime			
	Chinese Complex		Taiwanese Complex		Regime Stability		Democratic Reform	
	Yes	No	Yes	No	Yes	No	Yes	No
KMT voters	93 47.9%	101 52.1%	11 5.6%	184 94.4%	101 51.8%	94 48.2%	62 31.8%	133 68.2%
DPP voters	2 3.0%	64 97.0%	29 43.9%	37 56.1%	4 6.2%	61 93.8%	55 83.3%	11 16.7%
Total	95	165	40	221	105	155	117	144
Probability level of likelihood ratio statistic:	p<.000		p<.000		p<.000		p<.000	

Note: See Table 8.5 for item composition of each type of national identity and political
regime issues.

subcategories attracted as many KMT issue voters as DPP issue voters. It is
clear that in the eyes of the issue voters, the distance between the two parties
was measured on a scale of system legitimacy rather than a scale of policy
performance.

By now it has become evident that the electoral contest was centered
more around alternative views about the political system itself than around
the conflict of interest among clashing socioeconomic classes, a result
perfectly consistent with the result of our content analysis; this is especially

Table 8.9 The Salience of Five Types of Public Policy Issues to KMT and DPP
Voters (N = 260) in the 1986 Election

	National Development		Social Security		Postmaterialism		International Status		Administrative Reform	
	Yes	No	Yes	No	Yes	No	Yes	No	Yes	No
KMT voters	67	125	108	86	58	136	26	168	94	99
	75.3%	74.0%	73.5%	76.1%	74.4%	74.7%	60.5%	77.4%	73.4%	75.6%
DPP voters	22	44	39	27	20	46	17	49	34	32
	33.3%	66.7%	59.1%	40.9%	30.3%	69.7%	25.8%	74.2%	51.5%	48.5%
Total	89	169	147	113	78	182	43	217	128	131
Probability level of likelihood ratio statistic:	$p = .94$		$p = .73$		$p = 1.0$		$p = .03$		$p = .80$	

true for the issue voters. What is remarkable is that the conclusions are much
the same for the electorate at large as revealed by our multivariate log-linear
analysis.

Conclusion: The Prospect for Democracy in Taiwan

Our analysis has now come full circle. The contours of the electoral
competition laid out in the beginning of this chapter are well confirmed at
the level of candidate and individual voter. We notice some positive
developments for the transition to democracy. The level of partisanship has
risen, which will become a stabilizing factor for an institutionalized
competitive party system. We also ascertain that elections for national
lawmakers not only have increasingly acquired the normal function of
popular accountability and system legitimation in a representative democracy,
but in the transition they actually functioned as a catalyst of democratization
in Taiwan. Our content analysis and survey data all point to an interesting
dialectic process in which the DPP candidates mobilized the electorate
through their support of democratic reform and local identity, and, in turn,
the emerging electoral support for the DPP candidates has reinforced their
push for full democracy and majority rule. What is more remarkable is that
we detect a tacit alliance between the DPP and KMT candidates over the issue
of democratic reform. This possibility is more conducive to a democratic
outcome than anything else because it will force the KMT's national elite to
answer the democratic calling from within their own party, especially from
those who actually can secure continuous electoral success for the party.

We also notice some worrisome developments. The entanglement of democratic reform with identity issues created a potential source of polarized conflict. This entanglement cast a doubt on whether Taiwan can also follow the path of "transitions through transaction."[38] Not only might it create splits within the DPP camp, but it also might create obstacles for reaching a "negotiated pact" with the KMT elite on the basic rules of the game. There is only a thin line between a claim for Taiwan independence and the emphasis on Taiwanese identity and self-determination. Thus the more radical position on national identity issues that advocates an independent new nation entails an overhauling of the existing constitutional arrangements in which too many KMT elite, mainlander and Taiwanese alike, and their followers have vested interests. Radical changes in the political institutions will pose a grave risk and too much uncertainty to most KMT Taiwanese politicians whose gradual ascendance within the party and state apparatus is assured by the KMT-endorsed reform package within the existing regime. Under the self-initiated reform, they also stand a much better chance of playing a significant electoral and representational role in the subsequent regime.

Many structural factors are conducive to a democratic outcome. So far, emphasis on Taiwanese identity and self-determination has helped the DPP gain considerable electoral success and has given the DPP a clear political identity. But it is doubtful that this issue can help the DPP build up a winning electoral coalition in the future. As long as democratic reform and the process of Taiwanization within the party-state apparatus continue to proceed on their current course, the issue of regime legitimacy will gradually recede into oblivion. Once the Taiwanese identity issue is disentangled from issues of democratic legitimacy and majority rule, its all-class appeal will attenuate. However, as national elections become increasingly a real contest for the control of government and policy process, the salience of public policy issues no doubt will surface, and the emerging socioeconomic cleavages will also weaken subethnic cleavages. Finally, mainland China is another important factor not to be overlooked. Growing economic ties with mainland China will lead many business elites and the middle class to believe it is undesirable to have the great economic potential disrupted by Taiwan independence claims.

None of these generalizations exclude the possibility of historical accidents. In even the most carefully crafted of transitions, the indeterminancy of interactions, strategies, and the shifts in the configuration of interests is great.[39]

Notes

1. Two notable exceptions are Paul Drake and Eduardo Silva, eds., *Elections and Democratization in Latin America, 1980–1985* (San Diego: Center for Iberian and Latin American Studies, University of California, 1986); and Bolivar Lamounier, "Authoritarian Brazil Revisited: The Impact of Elections on

the *Abertura*," in Alfred Stepan, ed., *Democratizing Brazil: Problems of Transition and Consolidation* (New York: Oxford University Press, 1989).

2. For an elaboration of the concept of democratization, see Donald Share and Scott Mainwaring, "Transitions Through Transaction: Democratization in Brazil and Spain," in Wayne A. Selcher, ed., *Political Liberalization in Brazil: Dynamics, Dilemmas, and Future Prospects* (Boulder, Colo.: Westview Press, 1986). We share the view of Share and Mainwaring that democracy implies the possibility of an alternation in power. In this sense, a transition to democracy involves more than a liberalization of an authoritarian regime. Democratization refers to the establishment of institutional arrangements—free competitive elections, universal adult suffrage, freedom of speech, of press, and of political association—that make possible such an alternation.

3. The surveys for the 1983 and 1986 elections were conducted in February–June 1984 and February–June 1987. The number of respondents from the islandwide population twenty years of age and older in each of the surveys is 1,629 (1983) and 1,430 (1986) respectively. The data from the islandwide survey for the 1989 election were not ready for analysis when this chapter was being prepared. The surveys were based on multiphased quota sampling at the individual level. City/county, district/town (or village), and precinct were selected by probability-proportional-to-size criteria; then quotas by electoral turnout were drawn, utilizing both the official household registration data and the official elector registration record. For a detailed and more technical description of the sampling procedures, please refer to Hu Fu, Cheng Teh-yu, Cheng Min-tong, and Iou Yin-lung, *Voting Behavior of the Electorate* (in Chinese) (Taipei: Central Election Commission, Ministry of Internal Affairs, Republic of China, 1987), pp. 44–47; and Lin Chia-lung, "The Social Bases of Democratic Progressive Party and Kuomintung: A Comparative Study of Party Support Among Taiwan's Electorate, 1983–1986" (in Chinese) (M.A. thesis, Department of Political Science, National Taiwan University, 1988), pp. 67–79.

4. For an insightful discussion, see Edward Epstein, "Legitimacy, Institutionalization, and Opposition in Exclusionary Bureaucratic-Authoritarian Regimes," *Comparative Politics* 1984 (October), pp. 37–54.

5. See Thomas Gold, *State and Society in the Taiwan Miracle* (Armonk, N.Y.: M. E. Sharp, 1986), Chapters 3 and 4.

6. See Edwin Winckler, "Institutionalization and Participation on Taiwan: From Hard to Soft Authoritarianism," *China Quarterly* 99 (September 1984), pp. 481–499.

7. For an analysis of the mechanism for the co-optation of local elite, see Edwin Winckler, "National, Regional and Local Politics," in Emily Ahern and Hill Gates, eds., *The Anthropology of Taiwanese Society* (Stanford, Calif.: Stanford University Press, 1981).

8. See Tun-jen Cheng, "Democratizing the Quasi-Leninist Regime in Taiwan," *World Politics* (July 1989), pp. 471–499.

9. See Chu Yun-han, "Social Protest and Political Democratization in Taiwan," *Political Science Review* 1 (1) (March 1990), pp. 65–88.

10. Although it is very easy to tell the DPP candidates from the independent in the 1986 election, it is not quite so straightforward to differentiate Tangwai candidates from the independent for the elections before the forming of the DPP. Except for the 1980 and 1983 elections, credible sources can be readily found because in both elections, Tangwai candidates are formally united under some ad hoc national campaign organizations. Thus, for the 1980 election, Tangwai candidates are those identified by the "Statement of Identification" issued by the association of Tangwai Candidates for the Election of National Representative

Bodies. See Hsiao-fong Lee, *The Forty-Year Democratic Movement in Taiwan*, Taipei: Independent Evening News (in Chinese), 1988, pp. 164–166. For the 1983 election, Tangwai candidates are those endorsed by the Tangwai Candidates Campaign Support Committee. See Lee, *The Forty-Year Democratic Movement*, pp. 189–191.

11. In Taiwan, the election for national representative bodies is organized around a peculiar system of dual representation. Whereas most representatives are elected from the regional districts on the basis of more familiar geographic criteria, a disproportionally large number of seats are appropriated to six occupational districts on the basis of occupational criteria and two special districts instituted exclusively for the island's aborigines. This requires members of certain designated occupational associations and aboriginal voters to register on separate occupational or subethnic rolls and vote on separate ballots. For example, in the 1986 election, eighteen out of the total seventy-two elected seats were appropriated to the eight special districts, which, however, only accounted for 13.3 percent of total popular votes. In the nonsocialist world, Taiwan is perhaps the only case where geographic representation is combined with nongeographic representation in the electoral system.

12. To be more accurate, Tangwai contested in all electoral districts, because the twenty-three cities and counties were grouped into eight regional electoral districts.

13. The size of the entire chamber is dwindling steadily because of the natural elimination or voluntary retirement of the lifelong members. By the end of 1990, the overall size of the Legislative Yuan shrank to less than 256.

14. Of course, we don't rule out the possibility that this is also because more people become willing to express their party preference than before as a result of the general relaxation of the political atmosphere. But this hardly explains why we witness a corresponding growth of party preference toward the ruling party.

15. In this and following analyses, respondents who vote for independent candidates are excluded and only these voters who voted either for a KMT-endorsed candidate or a DPP-endorsed candidate are included for a clear-cut comparison.

16. Our items measure party preference, not party identification, which requires not just an attitudinal orientation toward a party but also the development of psychological attachment to a party. For a thorough discussion of different measures of partisanship, see Herbert Asher, "Voting Behavior Research in the 1980s: An Examination of Some Old and New Problem Areas," in Ada Finifter, ed., *Political Science: The State of the Discipline* (Washington, D.C.: American Political Science Association, 1983), pp. 354–360.

17. We do not mean by this that many voters choose a particular candidate solely because of his or her party preference. We recognize that the importance of party preference in vote decision needs to be compared with other factors. But a comprehensive analysis of modes of voting decision at the individual level is not of concern here; rather, we are interested mainly in assessing the significance of the rise in partisanship at the system level. For a comprehensive analysis of modes of voting behavior, See Hu et al., *Voting Behavior of the Electorate*.

18. Chinese complex refers to a value orientation that favors the ultimate unification of Taiwan with mainland China and insists on the inseparability of Taiwan and China both politically and culturally. Taiwanese complex, on the other hand, favors a separate identity for Taiwan both politically and culturally.

19. For the concept of postmaterialist values, see Ronald Inglehart, *The*

Silent Revolution: Changing Values and Political Styles Among Western Publics (Princeton, N.J.: Princeton University Press, 1976).

20. Only candidates who ran in the regional districts and who were officially endorsed by either the KMT or the DPP party are included in the analysis. This includes fifty-one KMT-endorsed candidates and seventeen DPP-endorsed candidates. In the KMT camp, party endorsement means that candidates had received either party nomination or party approval. There was no such distinction within the DPP camp. See Lee, *The Forty-Year Democratic Movement*, pp. 189–191.

21. A detailed tabulation of individual candidates' issue positions is available in Lin, "The Social Bases of Democratic Progressive Party and Kuomintung," pp. 275–277.

22. Because we base our content analysis only on the official campaign bulletin of the 1986 election, many issue statements concerning system maintenance that were widely adopted by KMT candidates in 1983 were dropped by most KMT candidates in 1986. This contrast is by itself a significant indicator of the sea change in the island's political climate taking place during the three-year interval.

23. Specifically, they are items 20, 22, 23, and 33.

24. The orientation to democratic values was measured on a ten-item scale developed by Professor Hu Fu and his colleague. The items are designed to measure the respondent's value orientation (approval or disapproval) toward five constitutive principles of democratic political systems, namely political equality, popular sovereignty and accountability, liberty, separation of power, and pluralism. For a thorough theoretical elaboration of the scale and an assessment of its measurement property, please refer to Hu Fu and Cheng Min-tong, "Political System and Voting Behavior: An Examination of the Construction of Theoretical Framework," in *Proceedings of the Conference on Voting Behavior and Electoral Culture* (in Chinese) (Taipei: Chinese Political Science Association, 1986), pp. 1–39. The original wording of all questions is available from the authors on request.

25. For attitude toward national identity, two questions were introduced: "Do you agree or disagree with the following statement that, for the larger goal of the unification of whole China, we should readily renounce localism?" and "Do you agree or disagree with the following statement that to build a better Taiwan is more important than the unification of China?" Before combining the two to yield a composite measure of the sentiment of national identity, a respondent's score on a Likert scale for the second question was inverted to be in alignment with the first question.

26. We classified by occupation each respondent into one of the six social class categories: farmer, labor, state employee, middle class, capitalist, and others. The farmer category includes rice farmer, dairy farmer, and fisherman. The labor category includes manual workers and rank-and-file white-collar workers in the private sector. The state employee category includes civil servants, the military personnel and police, employees of state enterprises, the KMT party and Youth Corps officials, and public school teachers. The middle-class category includes professionals, technicians, engineers, and managers. The capitalist category includes shop owners and large or small businessmen. Finally, the residual category includes housewives, students, the unemployed, and retirees.

27. Again, in this analysis, only the KMT voters and the DPP voters are included for a clear-cut comparison.

28. We reclassify the two attitudinal variables into dichotomous variables to simplify the dimensions of log-linear analysis.

29. For an introduction to the log-linear model, see Stephen E. Fienberg, *The Analysis of Cross-Classified Categorical Data*, 2d ed. (Cambridge, Mass.: The MIT Press, 1981).

30. Parameter estimates in Table 8.7 are calculated based on the best-fitted model [POD] [PC] [PI] [DC] [OC] where the letter P denotes party choice, O subethnic origin, C socioeconomic class, D democratic orientation, and I national identity. Based on a partitioning of the Likelihood Ratio Chi-Square Statistic, the stepwise procedures for model selection leads us to the aforementioned model as the "best" model. In identifying the suitable model, although the overall Likelihood Ratio Chi-Square Statistic (p = .994) suggests that the model might fit the data too well, the conditional test statistic indicates that the parameters that represent the pairwise association of [PC], [PI], [DC], and [OC], and those representing the second-order interaction effect of [POD], should be included. For an explication of the stepwise model selection procedure, please refer to L. A. Goodman, "The Analysis of Multidimensional Contingency Tables: Stepwise Procedures and Direct Estimation Methods for Building Models for Multiple Classifications," *Technometrics* 13 (1971), pp. 33–61; and Fienberg, *The Analysis of Cross-Classified Categorical Data*. Readers who are interested in the details of the model estimation and selection procedures can contact the authors for additional information.

31. Here a multiplicative parameter 1.752 means on average a voter is 1.752 times more likely to be a KMT voter and 0.571 means on average 0.571 times less likely to be a DPP voter. The two multiplicative parameters are derived from corresponding log-linear parameters (Lamda), which are not reported here, through an antilog function transformation.

32. Simply, 1.752 divided by 0.571 equals 3.07.

33. In log-linear framework, this is in terms of geometric means rather than arithmetic means.

34. Because the odds 1.69 describe only the departure from the baseline odds due to mainlander origin, *on the whole* a mainlander voter is more likely to vote for a KMT candidate than a DPP candidate with an odds of 5.19, where 5.19 is the multiplicative product of the baseline odds (3.07) and the effect of mainlander origin (1.69).

35. The cumulative effect of two or more social and attitudinal attributes can be calculated by taking the multiplicative product of relevant odds. For example, a voter with mainlander subethnic origin, being a state employee and taking a positive stand on national identity items, is relatively more likely to vote for a KMT candidate than a DPP candidate by a 3.99 odds, where 3.99 is the product of 1.69 (the effect of subethnic origin), 1.38 (the effect of socioeconomic class), and 1.71 (the effect of national identity). By taking into account the baseline KMT/DPP odds ratio (3.07), we can infer that a voter with the aforementioned sociopolitical attribute is on the whole more likely to vote for a KMT candidate than a DPP candidate by a 12.25 odds ratio! Take a more typical combination: a voter with Min-nan subethnic origin who is a member of the middle class and takes a negative stand on national identity items. This voter is on the whole more likely to vote for a KMT candidate than a DPP candidate by an odds of only 1.38, where 1.38 = 3.07x1.31x0.59x0.58.

36. Just as in the log-linear analysis, in the following statistical analyses only the KMT voters and the DPP voters are included for a clear-cut comparison.

37. For a comprehensive analysis of modes of voting decision among the electorate, see Hu et al., *Voting Behavior of the Electorate*.

38. For an elaboration on transition through transaction, see Share and Mainwaring, "Transitions Through Transaction"; and Donald Share, "Transitions

to Democracy and Transition Through Transaction," *Comparative Political Studies* 19 (4) (January 1987), pp. 525–548.

39. For an elaboration of the contingent nature of transition process, see Guillermo O'Donnell and Philippe C. Schmitter, *Transition from Authoritarian Rule: Tentative Conclusions About Uncertain Democracies* (Baltimore: Johns Hopkins University Press, 1986).

PART 4

Prospects

CHAPTER 9

The Effect of Taiwan's Political Reform on Taiwan-Mainland Relations

ANDREW J. NATHAN

The Taiwan experience has exerted an increasing influence on mainland China in recent years. Peking's coastal development policy, announced in January 1988, is explicitly modeled on the Taiwan experience. The still unimplemented idea of turning state-owned enterprises into joint-stock companies draws some of its inspiration from the success of the Taiwan model. In the political sphere, Chinese democrats have pointed to the reforms in Taiwan to argue that neither a Leninist party structure nor a Chinese cultural heritage is a bar to democratization.

Less noted and more complex are the effects that Taiwan's political liberalization, growing international self-confidence, and economic prosperity have had on Taiwan-mainland relations. These effects are the subject of this chapter. My argument is that political reform in Taiwan has changed the fundamental assumption on which China's Taiwan policy has hitherto been based—that the Kuomintang has the power unilaterally to negotiate the future of the island with the CCP. Democratization has so complicated the internal politics of Taiwan that it is now impossible for any deal to be struck with the mainland that does not command wide popular support in the island. Given the enormous risks that unification would pose for the people of Taiwan, this new political reality bodes ill for reunification on anything like the terms that have hitherto been offered by Peking.

Peking seems to have considered readjusting its strategy to take account of the new situation, but it has not yet made substantial policy changes and may no longer have any realistic options that will enable it to achieve its goal. The other actors in the drama—the KMT, the Taiwan electorate, and proponents of Taiwan independence—are also adjusting their strategies to take account of the changed situation on the island and to respond to the new strategies of Peking. All the actors see the United States as an important potential help or hindrance, but they often misunderstand the US position.

Mao Ze-dong used to say that it did not matter if Taiwan took a hundred years to rejoin the motherland.[1] But in a 1980 speech Deng Xiaoping expressed an increased sense of urgency about the Taiwan issue, listing reunification as one of the three great tasks of the decade.[2] Deng may have felt that Taiwan's importance for China's economic and security interests was greater than ever, given Taiwan's economic dynamism and China's growing aspirations as a regional power. And he may have felt that the completion of China's territorial unification was a historical mission of his generation of CCP leaders, which he was duty-bound to complete in his lifetime. Perhaps he realized that the passage of time would only make reunification harder to achieve.

Whatever his reasons, Deng has pursued reunification aggressively and imaginatively, building up pressure on the KMT to enter negotiations. His strategy has had two prongs. On the one hand, he has offered a series of radical concessions. In 1979 the National People's Congress Standing Committee issued "Letter to Our Taiwan Compatriots" seeking people-to-people contacts and peaceful reunification. In 1981 NPC Standing Committee Chairman Ye Jianying articulated Nine Points, offering Taiwan a high degree of autonomy in a reunified China. In 1983, in an interview with Prof. Winston Yang, Deng Xiaoping guaranteed Taiwan the right to maintain not only its own social and economic system but even its own military. And in 1984 Deng suggested the application to Taiwan of the notion of "one China, two systems," originally created for use in Hong Kong.

These concessions have not been merely tactical. They have in an important way altered, or at least rendered ambiguous, the substantive goals of the CCP's reunification policy. Deng's central goal remains that which the CCP has always pursued: to find some way of putting into practice the idea of "one China" that both the Taipei and the Peking governments officially recognize in principle, or, to restate the same thing, to implement Chinese sovereignty over Taiwan. In doing this, a second goal is also unchanged: to assert the higher, or national, status of the Peking government and to establish the lower, or local, status of the Taipei government. But a third and more concrete goal has become ambiguous: that of the establishment of actual physical control over the island. The idea of "one country, two systems" seems to suggest that such physical control is not an immediate aim of Chinese policy. (In this regard, Chinese authorities stress that Taiwan differs from Hong Kong.)

Yet, by extinguishing Taiwan's international persona, the first two elements of Deng's policy would lay the groundwork for the subsequent imposition of physical control at a time of the mainland's chosing. Its ability to do this would also be enhanced by the substantial economic integration that would be achieved between the island and the mainland under the one country–two systems policy. People in Taiwan are understandably cautious about handing over their bargaining chips to the people on the other side in exchange for a promise of respect for local autonomy.

Lending color to these concerns, Deng has unwaveringly maintained the second prong of his strategy, which is the threat of military force if Taiwan declares independence, obtains nuclear weapons, suffers from domestic insurrection, is subjected to foreign military intervention, or delays reunification beyond Peking's ability to be patient. The CCP leaders have been challenged over and over again, by the United States, by overseas Chinese journalists, and by the leaders of Taiwan to abandon this threat, and they have always refused.

A crucial element of the CCP's Taiwan policy has always been the insistence that its only interlocutor is the KMT, a rival political party that has emerged during the still unfinished Chinese civil war in control of some pieces of territory that include Taiwan as well as—the CCP has found it convenient from time to time to stress—some other pieces of territory that do not happen to be administratively part of the province of Taiwan.[3] For the CCP, almost any arrangement is conceivable between the two political parties so long as it does not entail a change in the status of Taiwan as a subordinate political unit under Chinese sovereignty. Peking regards this status as already settled and not open to negotiation (a position the KMT shares). Thus, Peking has always refused to consider dealing with Taiwan as a state or government, or with the people residing on Taiwan as a distinct people or nationality. To allow negotiations on any of these bases would risk abandoning the principle that the negotiations are intended to implement— Peking's sovereignty over Taiwan. Therefore, what the CCP seeks is negotiations not between the two "sides" but between the two (political) "parties."

CCP strategy has tacitly assumed that the ruling party in Taiwan is controlled by mainlanders committed to reunification, and that it has the power to resolve the fate of Taiwan. It is this set of assumptions that political reform has rendered untenable. Control of the party and of the island is tipping from mainlander to Taiwanese hands, and from the elite to the electorate.

The Taiwanization of the political system—initiated in the mid-1970s with the recruitment of increased numbers of Taiwanese into the upper ranks of the ruling party—has reached the highest levels of party and government. For the first time in Taiwan's history, the president is Taiwanese. The Legislative Yuan will come under the control of Taiwan-elected members by about 1992. Although mainlanders retain the highest positions in the party apparatus and the military, Taiwanese are moving higher and higher in both.

The new party and state elite still professes loyalty to the traditional party platform of one China in order to avoid a rupture with older mainlander party members and to avoid giving the PRC a casus belli. Yet they appear to be much less emotionally committed to unification than previous leaders and more committed to the interests of the Taiwan populace.

Party, electoral, representative, and public opinion institutions have developed to the point where the electorate is able to enforce considerable accountability and responsiveness upon the government. Elections are fiercely competitive despite structural constraints that load the dice in favor of KMT candidates. An aggressive print media keeps the government under a constant barrage of opinion columns, leaks, speculation, and second-guessing.

The Taiwan electorate seems to understand that a formal declaration of independence would be a costly and risky venture with few payoffs. The voters prefer to promote continued political reform at home that will increase their power in the political system, and innovative diplomacy abroad that will increase their government's international political profile and influence and hence their own convenience in traveling around the world and doing business. The electorate would probably not be averse in principle to some sort of formal reunification with mainland China provided that their rights and freedoms were credibly guaranteed and their access to international markets protected or enhanced. But the Taiwan electorate does not want to take even the slightest risk of coming under the actual physical control of the mainland authorities. This attitude is likely to continue even if the mainland regime substantially changes its political complexion. The islanders are unlikely ever to want to put their fate in the hands of outsiders, except in the unlikely event that the outsiders are much richer than they are.

All kinds of alternative futures for Taiwan are being publicly debated. Although it remains illegal to advocate Taiwan independence, members of the opposition party continue to bring up the issue in various forms. Numerous other proposals have been debated, such as "two countries, two systems," "the cultural approach," "one country under separate administrations,"[4] a "unification-pluralistic politics model,"[5] and "one country, two areas," a concept put forward by Taiwan's prime minister, Hau Po-tsun, in 1990.

Most of these proposals call in one way or another for legitimizing the governmental status of the Taipei authorities within the larger Chinese national entity and are therefore incompatible with the CCP's insistence on the Taipei government's illegitimacy. Peking views all such proposals as going down the road of Taiwan independence either intentionally or unintentionally.

Perhaps the most influential of these proposals has been Wei Yung's "multisystem state" model (tuo-t'i-chih kuo-chia), also known as the German model and multiple recognition, under which, pending eventual unification, the two sides would coexist on equal footing in the international arena, with neither reduced to the status of a local government. Both sides would continue to assert the notion of one China but would accept diplomatic recognition from countries that also recognized the other. Dr. Wei is a KMT member and government official and his proposal has been widely favored by influential politicians and academics in Taiwan. From time to time it has been rumored that his proposal was on the verge of official acceptance. The

CCP leaders view the proposal as a thinly disguised device to cement the de facto independence of Taiwan.

Beginning in late 1988, the Taipei government adopted a strategy of "flexible diplomacy" under which it has tried to increase its official presence in international organizations and foreign capitals by abandoning the all-or-nothing insistence on being the only Chinese government and on being labeled the Republic of China. (The strategy is influenced by, although not identical with, the multisystem state notion of Wei Yung.) On this basis Taipei was able to upgrade the level of nondiplomatic relations with several countries, including Canada, Britain, and France; expand trade and people-to-people relations with the Soviet Union and some Eastern European countries; and achieve full diplomatic relations with Grenada, Liberia, Belize, the Bahamas, Lesotho, Guinea-Bissau, Bolivia, and Nicaragua. (Some diplomatic partners were also lost—Saudi Arabia, Indonesia, and Singapore, with South Korea apparently set to follow—but these losses were sustained in spite of flexible diplomacy, not because of it.) Taiwan sent a high-ranking delegation to the Asian Development Bank meetings in Peking in May 1989, despite the fact that the delegation could not carry the label Republic of China there, and participated in the Asian Games in Peking in September–October 1990. Taipei has lobbied for admission to the General Agreement on Tariffs and Trade under the label of "Customs Territory of Taiwan, Penghu, Kinmen and Matsu."

Flexible diplomacy is connected with political reform. It is made possible by the Taipei government's newfound self-confidence in its democratic legitimacy within the island because it tacitly dispenses with the legitimizing fiction that the Taipei government represents all of China. And it is a sign of the government's increased responsiveness to the demands of the electorate, who are anxious to gain better access to and security within the international system. The CCP leaders see the new strategy as dangerous, because it aims to establish a viable international personality for Taiwan that will enable it to survive indefinitely outside the motherland's control.[6]

Taken together, the four developments just sketched mean that it is too late for any decision on the future of Taiwan to be taken over the heads of the people of Taiwan. The Taiwan electorate has entered the reunification game as a third player, indeed as the one that holds the most valuable cards and has veto power over any agreement. This development is far more threatening to CCP strategy than the obstacles it confronted in the past: the activities of the Taiwan independence movement, which the CCP correctly regards as having limited influence; the anticommunism of the mainlanders on Taiwan, which the CCP has always regarded as negotiable; and the economic and security interests of the United States in Taiwan, which the CCP believes it can preserve in a unified China. It means that the CCP's Taiwan strategy has failed.

Although bold and imaginative, the concessionary prong of CCP strategy failed to assure the Taiwan elites that their interests would be adequately protected in a future one country with two systems. The military prong of the strategy was never very credible and has become even less so over time, not only for directly military reasons but because China's domestic reform and new-look foreign policy have given it ever rising stakes in a peaceful Asian environment. Not only was the combination insufficient to induce the KMT into negotiations during the time when there were still only two players in the game, but in several ways the strategy gave added impetus to the emergence of the Taiwan electorate as the third player.

By continuing to place pressure on the KMT to solve the Taiwan problem in the near future, yet failing to provide a sufficiently attractive modality for doing so, the CCP provided a major incentive for the KMT to firm up its domestic legitimacy and stability by undertaking the political reform that has led to the emergence of the third player. The very imaginativeness and constant refining of Deng's proposals to the KMT helped unleash the flurry of alternative blueprints from scholars and politicians on the Taiwan side. The continuing threat of military force has helped the KMT reformers maintain stability through the risky reform process, because it has discouraged the opposition from appealing to Taiwan independence sentiment. The threat of PRC military intervention has helped to press both ends of the Taiwan political spectrum toward the vital center.

As recently as a few years ago, the CCP leaders seemed to believe that the people of Taiwan were yearning for the motherland's embrace and that only the KMT, with US support, was preventing this desire from being consummated. The CCP has now formed a more accurate impression of the Taiwanese state of mind based on several years of face-to-face contact between people from Taiwan and the mainland. Much of this has occurred on US campuses. In addition, starting in 1987, over one million people from Taiwan have visited the mainland, including representatives of the Democratic Progressive Party. The Chinese leaders have also had access to the reams of reportage published in Taiwan by journalists and other visitors to the mainland, which reflects the overwhelming impression that the mainland is far too backward for reunification to be desirable now.

Signs have emerged off and on since 1988 that the CCP leaders had begun to recognize the failure of their Taiwan policy and were exploring new ways of dealing with Taiwan. In the summer of 1988, a prominent Chinese-American professor of political science at New York University, James Hsiung, reported after meetings with senior Chinese leaders that the CCP would be willing to consider abandoning the right to use military force against Taiwan, establishing a coalition government of the two political parties, writing a new constitution that would not include the "four basic principles" (socialism, dictatorship of the proletariat, Marxism-Leninism-Mao Ze-dong Thought, and CCP leadership), and even changing the national name and flag.[7] When party general secretary Zhao Ziyang met with US secretary of state George Shultz on July 15, 1988, he stated that "both sides [the mainland and Taiwan] support the policy of one China. . . . Both sides hope for mutual cooperation. . . . Both sides want to carry on the fine tradition of China's national culture."[8] In August 1988, when CCP United Front Work Department chairman Yan Mingfu met with a group of Taiwanese, he stated that the CCP's refusal to rule out the use of military force in Taiwan was not directed against the Taiwan residents but only against potential foreign interference, and that the CCP would be willing to negotiate an agreement with the KMT that both sides would not use force against the other.[9] The official PRC journal *Outlook* elaborated that "the CCP will never use force against the patriots and those in favor of reunification of the motherland. If China must resort to force it will only be against aggressors and traitors."[10]

Such shifts of nuance, however, have failed so far to culminate in a substantial change of policy. A Central Commitee work conference on Taiwan affairs reiterated in December 1990 that the Taiwan issue must be solved through CCP-KMT negotiations.[11]

Meanwhile Taipei has challenged the CCP to up its ante. Taipei has given increasing leeway for cross-Strait travel, trade, and investment and has established a quasi-official organization, the Foundation for Exchanges Across the Taiwan Strait (FEATS) to handle what are in effect consular functions between the two sides. Yet Taipei preserves the "three-no" policy of no "official" contacts, negotiations, or concessions. President Lee Teng-hui has announced three rather tough conditions for initiating official talks—that Peking abandon its military threat against Taiwan, give up its four basic principles, and cease blocking Taiwan's activities in the international arena.[12] Through this combination of people-to-people flexibility and government-to-government inflexibility, Taipei has ingeniously seized the initiative from Peking, using the growth of unofficial relations not to diminish but to enhance its own viability as a regime, both domestically and internationally.

Political reform in Taiwan has strengthened the ability of the Taipei regime to conduct these intricate maneuvers by increasing the government's legitimacy and popularity in Taiwan and by demonstrating to the CCP that the Taiwan apple will not simply fall from the tree. But on the other hand, for the KMT as for the CCP, political reform has reduced its freedom of maneuver. Reform has placed new limits on the KMT's ability unilaterally to conclude a settlement with the Peking authorities if a mutually agreeable one could be negotiated. The third player confronts not only the CCP, but also the KMT.

But the impact of the Taiwan electorate on the KMT-CCP relationship has not been merely that of a potential veto power. The electorate's rising power in Taiwan gave it the ability to force the KMT into acts of flexibility that the regime initially viewed as risky. Before it embarked on the path of flexible diplomacy, the KMT faced great pressure from the opposition party, intraparty critics, members of the Legislative Yuan, and the press to find a way for Taiwan to reenter the international community. The electorate used the CCP's apparent flexibility as a goad to press the KMT to try for some new solutions to Taiwan's international isolation (so long as these would not involve a sellout of the Taiwan residents' interests).

Although the KMT's initiatives have proven remarkably successful so far, they are not without risk. Externally, they risk playing into the PRC strategy of "Hong-Kongizing" Taiwan. According to this scenario, Taiwan's economic ties with the mainland might create a powerful pro-unification constituency among Taiwan entrepreneurs, subject to manipulation from the mainland because of its economic interests held hostage there. At the same time, increased people-to-people and quasi-governmental contacts across the Strait could erode the international credibility of Taiwan's insistence on its legal personality as the sole legitimate government of China, leading to an erosion of foreign support.[13]

Internally, the major risk lies in the possibility that relaxation of tensions with the mainland will impair the KMT's claim to a privileged position within the Taiwan electoral system. Despite reforms, that system is still structured in such a way that the opposition cannot win control of the government no matter how many votes it gets. In a way that is legally intricate but politically simple, the structure derives its ultimate rationale from the fact of the civil war and the threat from the mainland. If this threat is seen to recede and the civil war to enter a twilight phase of informal peace, the question of why the KMT should not compete equally with the other parties, which has already been insistently raised, will become unanswerable.

Yet the net effect of the reforms has been to weaken the appeal of Taiwan independence as a political option. Although almost all the leaders of the opposition Democratic Progressive Party personally favor Taiwan independence, the mainstream of the leadership has decided that for the time being it is politically unwise to push for independence, mainly because of the anticipated strong reaction from the CCP. They have chosen to concentrate their efforts instead on pressing the KMT for more rapid democratization, in the expectation that this will not only bring them closer to winning power but in the meantime will strengthen the electorate's ability to block any unacceptable reunification settlement. So far, most of the DPP's electoral supporters seem to have accepted the democratization-first strategy. The openly pro-independence New Tide movement remains a small minority within the DPP and appears to have a relatively small base of support among the voters.

These developments have confronted the organized Taiwan independence movement, most of whose members are overseas, with a set of unappetizing political dilemmas. On the one hand, the Taiwan independence forces fear that political reform will legitimize and strengthen KMT rule. On the other hand, if they continue to hold aloof from participation in the political system, they risk becoming increasingly irrelevant in the eyes of the electorate. Increasing Taiwan-mainland contacts carry the risk of movement toward a negotiated settlement with the mainland that would make the success of the independence cause even more remote than it already is, but to oppose these contacts puts the independence movement at odds with the desire of most of the Taiwan voters for more flexible diplomacy. The independence movement fears both a weak KMT that fails to deal resourcefully with the CCP's smiling diplomacy and allows Taiwan to fall into a unification trap and also a strong KMT that wins political victories in the international arena and deprives the independence movement of much of its reason for being.

There has been much misunderstanding among Chinese on both sides of the Taiwan Strait about US policy toward reunification and the potential US role in shaping future Taiwan-mainland relations. The declared US policy remains that which was stated in the 1972 Shanghai Communiqué—that the United States "does not challenge" the position that "there is but one China and that Taiwan is a part of China" and that the only US national interest in the issue is "in a peaceful settlement of the Taiwan question by the Chinese themselves."

But this position is freighted with ambiguity. It can be read as saying that the United States agrees with the Chinese position that Taiwan is a part of China, or as saying that the United States does not necessarily agree but does not want to argue about the issue for the time being. Although no one involved in Taiwan is under the illusion that the United States now actively supports Taiwan independence, the ambiguity in the US position allows some to believe—with hope in the case of Taiwan independence leaders, with fear in the case of the PRC leaders—that the United States might swing its support to Taiwan independence in some future eventuality. Chinese on both sides of the issue are aware that influential congressional leaders such as Senator Claiborne Pell (chairman of the Senate Foreign Relations Committee), Senator Edward Kennedy, Representative Stephen Solarz, and Representative Jim Leach, are sympathetic to the goals of the Formosan lobby in the United States, which supports preservation of Taiwan's autonomy even though it is split on the question of whether to promote an immediate, open declaration of independence.

Among some pro-independence Taiwan politicians, the opinion is prevalent that, as one such person told me, "if Taiwan declares independence, I believe the US will support us. Taiwan's strategic value as an 'unsinkable aircraft carrier' is too great for America ever to abandon it. America will welcome an independent Taiwan that is friendly to its interests." In mirror-image fashion, as the prospect of reunification recedes, Peking tends to blame US arms sales for emboldening the KMT, to see the US hand behind KMT reforms, and to perceive a hidden US agenda of protecting its economic and strategic interests in Taiwan by preventing reunification. A November

1988 article in the official weekly *Outlook*, which was subsequently withdrawn, charged the United States with "increasing its interference in Taiwan's affairs, strengthening its political, military, and economic infiltration and control with a view to consolidating the situation in the Taiwan Strait of no peace no war, no unification no independence, no economic rapprochement or estrangement."[14] A December 1989 commentary blamed the rise of Taiwan independence forces on the United States.[15] In July 1990 a mainland specialist on Taiwan affairs argued to me that the United States opposes reunification because a united China would have great enough economic and political influence in Southeast Asia to challenge the United States role there. Although these charges are off the mark, it is true that the United States has contributed in an important way to the frustration of PRC goals by asserting a national interest in peaceful resolution of the Taiwan issue and by selling arms to Taipei to assure its capability for self-defense.

While deploring US involvement, the PRC has called upon the United States to take active steps to achieve the peaceful resolution of the issue that it says it wants by pressing the KMT into negotiations, or even by serving as a mediator. The Chinese placed great hopes in a reformulation of the US position that was offered by Secretary of State Shultz in Shanghai in April 1987. The secretary stated that "our steadfast policy seeks to foster an environment in which such developments [toward a relaxation of tensions] can continue to take place."[16] The PRC interpreted the Shultz statement as a new moral commitment to take active steps to encourage peaceful resolution of the unification issue. US officials insisted it was nothing more than a restatement of existing policy, politely rephrased to take note of Peking's sensitivities.

On my reading, the hopes and apprehensions on both sides of the Taiwan Strait about a US secret agenda or a change of policy are misguided. Despite a mix of intended ambiguities, policy countercurrents, confusion engendered by the separation of powers, and occasional reformulations in wording, US policy remains what the government says it is: the United States does not care whether Taiwan is eventually reunified with China or becomes independent, just so long as the issue is resolved peacefully. If this analysis is correct, then the United States is unlikely to play an active role in future reunification politics except in the improbable eventuality of rising military tensions in the Taiwan Strait.

The future prospects for Taiwan-mainland relations can be sketched in terms of three scenarios. The first scenario is of increasing tension. This would come about at the initiative of either the Taiwan or the mainland side. On the Taiwan side, it could be engendered if Taiwan acquired nuclear weapons, if there were a military coup or widespread social disorder, or if the independence forces gained much strength. On the mainland side, this scenario would be triggered if the Peking authorities decided for some reason to step up efforts to isolate Taiwan diplomatically and to increase the level of military threat. But for reasons implicit in the foregoing analysis, all these events are highly unlikely.

The second scenario is for an eleventh-hour negotiated agreement between the KMT and the CCP that legitimizes the de facto independence of the island under the thin disguise of an affirmation of China's unity.[17] Such an agreement might contain the following essential points. Both sides would agree that there is only one China and that Taiwan is part of that China; that fellow Chinese on both sides of the Taiwan Strait will not use military force against each other; and that fellow Chinese on both sides of the Taiwan Strait will not interfere with one another's participation in international organizations or diplomatic activities with foreign countries. The two political parties would agree to settle once and for all on paper the question of Taiwan's status, thus seeking to strengthen existing legal and political barriers to de jure Taiwan independence. The agreement would help to assure the mainland authorities that Taiwan would not fall under the influence of a hostile power, and it would make it easier for the PRC to gain access to Taiwan's capital and technology. But the CCP would make major concessions in agreeing not to use force against Taiwan and to allow Taiwan to conduct its activities in the international arena. The question of the form of Taiwan's association with the mainland would be left to the future to resolve, and Taipei would be under less pressure than before to resolve it on Peking's terms. Thus, such an agreement would serve the KMT's interests more than those of the CCP. For this reason, such an agreement cannot be considered a strong likelihood.

An agreement of this sort could only be effective if it won the support of the Taiwan electorate. Under the present disposition of public opinion in Taiwan, such support is certainly not guaranteed, but it is possible. Although a major motivation for the two political parties to reach such an agreement would be to block the Taiwan independence option, the residents of Taiwan would not necessarily see the agreement as working against their interests. It would remove the threat of PRC military action against Taiwan and would increase the ease with which Taiwan residents could conduct their international activities. In these ways it would increase the ability of Taiwan to survive and prosper. In the long run it would make it even more difficult for the mainland authorities to impose their control on the people of Taiwan against the will of the residents.

The third scenario is for the maintenance of the current situation—one of de facto independence—which is growing increasingly viable economically and diplomatically, despite continuing political tensions over it, but remains unofficial. This scenario has to be accounted most likely, because the CCP authorities continue to argue adamantly against Taiwan's flexible diplomacy and against the idea of dual recognition, refuse to abandon the threat of the use of military force, and continue to work against Taiwan's attempts to reenter international society under any rubric but that of a local level of Chinese goverment.

According to the analysis presented in this chapter, this last scenario offers no realistic chance of achieving reunification unless there are momentous changes in the international environment or the situation within Taiwan. Yet, so far the PRC leaders prefer it. This policy at least keeps the Taiwan problem open, and with it the possibility that the strategy may somehow still encounter the improbable historical circumstances that will allow it to succeed. Moreover, keeping the Taiwan strategy of the 1980s in place postpones the domestic political costs of acknowledging its failure. Perhaps not until Deng Xiaoping's passing can the Chinese leadership afford to come to terms with the fact that winning back Taiwan, if it can be done at all, may turn out be a more time-consuming process than even Mao Ze-dong foresaw.

Notes

An earlier version of this chapter was published in *Issues and Studies* (25:12) (December 1989), pp. 14–30.

1. Henry Kissinger, *White House Years* (Boston: Little, Brown, 1979), p. 1,062.

2. "The Present Situation and the Tasks Before Us," in *Selected Works of Deng Xiaoping* (1975–1982) (Beijing: Foreign Language Press, 1984), p. 225.

3. The significance of this is explained by Thomas E. Stopler, *China, Taiwan, and the Offshore Islands* (Armonk, N.Y.: M. E. Sharpe, Inc., 1985).

4. An informative discussion (and refutation) of these and additional proposals may be found in Li Jiaquan, "Again on Formula for China's Reunification," in *Beijing Review* 31 (13) (March 28–April 3, 1988), pp. 23–27.

5. Proposed in a Taiwan magazine by John Quansheng Zhao, a scholar from mainland China teaching in the United States: "Yi-ke 't'ung-yi-tuo-yuan cheng-chih' mo-shih de t'i-ch'u," ["To Proffer a Model of a 'Unified Pluralist Political System'"] *Chun-kuo lun-t'an [China Tribune]* 26 (5) (June 10, 1988), pp. 47–57.

6. For the comments to this effect of the PRC Foreign Ministry spokesman, see *Jen-min jih-pao, Hai-wai pan [People's Daily, overseas edition]* (December 20, 1988), p. 1.

7. Among numerous sources, see Shih-pao chou-k'an (New York), no. 182 (August 19–25, 1988), pp. 22–26; and Professor Hsiung's own account of the incident in *Shih-pao chou-k'an [China Times Weekly]* (New York), no. 185 (September 9–15, 1988), pp. 54–55.

8. *Beijing Review* 31 (30) (July 25–31, 1988), pp. 9–10.

9. Reported in *Hua-ch'iao jih-pao [Overseas Chinese Daily]* (New York) (September 14, 1988), p. 10, as reprinted from *Ch'ien-chin cho-k'an [Progressive Weekly]* (Taiwan) (August 27, 1988).

10. Chen Bing, "Thoughts Associated with 'Chen Li-fu's Proposal,'" *Liaowang*, overseas edition (September 12, 1988), in *FBIS-CHI-88-177* (September 13, 1988), p. 64.

11. *China Daily* (December 13, 1990), p. 1.

12. E.g., most recently, President Lee's interview with *Reader's Digest* editors, reported in *Lien-ho pao*, [*United Daily News*] overseas airmail edition (October 27, 1988), p. 1.

13. See Kao Ying-mao, "'K'ai-fang'yu 'cheng-t'i li-yi' ping-chin ti da-lu cheng-ts'e," ["A Mainland Policy that Sustains 'Rapprochement' and 'Collective Interest'"] and T'ien Hung-mao, "Chung-kung 't'ung-chan ts'e-lueh tui T'ai-wan an-ch'uan ti wei-hsieh" ["The Threat that Communist China's 'United Front Strategy' Poses to Taiwan Security"] (Paper presented at the conference on "Ta-lu cheng-ts'e ying he-ch'u ch'u?" ["Where Should the Mainland Policy Lead?"] Taipei, December 29–30, 1988), p. 11.

14. Zhang Jinxu, "U.S.-Taiwan Relations and Peaceful Reunification Across the Strait," *Liaowang*, overseas edition, no. 45 (November 7, 1988), in *FBIS-CHI-88-216* (November 1988), pp. 5–8; I have corrected the translation.

15. Guo Xiangzhi, "Internal and External Political Factors That Encourage Explosion of 'Taiwan Independence' Forces," *Renmin Ribao*, overseas edition, (December 16, 1989), in *FBIS-CHI-89-241* (December 1989), pp. 3–4.

16. Cited in Dennis Van Vranken Hickley, "America's Two Point Policy and the Future of Taiwan," *Asian Survey* 28 (8) (August 1988), p. 889.

17. Compare Andrew J. Nathan, "Ch'iu-t'ung ts'un-i: shih wei Hai-hsia liang-an kuan-hsi hsun i ch'u-lu," ["Search for Commonalities and Tolerate Differences: Finding a Way Out for the Relationship Between the Two Sides of the Taiwan Strait"] *Lien-he pao* [*United Daily News*] (Taipei), June 14, 1988.

CHAPTER 10

Taiwan Transition?

EDWIN A. WINCKLER

In 1990 Taiwan was halfway through transition—neither authoritarianism nor democracy, but rather a jumble of both. Taiwan had liberalized authoritarianism but not yet institutionalized democracy. Transition was likely to continue as it had begun—protracted struggle between conservatives and progressives, producing tortuous but cumulative change. Taiwan has long had most of the prerequisites for democratization identified by comparative analysis. However, it still lacked some prerequisites that some would consider essential, such as basic agreement, both domestically and abroad, on what kind of a political entity Taiwan is.

Thus, in 1990 the most basic negatives remained the refusal of the PRC to let Taiwan be just Taiwan, and Taiwan's own lack of consensus about the definition of Taiwan as a political community. Consequently, the Nationalist military insists on maintaining some controls over political discourse, and some Taiwanese insist on asserting Taiwan's independence from China. Less basic, postdictatorial struggles over power and policy continued within the establishment, and the opposition struggled to organize itself and define its role. Thus, though one could be guardedly optimistic, the outcome of Taiwan's transition remained in doubt—consolidation of a liberalized authoritarianism, as some conservatives still hoped, or negotiation of a democratic system, as most others wished?[1]

It is worth dwelling for a moment on the characteristics of this transitional zone. On the one hand, "residual authoritarianism" remains strong. The Nationalist military still limits politics and the Nationalist party still pervades the state. One still looks to the Nationalist establishment for the planning and implementation of reform. On the other hand, "anticipatory democracy" intermittently flares. Progressive politicians strive to realize a democracy that is not yet in place but seems just about to be installed. The Nationalist establishment no longer offers firm direction, and the opposition and public increasingly affect outcomes. In this transition zone, the roles of institutions and consequences of actions abruptly switch between regressive and progressive—authoritarians exploit democratic opportunities and democrats revert to authoritarian modes. Nor is transition the only game in town: the political landscape is riven by coalitions for and against President Lee, turf wars between state institutions, and the personalistic factions of Chinese politics. Given that the rationale for authoritarianism is no longer credible, and the procedures for democracy are not yet operative, what is remarkable is that the government continues to work so well and that most politicians exude such confidence that transition will proceed. One cannot, and should not, believe one's eyes. An acute but commercialized political journalism quickly abandons each old, and inflates each new, development. Nationalist spokesmen have always been eager to proclaim that true democracy has finally arrived, but by midtransition opposition politicians too have a stake in believing so.[2]

This conclusion has three main themes. One theme, of "transition paths," takes political change on Taiwan as a "dependent variable" and identifies some distinctive characteristics of Taiwan's transition. A second theme, of "regime types," explores the proximate causes of that transition path in the particular type of authoritarianism from which Taiwan began and the alternative types of democracy toward which it may move. The third theme, of "contextual processes," relates national institutional change to contemporaneous changes in both the supranational world and subnational society and to Taiwan's distinctive sociocultural heritage. The next section provides an overview of these three themes. The body of the chapter explores them in five sections: supranational environment, leadership, institutionalization, participation, and subnational environment, identifying past processes that will continue to shape Taiwan's future. A final section on prospects briefly explores the pace, dynamics, and direction through which Taiwan may evolve.[3]

Problematique

Transition Paths

Our first theme is identifying what is distinctive about the course of political change in Taiwan.

At the most general level, the comparative literature has outlined a generic transition path. The first half, "from authoritarianism," liberalizes civil society and dismantles controlling institutions. The second half, "to democracy," constructs representative institutions and formulates social policies. A complete transition surmounts a sequence of military, political, and socioeconomic "moments," in the course of which the elites involved negotiate pacts to reduce uncertainty and protect their vital interests. Meanwhile, the masses go through a "mobilization cycle"—some public involvement is necessary from time to time to push transition forward. In these terms, Taiwan's transition "from authoritarianism" has been quite peaceful, with high levels of elite civility and low levels of mass involvement. However, many basic issues remain unresolved: the role of the military and the form of politics, Taiwan's external status and internal policies. Around 1990, authoritarian dynamics were reflected in Nationalist conduct of the indirect 1990 presidential election and in the appointment of conservative General Hau as premier. Democratic dynamics were reflected in a strong showing by the major opposition party in the 1989 parliamentary elections and in President Lee's convening of a reformist National Affairs Conference in 1990.[4]

At a slightly less general level, transition theory stipulates that the political key to successful democratization is maintaining a coalition of centrists (establishment progressives and opposition moderates) against extremists (establishment conservatives and opposition radicals). In Taiwan, interaction between these four tendencies has long been the staple of political journalism, and in the course of transition these interactions have become both more visible and more intricate. Despite ups and downs, cooperation between the centrists has gradually strengthened and, despite starts and stops, they have so far always succeeded in regaining some initiative. Centrist détente reached a high point between progressive KMT president Lee and the DPP's moderate Formosa faction during the 1990 National Affairs Conference. However, the extremists too remain strong. Among establishment conservatives, the dwindling cadre of mainlander elders adamantly reaffirm their Nationalist mission. The Nationalist military will not wither away, and it has good reasons for urging restraint on civilian politicians. Rivalry with President Lee has allied some formerly "progressive" Nationalists (both mainlanders and Taiwanese) with establishment conservatives. Among opposition radicals, the emotional issues of Taiwan independence and constitutional revision give the DPP's New Tide faction enough clout to insist that DPP moderates maintain some distance from KMT progressives.[5]

At a still less general level, the comparative literature has distinguished variant transition paths, most frequently from above, less often from below. So far, Taiwan's transition from authoritarianism has been a successful case of transition through transaction—the negotiation between a still robust establishment and an increasingly strong opposition of mutually acceptable rules for political competition (as earlier in Spain and Brazil). This contrasts with democratization resulting from the breakdown of an authoritarian regime (as in the Philippines and most recent East European cases) or from the violent overthrow of an authoritarian regime by armed rebellion (as in some Latin American cases and Romania). Transition through transaction is attractive for its gradualism of process, centrism of elites, and moderation of masses. Nevertheless, this transition path does have its drawbacks— progressives must keep pushing to prevent transition from stopping, because conservatives keep obstructing long into the process. There is no decisive moment when conservatives are exorcised, particularly the military in an ostensibly civilian regime.[6]

Regime Types

Our second theme is that transition paths are defined most immediately by the particular types of regime between which the transition occurs.

Aristotle distinguished between malign and benign regimes—those that serve the rulers and those that serve the ruled. To a remarkable extent, Nationalist authoritarianism has served both. External competition with Chinese communism, reinforced by American pressure for successive reforms, has compensated for the lack of internal competition with an opposition party in Taiwan. The result is a developmental performance that was not only fairly well intentioned but also extraordinarily successful. The legacy for transition is negligible bitterness between establishment and antiestablishment elites and considerable public tolerance for continuing authoritarianism. The elite amity facilitates maintaining the centrist coalition promoting democratization. The public tolerance may have contradictory effects: it permits authoritarianism but, from the point of view of the authoritarians, does not require it. They can relinquish power without facing vengeful mobs.[7]

Modern comparison has directed attention to authoritarian regimes as a distinct segment of the political spectrum. Juan Linz distinguishes between "organicist-statist" and "pseudodemocratic" authoritarian regimes, here abbreviated as "hard" and "soft." Truly hard authoritarianism denies any need for popular mandate and rules through some combination of nationalist legitimacy, military coercion, and remunerative benefits, forbidding the organization of opposition. Soft authoritarianism proclaims popular sovereignty and permits rival parties, but the "ruling party" retains an overwhelming advantage in political resources and so always wins. In these terms, the Nationalist regime on postwar Taiwan evolved from decreasingly coercive hard authoritarianism (1945–1960) through increasingly remunerative hard authoritarianism (1960–1975) toward still unlegitimized soft authoritarianism (1975–1990). The shift from hard to soft authoritarianism began about 1975, reversed about 1980, resumed about 1985, and was largely complete by 1990. However, it was not by then a stable system, and it appeared likely to slip forward into democracy. Consequently, most observers regard 1985 as the beginning of a transition to democracy.[8]

At the most specific level, the best postwar literature on types of authoritarian regimes (by Juan Linz and Amos Perlmutter) distinguishes them by the mix of institutions involved and the distinctive political dynamics that mix entails. Almost alone in recent transition theory, Al

Stepan has reiterated the need to define specific transition paths in terms of the particular mix of authoritarian institutions from which the system starts, particularly the military. Here the basic point about Taiwan is that, contrary to most treatments of it as a "Leninist party" or "developmentalist state," the authoritarian Nationalist regime was basically a "leaderist" dictatorship with a primary reliance on the security sector (external military and internal police). In these terms, a basic cause of political change in Taiwan has been that the more the Taiwanese majority manned the security sector, the less the mainlander minority could rely on force to maintain its rule. Unfortunately, this does not preclude a joint mainlander-Taiwanese, or largely Taiwanese, authoritarian regime. In any case, the basic problem of the transition from authoritarianism in Taiwan is to deinstitutionalize leaderism while containing the military without provoking it into blocking further reform. The basic problem of the transition to democracy is to institutionalize a democratic form of civilian control over the security sector.[9]

Contextual Processes

Our third theme is that transition paths are intimately shaped by surrounding processes—supranational, subnational, and historical.

Transition theorists acknowledge the sometime role of supranational processes. However, most treat them as secondary, mostly to deny radical claims that national political transition is a function of global capitalist development. Nevertheless, supranational processes are quite salient for Taiwan, which has been heavily impacted by Japanese colonialism, Nationalist occupation, Chinese threat, American influence, and expatriate involvement. From this point of view, it was the American security commitment that consolidated the Nationalist security state in Taiwan (1945–1960), the American economic connection that transformed it from coercive to remunerative hard authoritarianism (1960–1975), and the withdrawal of the American security commitment that required Nationalist transformation from hard to soft authoritarianism (1975–1990). By 1990, maintaining ties with the United States, and expanding ties with the rest of the world, required steady but stable democratization. Thus, like Japan, Taiwan presents the problem of "democratization from above." Externally installed in the early postwar period, a conservative party has since provided developmental leadership. Opposition parties cannot command majorities because they lack public support, which requires access to state resources and governing experience, which the opposition cannot get because it lacks public support. In Taiwan this historical problem is aggravated by another external factor, the PRC, which holds the Nationalists responsible for keeping the Taiwanese opposition under control.[10]

Transition theorists make more of subnational influences than supranational ones, but most emphasize the partial autonomy of national politics from subnational socioeconomic change. Taiwan shows why. It is true that by 1985 it was largely socioeconomic modernization that finally forced political democratization on a reluctant Nationalist state. It is also true that political change lagged economic change by several decades, for largely political reasons. Nevertheless, the lagged correlation between socioeconomic modernization and political democratization does not mean that there has been no contemporaneous relation between Taiwan's evolving postwar economy and its politics. Taiwan's remarkable postwar prosperity facilitated stable authoritarianism by preoccupying people with advancing themselves. Then, after they "arrived" and began demanding democratization, economic prosperity facilitated that too by relieving politics of hard economic choices. Few political transitions can be so economically fortunate. But the political-economic fit goes further than just prosperity. More than most observers understand, the political stability of the Nationalist regime has relied on myriad deals between the mainlander Nationalist state and Taiwanese local elites. The content of these deals has reflected the successive stages of Taiwan's political-economic development. How to renegotiate these deals in terms appropriate to economic internationalization and political democratization will be central to Nationalist performance—electoral and parliamentary—in the 1990s.[11]

Finally, transition analysis must confront sociocultural distinctiveness. This should not mean abandoning political-economic analysis, nor should it mean reducing "distinctiveness" to a disembodied, preexisting, immutable "political culture." A signal contribution of transition theory has been to argue that political actors construct political culture as they go along, and that "rules of the game" are a product, not a precondition, of transition. Accordingly, the use of the term "sociocultural" here is deliberate, referring to a socially constructed "culture" that is embedded not in cognitions but in institutions. Thus in running states and markets, Eastern societies make more obvious use of personal networks than do Western ones. Eastern networks are more strongly stratified in terms of gender, age, and authority than Western ones. The sophistication of Eastern sociocultural infrastructure affects everything—why leadership remains personal and elite politics remains confidential, how publics relate to the state, and how Chinese mold foreign perceptions of their politics. Thus, subnationally, again like Japan, Taiwan presents the problem of a network society. Public participation has been mobilized indirectly by local political elites, through an elaborate exchange of favors between state elites, local elites, and local constituents. This has similarities to old-fashioned Western machine politics, and to the increasing emphasis on constituency service even in newly refashioned Western "good government" politics. Nevertheless, the proportion of votes mobilized through network obligations remains significantly higher, and the proportion of votes "autonomously" decided on issue grounds by individuals in the voting booth remains significantly lower.[12]

Supranational Environment

Domestic political development in Taiwan responds to global processes—
geopolitical, political-economic, and sociocultural. These processes, mostly
emanating from such core countries as the United States and Japan, have
contradictory effects, both retarding and promoting democracy. Into the
1970s, the effect of the core in bolstering the Nationalist elite outweighed the
effect of the core in fostering democracy. By the 1980s, the net effect of the
core favored liberalization, if not full democracy. In the 1990s, the net effect
of the core may again be restraining, particularly of Taiwan independence.

Geopolitics

The most basic external political process affecting Taiwan's domestic
political development will remain PRC claims to Taiwan and US
geopolitical disengagement from Taiwan. Taken together, these require
Taiwan to achieve a self-reliant defense against the PRC and make it difficult
for Taiwan to achieve a viable diplomatic posture toward the rest of the
world. These foreign policy issues have always interacted strongly with
domestic politics, and will continue to do so. Centrists try to delink external
status from internal politics. They have gained legitimacy from confident
handling of mainland contacts and aggressive pursuit of international
participation. Extremists, in their opposite ways, insist on the link between
external status and internal politics. The issue remains their biggest
preoccupation and biggest resource.[13]

PRC threat provided the main excuse for authoritarianism, and it may
still provide the main obstacle to democratization. Conservative Nationalists
still consider soft authoritarianism necessary to prevent Taiwanese
nationalism from provoking the PRC. At a minimum, the need to placate
the PRC complicates democratization. Through the 1980s, Nationalist
conservatives thought the best way to deal with the mainland was to avoid it.
Nationalist progressives thought the best way is to engage it, albeit
unofficially. By 1990 conservative avoidance had somewhat yielded to
progressive engagement. Then conservatives and progressives switched
emphases: suddenly the conservatives advocated engagement, to combat
Taiwanese independence, while progressives cautioned prudence, to retain
Taiwan's autonomy. Meanwhile, tourism, trade, and investment has
flourished. Increased contact with the mainland has reaffirmed the centrist
domestic consensus that, for the foreseeable future, neither unification nor
independence is feasible. Nevertheless, some possibilities—direct travel, large
investments, and official contact—remain controversial. Nationalist
conservatives warn that economic transactions with Taiwan may give the
PRC leverage over Taiwan's external economy and internal politics.
Opposition moderates downplayed discussion of independence until they were

embarrassed by Lee's emphasis on unification. Opposition radicals discount any PRC threat and insist that external political independence is necessary for internal constitutional reform.

The dwindling of formal diplomatic relations has long been an emotional humiliation and practical nuisance for Taiwan. Its ingenious cultivation of informal relations through "practical diplomacy" has only partly compensated. The PRC still opposes official participation by Taiwan in the international community, with much effect. However the collapse of communism and the intransigence of China have increased support for prosperous and pragmatic Taiwan. The international community increasingly welcomes Taiwan as an informal participant. Progressive nationalists are pursuing an activist foreign policy, both formal and informal. By formally reaffirming the diplomatic viability of the Republic of China, and establishing a National Unification Commission, President Lee hopes to reassure Nationalist conservatives that Taiwan will remain part of China. They still accuse him of begin an autonomist. By informally expanding Taiwan's actual participation under other titles, President Lee hopes to preempt demands from opposition radicals for Taiwan's independence. Nevertheless, their preoccupation with independence persists.

Political Economy

The basic external economic process affecting domestic political development is that further upgrading Taiwan's role in the global economy requires further increase in the sophistication of its elite policy process and mass economic activities. Increasingly, from 1960 to 1975, the degree of internationalization required was no longer compatible with a garrison state isolated from external influences. Increasingly, from 1975 to 1990, the number and diversity of initiatives required could not be processed through government planners but instead required a more active and independent role for both business and labor. This required at least soft authoritarianism but may not require full democracy.[14]

By 1990 Taiwan's growing international economic role had produced new economic prosperity and political confidence, but it had also led to new problems of success, both abroad and at home. The Nationalist state was frequently caught between American trade demands and domestic economic interests. Taiwan reluctantly surrendered long-standing economic advantages—an exchange rate favoring exports, unrestricted access to the American market, and protection of Taiwan's domestic market. The Nationalist state reluctantly abandoned treasured controls of external transactions—flows of information, capital, and even workers. Trade surpluses produced excess money that fueled speculative investments and domestic inflation. Still, remarkably, the economy appeared to remain basically sound, and there appeared to be little effect on political transition.

In the 1990s Taiwan may well have to adapt to a lower overall growth rate, partly because of slower growth of export opportunities and partly because of the faltering of the postwar domestic construction boom. Thus not only will Taiwan have to substitute internal for external sources of growth, but it will also have to replace old internal sources of growth (such as construction) with new internal sources of growth (such as services). In addition, Taiwan will have declining industries such as textiles and footwear. These economic adjustments will impose new burdens on the political system, requiring a new relationship between government, business, and labor. In the 1990s the Nationalists may install some elements of a continental European welfare state to ease these adjustments. Once again the opposition could be left without its own program, though it deserves credit for scaring the Nationalists into reform.

Society-Culture

The main external sociocultural process affecting domestic political development in Taiwan will be the increasing preponderance of cosmopolitanism over nationalism and provincialism. Cosmopolitanization does not mean merely Westernization, but rather Chinese participation in global culture. Neither mainlander nationalism emphasizing the Chinese cultural heritage nor Taiwanese provincialism emphasizing the island's distinctive history are adequate for formulating a new cultural identity for Taiwan. Such an identity is not a cultural luxury, but rather an intrinsic part of deciding basic political and economic policies. Already in 1960–1975 Taiwan's increasing involvement with the outside world increased its cosmopolitanism. However, in 1975–1990 this accelerated, particularly after 1985 when progressive Nationalists encouraged cosmopolitanism to preempt Taiwanese provincialism. Meanwhile, progressive Taiwanese, arguing that islander Taiwanese are inherently more cosmopolitan than continental mainlanders, also began formulating a future Taiwanese identity emphasizing cosmopolitanism.[15]

By 1990 Taiwan's external sociocultural links had proved to be valuable political-economic assets. Expatriate Chinese took an active role in both economic internationalization and political reform. The media were a continuous seminar on economic and political theory, including astute analyses of the latest foreign developments. Intellectual fads were wide in range and rapid in turnover—neomarxism, neoclassicism, postmodernism, deconstructionism. Private institutes for policy research, staffed by returned students and stocked with foreign journals, canvassed the world for relevant models and adapted them for Taiwan.

In the 1990s the sociocultural terms of political debate should shift from the old confrontation between mainlander nationalism and Taiwanese provincialism to rival versions of cosmopolitanism. This should be less explosive, because a cosmopolitan provincialism must incorporate mainland Chinese culture. An opposition based largely on appeals to Taiwanese provincialism would remain a minority, because most Taiwanese still value their Chinese heritage and most realize that political independence is impossible. Besides, it would be counterproductive, given the economic opportunities that have opened up on the Chinese mainland.

Leadership

Leadership is the first of the three main political processes shaping Taiwan's transition, and one that deserves more attention from transition theory. In Taiwan, leadership includes three related components: the Nationalist ideology of Sun Yat-sen (Sunism), the führerist leaderism of Chiang Kai-shek and Chiang Ching-kuo (CKS and CCK), and generational succession by the mainlander followers of Chiang Kai-shek. It was these components taken together that made the central pillar of Nationalist authoritarianism not merely the personal power of a particular leader but an institutionalized role of preeminent leader. Transition requires change in all three components, reducing the dominance of leadership over institutions and participation. At the same time, transition itself requires leadership. In fact, as of 1990, President Lee remained pivotal to further transition. On the one hand, he appeared committed to achieving significant democratization before retiring in 1996 and could expect public support for virtually any action that he might take in that direction. On the other hand, he appeared constrained, by both constitutional scruples and political calculations, to proceed with caution. One could only hope that he knew what he was doing and would act decisively when opportune.[16]

In Chinese political culture the leader defines the ideology and the ideology legitimates the leader. Followers commit themselves to leaders so long as the leader's ideology works, in exchange for which the leader supports the followers so long as they remain loyal. These commitments placed real constraints on CKS and CCK but are less binding on Lee, facilitating transition from hard to soft authoritarianism. However, like Lee, successors will probably consider it prudent to affirm their commitment to Nationalist orthodoxy and necessary to cultivate good relations with Nationalist elders, inhibiting transition from authoritarianism to democracy.

Ideologism

Ideologism is the ideological tenet that ideology is a particularly necessary and effective means of political struggle. The Nationalist political system remains somewhat ideological in style, but decreasingly ideological in content. We briefly consider old Nationalist formal ideology, old Nationalist informal political culture, and Taiwan's emerging national political culture. Nationalist ideology is sufficiently vague to accommodate a shift from hard to soft authoritarianism, but the party's insistence that its Nationalist mission remains above public opinion inhibits a transition to democracy.[17]

Formally, the Nationalists' ideology is Sunism. Externally, in the 1990s, Sunism could provide the ideological grounds for some reconciliation between Taiwan and the mainland. The main effect of external ideological struggle on internal political development will remain the Nationalists' insistence on maintaining institutions representing all of China. Internally, Sunist constitutionalism provided the rationale for the transition from hard to soft authoritarianism, and Sunist welfarism will provide the rationale for a shift in state priorities from development to distribution. Nevertheless, Sunism will continue to maintain that conservative social values are the foundation of social stability, and that stability is the prerequisite for change. This conservatism will continue to restrict the extent to which society can assert itself against the state. The party's Leninist organization remains remarkably successful at winning elections, managing the economy, and providing welfare.

Informally, as Mark Pratt has aptly said, the elite Nationalist party originated as the social club of the Chiang dictatorship's hangers-on. Through the 1980s, this club performed the useful function of socializing new entrants to the core of the political system into norms of loyalty to leaders, respect for elders, cautious accomplishment, and personal probity. Scrutiny for these values may even intensify as the party assumes more responsibility for personnel appointments, including selection of the leader himself. Stringent criteria of personal character, party loyalty, and administrative experience will leave few candidates for top posts—for example, mainlanders Ch'ien Fu and Ch'en Li-an or Taiwanese Lien Chan and Shih Ch'i-yang.

However, in the 1990s the club's culture will be under relentless assault—from both new cohorts of Nationalist Taiwanese politicians and new waves of opposition entrants, both mostly brash businessmen. Arguably the transition will be from a political culture of authority to a political culture of parliamentarism. At least so far, the National Legislature has been the most conspicuous forging ground for new rules of elite conflict.

Leaderism

Through the 1980s the Nationalist regime remained largely a leaderist (führerist) rather than a party (Leninist) system. Leaderism was one institution among many but, until the death of CCK, it was the critical one. As under Stalin and Hitler, under CKS and CCK the leader, not the party, directly controlled the major institutions and maintained power by playing them off each other. Transfer to Taiwan gave Chiang Kai-shek a dominance over the Nationalist state even more complete than on the mainland, grafted onto the already supreme office of Japanese governor-general. At CCK's death, Taiwan had a strongman system without any prospect of a strongman to lead it. Evidently that is what CCK wanted—to force Taiwan, after him, to make the transition from führerist to merely presidential leadership.[18]

Nevertheless, the leaderist system remains strongly entrenched. The 1946 Constitution, a compromise between presidentialists and parliamentarists, does not preclude leaderism. The 1948 Temporary Provisions, in which presidentialists gained back what they had conceded parliamentarists, facilitated leaderism. Subsequent amendments to the Temporary Provisions, particularly emergency powers that CKS had the National Assembly assign the presidency and National Security Council in 1966, further extended leaderism. It was these powers that enabled CCK to initiate the transition from hard to soft authoritarianism. Lee's dilemma is whether to use these authoritarian powers to push democratization, breaking impasses, or to eschew authoritarian methods for democratic ones, risking stalemate. Evidently he intends to eschew them, having rescinded the Temporary Provisions in May 1991.

In 1990 Nationalist conservatives fielded candidates against Lee and his vice-presidential choice. On the one hand, this challenge was an authoritarian ploy to hobble Lee, who may have made substantial concessions to the conservatives to negotiate their withdrawal and restore an appearance of Nationalist unity. On the other hand, the conservative challenge did further intraparty democratization.

Defining a reduced but effective leadership position will be both facilitated and complicated by the fact that even the 1946 Constitution does not really specify who, formally, should lead. (The Nationalist party constitution assumes it will be the party chairman.) As often observed, the Constitution combines elements of both presidential and parliamentary systems, allowing either the president or the premier to act as leader. Thus Taiwan is a mixed system and likely to remain so. In the past this mixed character gave the leader flexibility in adapting the system to his requirements; in the future it should give contending forces flexibility in adapting it to their needs. However, this mixed character also means that the mix remains up for grabs, changing paradoxically with the balance of personalities, institutions, and circumstances. Thus in 1990 conservative Nationalists favored a parliamentary system (formerly advocated only by liberals) to combat President Lee. Lee and the DPP favored presidentialism (formerly the bastion of conservatives)—Lee because he was president, the DPP because it sees winning the presidency as a shortcut to power. Nevertheless, Lee's appointment of a strong premier strengthened the premiership.

The most likely outcome is the division of labor that has repeatedly emerged between president and premier. The president remains above most issues of current policy, preserving his legitimacy to lend continuity to the system. The premier runs daily government affairs, and he can be changed as necessary. Such a division could be quite adaptive for Taiwan's needs. Neither the president nor the premier is likely to be elected by popular vote or parliamentary majority in this century. Probably they will emerge from orderly processes within the political elite, and probably that will remain acceptable to most of the public. Probably the president will be Taiwanese, except when a mainlander vice-president succeeds upon the death of the incumbent.

Succession

Intergenerational succession is a constant preoccupation of Chinese politics, involving not only the leader but also the entire generation of advisers and supporters surrounding him. For example, Li Huan made an attractive premier because, aside from providing mainlander representation and policy continuity, as the architect of party reform, he had the most protégés. For both cultural and rational reasons, in China the process of succession is surrounded by anxiety and hedged with cautions. Consequently in Taiwan many still prefer that elite succession continue to be managed from within the state, not thrown open to choice by society. [19]

Culturally, in China, elders provide and control resources, and youngsters should be grateful and submissive, even as adults. Traditionally, with few resources and many claimants, property passed from father to son, and maneuvering between brothers could occupy much of life. Chinese politics borrows heavily from such family processes of succession and inheritance. Political succession is a protracted game in which elders retain power as long as possible, with no formal mechanism for removing them. In Taiwan, the refusal of mainlander parliamentarians to resign would seem even more illegitimate in a less gerontocratic political culture. For youngsters, the long-run impressions of elders have been more important for eventual promotion than administrative accomplishment or electoral base. Family background has counted, on the belief that a good son makes a good minister. Not only have aspirants had to demonstrate loyalty to the leader himself, but they have also had to show respect for political elders in general. The policy process has had two tiers, retiring older advisers continuously reviewing initiatives from younger incumbent administrators. These norms may be weakening, but they are likely to persist at least through the next generation.

Rationally, Chinese succession behavior attempts to reduce uncertainty. Taiwan's political system is moving from a more traditional to a more modern mix of procedures for avoiding unwelcome political surprises. Thus hereditary succession is one way of reducing uncertainty still broadly applied in Chinese society, for example in family firms. Family inheritance was one of the principles underpinning the succession from CKS to CCK, but CCK stipulated that none of his family would succeed him as president. Nevertheless, there remains a strong tendency for sons of previous leaders to emerge, and family credentials could be significant in differentiating between first- and second-rank leaders in the 1990s. For example, Chen Li-an, the able son of mainlander former general and vice-president Chen Cheng, could provide an attractive focus for military and mainlander loyalties.

A minimal departure from hereditary succession is to allow the incumbent to pick his own successor. CCK exercised this prerogative in designating Lee Teng-hui. The Nationalist leadership might want to continue the practice for another term or two as, at least informally, in Mexico. So far, constitutional procedures have functioned largely to implement successions arranged by elites. Yen Chia-kan could succeed Chiang Kai-shek as president because it was understood that real power went to Chiang Ching-kuo as premier. Lee Teng-hui could succeed Chiang Ching-kuo as president because it was understood that he would largely continue existing policies. By 1990, pollsters were already probing whom the public might favor in direct elections for governor and president, and this mass input may increasingly affect elite arrangements. Nevertheless, these polls, aside from questionable reliability, still largely reflect the prestige of official position, not produce it. For example, in 1990, President Lee chose a premier whom neither the pollsters nor the public had even considered, and that premier quickly became quite popular.

Institutionalization

Institutionalization is the second of the three main political processes shaping Taiwan's transition. It includes three main sectors and a problematic process in each. Most fundamental is the security sector (external military and internal police) and the accompanying problem of civilianization. Also central is the legitimation sector (parties and media) and the accompanying process of party building. Third is the development sector (finance and economy) and the accompanying issue of technocratization.[20]

Though it is a "strong state," the Nationalist regime remains underinstitutionalized. The main problem is that the decline of control by leadership over institutions leaves the question of how military, party, and government should relate to each other. Turf battles have been an endemic feature of the transition to soft authoritarianism. This could facilitate democratization, but only if participation can assert popular control from below. This raises a second problem, that many of Taiwan's administrative arrangements lack statutory basis (for example, the provincial government), and many policy areas lack detailed legislation (for example, urban development). A further problem is weakness in both government enforcement of, and public compliance with, the law. These problems required reform, helping drive the shift from hard to soft authoritarianism. However, in the early 1990s deadlocks between institutional interests over how to solve them are delaying democratization. For example, bold proposals to redistrict Taiwan into metropolitan and intermetropolitan regions (three big cities and three small provinces) were soon defeated by the status quo (one big province and two big cities).

Security

The military and police remain largely behind the scenes in the Nationalist system, causing most observers to regard them as civilian controlled. However, this ignores the fact that both CKS and CCK based their personal power over the state in the security sector and used the security sector to maintain the state's power over society. Security crises provided the grounds for exceptional grants of power to the president and National Security Council, which provided the legal basis for the hard-authoritarian state. The leader himself has maintained control of the military and security apparatus only through immense personal prestige and adroit personnel maneuvering. Military officers have long enjoyed high prestige and high position in party and government, and the military itself remains largely immune from either party or government control. The internal security agencies too remain, not least as a check on the military, and as an alternative to a domestic military role. The transition from hard to soft authoritarianism has required a reduction in the public authority of security agencies and an expansion in the public authority of civilian law. However, the issue of Nationalist influence over the police and courts remains. Having resisted the transition from hard to soft authoritarianism, the security sector is likely to veto any precipitous transition to democracy.[21]

CCK's own preparations suggested the magnitude of the problem. He had both military and security leaders promise publicly to uphold the constitution and obey any future civilian leaders. Probably they will do so, provided that security matters continue to be managed as the security specialists prefer. The support of CCK's chief military aide, General Hau Pei-ts'un, was essential to Lee Teng-hui's successful succession. Lee's later appointment of Hau as premier again underlines the continuing centrality of the security sector to Taiwan's future political development. After becoming president, Lee, the leading government technocrat, found himself at odds with Li Huan, the leading party administrator, whom he had appointed as premier. So, after his reelection as president, Lee turned to the main structural alternative, leading military figure Hau. Hau has proved an aggressive premier, reasserting law and order using military organizations, with some social results and much public approval. One hopeful sign has been the military's willingness to participate in, not stand against, elections, running candidates on an equal basis with other contenders. One alarming sign is

Hau's attitude that Taiwan's environmental and other social movements are troublemakers.

Thus civilianization remains problematic in Taiwan. One side of civilianization is keeping the military out of civilian affairs. It was only in the 1970s that CCK removed the older, more nationalistic generation of mainlander officers from the political roles to which CKS had appointed them. The incumbent, more Americanized generation of mainlander military officers evidently believe the military should remain behind the scenes. What the next generation of Taiwanese officers think is a significant question mark. Probably they will regard themselves as guarantors of the Constitution, intervening only if civilians fail. However, like most militaries, they probably have a conservative definition of how much popular instability would be a threat to the Constitution. Regional developments, as in Korea and the Philippines, are influential—past military withdrawal there encouraged military restraint in Taiwan, but future civilian failures there could encourage military activism in Taiwan.

The other side of civilianization is civilians' gaining control of military affairs. The military in Taiwan still has its own defense plans, its own defense budget, and its own party-security system. It has reported to a military leader, not to the civilian party or government. Presumably any civilian attempt to manage these matters would provoke one of the running battles of the 1990s. The more likely course is that the military will exchange support for either the party or government, or noninterference in both, for civilian noninterference in security affairs.

Legitimation

The Nationalists continue to proclaim themselves the ruling party and extensively supervise both state and society. Nevertheless, as argued above, the Nationalist polity falls short of being any kind of party system—never quite Leninist, and certainly not yet parliamentary. Constructing a genuine parliamentarism is the main challenge facing the Nationalist party. The elite Nationalist party has been fairly Leninist in its monopolization of political legitimation functions and penetration of state organizations. The mass Nationalist party, though formidably organized and penetrating society to local elites, was never fully Leninist in mobilizing society to its grass roots. However, the basic reason the system was not Leninist is not that the Nationalist party was not sufficiently Leninist, but that the political system was not sufficiently partyist.[22]

Thus one reason why the system under CKS and CCK was not fully Leninist was that it was the Leader who produced the party, not the party that produced the leader. The Leader made his own personnel arrangements, including the composition of party councils, which then passively approved his arrangements. In the 1990s these party councils may play a key role in the political system by actively deciding top personnel appointments. This will be a major change, particularly if the composition of the party councils reflects the preferences of the party's own membership.

Another reason why the system was not fully Leninist was that it was the Leader, not the party, that controlled state institutions. As noted above, the military had its own internal party system, directly supervised by the Leader and largely separate from the civilian party's control. As for the government, despite the fact that all government policies must be adopted concurrently by the party, and the fact that all key government personnel are concurrently party members, in the final analysis it was the Leader who has decided both policies and personnel, albeit through party channels. Moreover, economic success has made government technocrats themselves increasingly assertive. Though the party has always claimed to set the general direction of government policy, it has never had the staff to specify the details. One could even argue that the party's influence has declined in its own area of primary responsibility—elections, media, education, and culture—with the proliferation of non-Nationalist alternatives.

Thus the process of party building, an essential aspect of modern political systems, also remains somewhat problematic in Taiwan. In the 1980s the Nationalist party tried reforming both its elite Leninist functions (retaining control of the state) and its mass parliamentary function (retaining support of society). Taken together, these reforms led to soft authoritarianism, not democracy. The purpose of the KMT's reform of its elite functions was to reclaim the party's capacity to dictate government policy and to reassert its supervision of policy implementation. In the short run, making the government responsive to the party was intended to bolster incumbents against opposition by improving the effectiveness of public policy. In the long run, however, it could facilitate transfer of state power from incumbents to opposition by making the government responsible to whatever party wins elections. In any case, by 1990 decisionmaking had again drifted away from party organs, to the presidency and the cabinet.

The purpose of the KMT's 1980s reform of its mass functions was to ensure that it could still win elections even after the Nationalists lose their monopoly of party organization and media access. This too was intended to make the Nationalists more difficult to dislodge, but eventually it too could help produce a cabinet responsible to the people through a majority party in parliament. Indeed, by 1990, Nationalist parliamentarians elected from Taiwan were already challenging the control of parliament, not only by retiring mainlander representatives, but also by Nationalist party headquarters. The KMT's Central Policy Committee again strengthened committees steering major policy areas; Nationalist parliamentarians responded boldly with parallel committees of their own. Even if the "mass" KMT lost control of representative bodies, it is not obvious how the 1947 Constitution would require the "elite" KMT to yield control of the government.

Development

Taiwan has been exceptionally successful at the "easy" stages of development. A stable investment climate has long combined with government incentives to enter new industries was enough. Many observers, particularly those preoccupied with development issues, assume that Taiwan was a technocracy, ruled by experts. This captures the fact that the state, not society, made economic policy, but it overlooks the fact that Taiwan's economic administrators did not constitute a strongly institutionalized elite corps of autonomous bureaucrats, as in the French case from which the term technocracy derives. Under hard authoritarianism, it was the leader's design that government technocrats should recommend development policy, with conflict between extraconstitutional planning agencies and constitutional ministries providing some intragovernmental policy debate. Taiwan's would-be technocracy was a collection of individuals manipulated by the leader, penetrated by the party, and divided by bureaus. Hence doubt that the government bureaucracy could provide the power base for a future leader, and the assessment that Lee Teng-hui was "only a technocrat."[23]

Taiwan is now in transition to high technology and high finance, which require more sophistication by the state and more initiative by society. Taiwan now has huge resources, so in the 1990s it is likely to achieve some success. However, the process will expose many strains in government— between the few officials who understand these new problems and the rest, between the high-productivity extraconstitutional planning agencies and the low-productivity ministries, and between the relatively autonomous central government and politically constrained local governments, among others. Nor is it clear that the government can maintain its control of development policy. Already, under soft authoritarianism, the government has had to defend its policy prerogatives from both party and parliament. Democratization will further challenge these prerogatives and raise the question of to whom the cabinet should be responsible—the president who appoints it, the parliament that approves it, the party that staffs it, or the people that suffer it. Transition also raises the issues of technocratic versus populist government, and of the different effects on administrative efficiency of different modes of politicization.

Thus the process of technocratization too remains problematic in Taiwan. In the 1980s the policy process was politicized by power struggles anticipating CCK's departure. In the 1990s it may well be politicized by parliamentary party politics. In any case, Taiwan needs a neutral, professional civil service. Economically, it must be professional enough to shift from direct control to indirect regulation. This is already occurring. Politically, it must be neutral enough to serve whatever president or party wins an electoral majority. This seems unlikely soon. Democratization would require Taiwan to dismantle domestic monopolies and controls that were important resources for hard authoritarianism but have now become both economic obstacles and political embarrassments. Because these resources are part of the KMT's soft-authoritarian advantage, it is not surprising that the KMT is reluctant to relinquish them.

In any case, in the 1990s major economic initiatives will no longer be so exclusively the province of state elites. The state will finally include more business and labor leaders in its own policymaking. Business and labor will increasingly take their own initiatives to solve their own problems. The pace of change will have long since outrun the bureaucracy, and Taiwan's businessmen will be sufficiently modernized to assume a more equal partnership with the state. The result will be a still more dynamic economy than one overreliant on the state, and a still livelier politics, resulting from the broader participation in policymaking and the wider distribution of political resources.

Participation

Participation is the third of the three main political processes shaping Taiwan's transition. Though formerly weaker than leadership and institutionalization, from 1975 participation gained sufficient momentum to carry the system forward to soft authoritarianism. We discuss three subprocesses—representation through elections, incorporation through mass organizations, and opposition through parties, criticism, movements, and demonstrations. Each of these was weak in both traditional and early to modern China, and each remained weak in Taiwan until the 1980s. Each has changed from passive to active with the transition from hard to soft authoritarianism. Under hard authoritarianism the Nationalists tried to immobilize social forces by encapsulating them in state organization. For soft authoritarianism the Nationalists advocated a plural society in which the KMT would umpire contending social forces. Democratization would require the KMT to relinquish its posture as a permanent "ruling party" and either compete equally with other parties or govern in consultation with its main opposition. These changes in turn involve trade-offs between legitimacy, autonomy, and effectiveness. Increasing participation increases the legitimacy of the Nationalist state but reduces its autonomy and, some fear, its effectiveness.[24]

Representation

Of our three forms of participation, representation has achieved the most complete acceptance in Nationalist China. The problem of national representative institutions in Taiwan has not been whether they should be representative or not, but in what proportion they should represent the mainland versus Taiwan. What has been authoritarian about representation in

Taiwan, through 1990, is that residents of Taiwan have had no way to gain control of the National Legislature or National Assembly, let alone influence the selection of premier or president. What may remain authoritarian about representation through the 1990s is that the Nationalist party's inherited advantages will enable it to maintain control of central representative organs, even after those organs are restaffed from Taiwan, and to decide who will be premier and president even before the issue reaches those bodies.[25]

Students of comparative legislatures have long argued that one should not dismiss apparently rubber-stamp legislatures because most exert some influence in exchange for their approvals. Taiwan's representative bodies, particularly the National Legislature, have demonstrated how much leverage even a small group of opposition legislators can get out of even a modest legislative platform, if they make bold use of it, so long as they are allowed to do so, and so long as the media reports their activities. Progressive Nationalists and opposition legislators have succeeded in embarrassing the government into action on a variety of issues—environment, labor, even institutional reform and mainland relations. The opposition long demanded complete reelection of all central representatives. In the late 1980s the Nationalists adopted voluntary retirement of old representatives and phased addition of new ones, leaving for later the question of how many seats might be reserved for mainlanders. However, the oldsters refused to retire. So in 1990 the Nationalists had the High Court order retirement of all original representatives in 1991 and complete reelection of new ones by 1992. The Nationalists intend a two-stage constitutional reform in which first the original National Assembly returns the country from emergency to constitutional government, then the new National Assembly amends the constitution to adapt it to Taiwan. The opposition intends to attack through the National Legislature, gradually rendering such Nationalist preserves as the National Assembly and Control Council simply irrelevant.

"Complete reelection" should finally produce operating majorities for Taiwan and at most symbolic representation for the mainland. One hopes this will enable national representative institutions better to perform such functions as raising revenues, reviewing legislation, and monitoring administration. One hopes too that it will enable the opposition finally to go beyond political-constitutional demands to substantive policy issues. However, one fears that reelecting representative institutions from Taiwan will result in business dominance of a "money politics," in both KMT and DPP. One fears too that mass demands could become the occasion for elite demagoguery, deadlock, and deficits. In any case, the National Legislature will increase its influence over the bureaucracy. Whether this will lead to parliamentary democracy, the existing Constitution does not fully specify. The president appoints the premier but the parliament must approve him. So far the parliament has always accorded a new president the premier and cabinet of his choice, making the system effectively presidential. So long as the same party controls both the presidency and the parliament, the constitutional relationship of premier to parliament is likely to remain ambiguous. If different parties control them, in principle the parliament could insist on a premier and cabinet of its choice, making the system effectively parliamentary. What will happen in practice may depend much on the personalities and issues involved.

As for subnational executives, the Nationalists have promised to make the mayors of Taipei and Kaohsiung elective again by 1993, partly because appointed mayors have not had the political clout to impose constructive programs on fractious city councils. The Nationalists were long reluctant to allow direct election of the provincial governor, lest it provide a platform for an opposition politician to assemble an islandwide following. Nevertheless, in 1990 President Lee endorsed a gubernatorial election, and two top KMT and DPP politicians (both Hakka) soon began a friendly rivalry, also with a late 1993 showdown. (The incumbent appointed governor declared he too could win election.) As for the presidency, given the large powers attached to that office, it is hard to imagine the Nationalists throwing it open to direct popular election, particularly since the current practice of indirect election by the National Assembly is what the Constitution specifies. "Direct election of the president" may be to the 1990s what "complete reelection of central representatives" was to the 1980s. Nevertheless, indirect election, though somewhat old-fashioned, need not be undemocratic. A lively contest between equal parties within the National Assembly could provide an acceptable substitute for direct election.

Incorporation

Incorporation is the state strategy to coopt social groups by drawing them into organizations under state control. It is a strategy typical of authoritarian regimes, and the Nationalists have employed it since the 1930s. In Taiwan, elections reserve seats for such groups as aborigines, overseas Chinese, occupational groups, and women. Within society, corresponding organizations reach the employed male population through occupational associations (industry, commerce, labor, farmers, and fishermen), and the rest of the population through other functional associations (women, youth, and retired servicemen). By 1990 these corporatist associations had shifted from passive toward active.[26]

Under hard authoritarianism, the main function of corporatism was to prevent anyone from organizing social forces to challenge Nationalist rule. Because the Nationalists allowed only one organization for each social category, and maintained that organization themselves, there could be no rivals. After their defeat on the mainland, the Nationalists were particularly wary of workers and students—urban groups concentrated in large organizations, with a high potential for political activity. The Nationalists particularly feared cross-local alliances between such groups. As is well known, they kept unions small in scale and weak in power, more mediators from management than spokesmen for workers. Intellectuals too were kept firmly under wraps. Schools were elaborately supervised by the Ministry of Education and extensively penetrated by party, military, and security organizations.

However, in the 1980s social problems arose whose solution required active social organizations, giving rise to the three movements of workers, students, and environmentalists. Electoral defeat of Nationalist labor leaders in 1986, for what previously were considered safe seats, propelled the Nationalists into strengthening state labor administration and encouraging private labor unions. Meanwhile, some university students began asserting their interest in politics, not only promoting campus discussion of sensitive political issues, but also extending organization between universities and to labor. Finally, for the new middle class, quality of life became a concern, with issues ranging from protecting consumers against faulty products and hazardous wastes to preserving cultural antiquities and the natural environment. The Nationalist response was remarkably sophisticated, supporting social groups with worthy causes so long as they remained within the law. Organized conflict within civil society need not challenge soft authoritarianism, but rather could provide new bases for state autonomy. In the 1990s, the Nationalists will attempt to give at least the appearance of umpiring the system from above the fray, continuing their role as mediator between social forces. To what extent social mobilization will promote political democratization depends on the extent to which social issues can be settled through mediation behind the scenes, rather than as electoral or parliamentary issues between competing parties.

During the 1990s, probably Taiwan will adopt a mixture of Asian, American, and European solutions to such social problems as congestion, unemployment, retirement, deviance, and alienation. Drawing on the strengths of Chinese society, the Nationalists are trying to get the family and community to handle as many problems as possible. At the same time, the Nationalists are granting unions a more adversarial role and requiring employers to contribute to unemployment insurance, pension funds, pollution controls, and environmental cleanup. Alarmed by the deficits that welfare programs have produced in Britain and the United States, the state will keep its own welfare role as small as possible, focused on those without family or employment. Taiwan may imitate the continental European small-state model of "democratic corporatism." Like Taiwan, these small states are subject to constant shifts in their external terms of trade and rely on constant consultation among corporatist associations to redistribute the resulting costs and benefits internally. If successfully installed under soft authoritarianism, such a system could constitute an important precondition for further transition to democracy by demonstrating that corporatist consultation could handle difficult social issues under democracy as well.

Opposition

Opposition is a broad process including not only party politics but also public opinion and personal petitions—any activity that pressures the Nationalist establishment for power sharing or policy change. Among our three forms of participation, opposition is the least firmly legitimated in modern Nationalist China. Conservative Nationalists thought Taiwan would be better off without any opposition activities, even those allowed by the Constitution. Hard authoritarianism allowed only token opposition to let off steam in order to avoid change. Progressive Nationalists prevailed with the view that it was no longer politically feasible to suppress opposition but that it was feasible for the Nationalists to continue to defeat the opposition through elections. Soft authoritarianism has allowed much substantive opposition to facilitate necessary policy change in order to preserve the existing power structure. However, probably the conservative party elite running the state has still held the progressive mass party managing society responsible for continuing to deliver roughly the old Nationalist electoral majorities. Although the progressives have not done quite that well, they have done well enough to sustain their strategy.[27]

In 1975–1990 the divided development of the opposition movement favored progressive Nationalists, facilitating transition from hard to soft authoritarianism. Through the late 1980s, more than half the public remained uncommitted—more than a third reported identification with the KMT but at most a tenth admitted commitment to the DPP. The KMT claimed nearly 2.5 million members, the DPP at most a few tens of thousands. However, the consolidation of public support behind one major opposition party in the 1989 elections was a major development, propelling the system forward toward democracy faster than many had expected. The DPP fielded an effective 1989 strategy and the public endorsed it with about 30 percent of the vote. Thus a major question is whether in subsequent elections notoriously fickle Taiwan publics, having observed DPP performance as central parliamentarians and local executives, will renew that endorsement. Even if the public does, the DPP will require many years for its diverse wings and headstrong personalities to coalesce into a disciplined party. Unfortunately, a continuation of individualistic opportunism remains a possible alternative direction of development.

In the 1990s, transition will require the opposition to present the electorate with an alternative program of public policies, something it has not yet done. Minimal democracy will also require that it be at least legally possible that, in a fair election, an opposition party (or coalition of parties) could defeat the incumbent party and replace it in power. Western theoretical criteria for full consolidation of democracy usually require several electoral alternations in power between government and opposition. This criterion is problematic, however, because it is not met by some countries generally considered democratic, such as Italy and Japan. There, instead of alternation between incumbents and opposition who exclude each other from political spoils, incumbents include the opposition in the distribution of political goods. Taiwan is already such a system in part and may become one in full with a publicly strident but privately accommodating permanently out-of-power opposition. In any case, weaker criteria of opposition access may be more appropriate for Eastern systems: a strong record of electoral alternation in subnational governments, and several national elections in which everyone agrees that the opposition could have assumed power if it had won, even though it did not win.

The likely course of unorganized opposition also deserves comment. Such protests and petitions occur whenever there is some combination of social concentration (factory, campus, or community) and political grievance (layoffs, censorship, or hazard). Temporary groups facing sporadic problems will create disconnected incidents through the 1990s, too numerous and transient to coopt. Nevertheless, the Nationalist state is gradually learning to view lawful "self-help" protests with sympathy rather than alarm. However, what it tolerates is private individuals bringing their problems to public attention, not private individuals attempting to impose their preferred solutions on society. There are issues here that will receive debate in the 1990s. For example, under what circumstances and to what extent is minor civil disobedience justified? Under what circumstances can how much redress be sought from the normal terms of economic contracts in a capitalist society? Where does freedom of expression leave off and deviance—including libel and obscenity—begin?

Subnational Environment

Stepping outside the political system again, it is worth noting some major processes in domestic society that will affect Taiwan's transition. Some, such as class formation and cultural change, are largely domestic extensions of global processes. Others, such as ethnicity and familism, originate largely within Chinese society itself. Some are unifying, some divisive, some both. Here we discuss ethnicity, class, and networks.

Ethnicity

Most political systems contain sociocultural cleavages such as race, religion, language, and customs. In comparative perspective, such differences in Taiwan are not ethnic but subethnic—hardly any of race and religion, only some of language and customs. Moreover, even this subethnic conflict between Taiwanese and mainlanders has really been not sociocultural but political-economic—mainlanders have had greater political access to the state, and depended more on it economically, than Taiwanese. In addition, the Nationalists promoted mainland language, culture, and history, while they suppressed their Taiwanese counterparts. Not surprisingly, the overwhelming majority of mainlanders still support Nationalist candidates while a significant minority of Taiwanese voters still adamantly oppose them. In electoral studies, subethnic origin consistently emerges as the strongest influence on party identification and voting behavior. Nevertheless, the Nationalists have always won most seats, partly because most Nationalist candidates are Taiwanese. Some opposition politicians covertly appeal to ethnic grievances and will continue to do so until anything that can be regarded as political discrimination has disappeared. Fortunately, both politicians and publics have raised the issue as one of procedural fairness not ethnic revenge.[28]

Nevertheless, for the foreseeable future, mainlanders will remain overrepresented in state and party leadership, with disproportionate access to state economic resources. Taiwanese culture has become a media fad, but the coverage of Taiwanese history in educational curricula is still inadequate. So, there remains plenty for Taiwanese politicians to complain about, and solving these problems will require much struggle. If badly managed by political leaders, ethnic politics could turn nasty and even damage now cordial social relations. One hopes that the Chinese preference for civility, and long experience at managing this issue, will enable Taiwan eventually to supersede it. The smaller ethnic differences within the Taiwanese between Hokkien and Hakka, and the larger ethnic differences between Chinese and aborigines, do not play a major political role. The solidarity of the minority Hakka is still expressed in local elections. Aborigines, at only 2 percent of the population, have negligible impact.

Class

Most political systems contain political-economic cleavages that supplement, but do not supersede, sociocultural cleavages. In Taiwan these too are relatively mild. Some Taiwan electoral studies show some tendency for voters with more education and higher class to support the KMT, and for those with less education and lower class to support the DPP. However, the influence of class is not so strong as that of subethnicity. Developing countries typically contain not one stack of classes, but several—rural, state, and urban—through which the population shifts forward as development proceeds. In Taiwan, what is politically most salient are the distinctions between these systems, not the distinctions within them. The Nationalists dominate all three, but they are more dominant in the rural and state sectors and less dominant in the urban private sector, where the opposition does best.[29]

Rural stratification involves relations between farmers and local elites—in Taiwan, first landlords and then community officials. The Nationalists long depended on Taiwanese local elites for mobilizing rural votes, and only a small minority of rural factions and rural voters were consistently anti-Nationalist. By 1990, however, most population and economic activity had shifted from rural to urban sectors. The Nationalists were struggling unsuccessfully to reduce their reliance on local factions, and more local factions and rural voters were openly supporting the DPP. The state constitutes a stratification system in itself, in Taiwan stretching from mainlander military leaders through Taiwanese civil servants to retired mainlander servicemen. State employees long provided the Nationalists with "iron votes" that were not only reliable but also reallocable between Nationalist candidates as electoral exigencies required. By 1990 these votes were less reliable—bureaucrats, educators, and even servicemen had become more independent minded, and workers in state firms were among Taiwan's most militant. Urban stratification involves private capitalist relations between owner-executives, white-collar staff, and blue-collar workers. In Taiwan, this is the increasingly dominant sector, combining "national capitalist" and "foreign-oriented" private economies. By 1990, most of the island's population had crowded into the expanding suburbs of a few large metropolitan regions. Metropolitanization converted local elites from rural political patrons to suburban political machines, and local masses from mobilized to autonomous voters.

Cleavages between capitalists and workers have emerged slowly, and they are only beginning to be politicized. In a country of small family firms, many are managers, and few workers consider themselves permanent proletarians. Postwar prosperity has allowed most people to regard themselves as middle class, implying a low level of conflict between owners and workers and political support for the Nationalist Party that brought them to this happy condition. Nevertheless, even in Taiwan, repeated or prolonged recession would lead employees, both blue collar and white, to discover the inconvenience of not owning income-producing property. Nevertheless, economic adversity need not translate into political repudiation of Nationalist rule. Past recessions have reminded businessmen of their dependence on the Nationalist state and reminded everyone that the Nationalists have much more experience running an economy than the opposition.

Thus the upper, middle, and lower strata of Taiwan society contain fractions from each of these stratification systems. In the upper stratum, the older rural-based Taiwanese "big families" have long since either gone abroad or joined the Nationalist establishment. The mainlander state political elite remains distracted between maximizing returns from Taiwan, preparing a retreat to the United States, and hoping for a possible future role in the development of the mainland. The new Taiwanese money remains dependent on the Nationalist state and uncertain about its international capitalist future. Although old and new Taiwanese elites may aspire to lead the state as well as the economy, neither can be sure that their position would remain as secure in a democratized Taiwanese state as it has been under authoritarian Nationalist rule. Some Taiwanese big businessmen may resist full democratization, fearing mass demands for redistributive policies.

The large middle stratum too contains diverse fractions. The old, politically committed fractions are dwindling. One is the small anti-Nationalist, old-Taiwanese petit-bourgeois middle class, which still resents early postwar Nationalist repression. The other is the small pro-Nationalist old-mainlander middle class, which still depends on the Nationalist state. The large new white-collar middle class, though certainly preferring political and cultural liberalization, still mostly supports the Nationalist party, partly because of genuine awareness of the many benefits conferred by Nationalist rule, partly because of a skepticism about the practical benefits offered by opposition candidates. Intellectuals will continue to back their favorite local opposition politician, but most of the middle class will continue to support the Nationalists so long as they do a good job.

The large lower stratum offers the most promising targets for opposition recruitment, particularly industrial workers. Agriculture has already shrunk, and will continue to shrink, given its falling comparative advantage and falling profitability. Despite the resulting farmer protests, the Nationalists are unlikely to lose much of their electoral hold on the countryside because the state still controls rural associations. In any case, by 1990 there were few pure farmers, most rural families earning much of their income off-farm. Thus industrial workers are now numerous and have the intermediate levels of education and uncertain economic prospects to which the opposition appeals. However, the proportion of industrial workers in society will not increase. The real growth will be in service workers, who now consider themselves middle class but could be radicalized by unemployment.

Networks

The family has always been a strong institution in Chinese society, and much of Taiwan's success at both development and distribution depended on it. Chinese familism is compatible with any political system that affords it ample economic opportunities. However, the low priority it accords political involvement, and the high priority it gives orderly behavior, may favor authoritarian stability over democratic uncertainty. The Chinese family system is designed to manage property and pass it from generation to generation. For this purpose it emphasizes parental control of resources, training of children in obedience, and investment in education and entrepreneurship. Retaining its rural farm or urban business base, the family can always reabsorb members who are temporarily unemployed. In return, children remit money to the family "corporation" and support their parents in old age. The result is not only a nation of hard workers and loyal citizens, but also high savings and aggressive investment, social welfare and even social civility. The state has to worry about only those who do not have family to take care of them. Feminism is not an issue—most women remain content with their roles as managers of their households, and they can work outside the home if they wish.[30]

The question for the 1990s is how long, in the face of the rapid modernization of everything else about Taiwan society, this paragon will continue. So far, the family's socialization and entrepreneurial functions appear alive and well. As for the family's welfare role, private savings should support most of the currently employed generation when it retires. After that, however, a declining proportion of young workers must support a rising proportion of retired elderly. The government has even switched from discouraging births to encouraging them, to enlarge the economically active population after 2000. Meanwhile, the elderly are rapidly becoming a political lobby and the Nationalists are strengthening programs for them accordingly.

Meanwhile Chinese reliance on non-kin networks also persists, because it works. Politically, networks make transition less urgent, less abrupt, more subtle, and more stable. Networks are fundamental to how Taiwan is linked to its supranational environment, providing the sociocultural infrastructure for informal contacts with formally inaccessible enemies and friends. Networks are fundamental to how conflict is organized within the national state—they provide the informal links between formally separate institutions. Networks are fundamental to how the state is linked to society—they provide citizens with more informal access than formal participation suggests. Networks are also fundamental to Chinese discourse about politics. This emphasis on informal organization reflects a continuing discrepancy between formal institutions and actual processes, and fosters distinctively Chinese concepts of authority and democracy.

Prospects

In conclusion, looking forward to Taiwan's transition to democracy, we treat three dimensions of possible outcomes: pace of transition, balance of parties, and type of democracy. As regards pace, a full transition from authoritarianism to democracy is likely to accelerate only in the mid-1990s and culminate in the first decade of the next century. As regards balance, in the long run, equal competition between parties is a more likely outcome than dominance by either KMT or DPP. As regards type, Taiwan may grope toward a Chinese adaptation of some compromise between Japanese "fiduciary statism," American "interest pluralism," and European "consultative elitism."[31]

A broad theme underlying these dimensions and informing Taiwan's transition is the tension between "hard" and "soft" democracy. This slogan provides a convenient rubric for collating distinctions by diverse authors regarding ideology, institutions, and publics in democracies. Thus the "hard" tendency is toward programmatic clarity, institutional responsibility, and political exclusion. Voters should have a clear choice between incumbents and opposition. Popular mandate should dictate who governs and with what policies. Incumbents largely exclude the opposition from participation in policymaking and policy benefits. This hard tendency predominates in Anglo-American systems—strong executives, competitive parties, and majoritarian elections. It also predominated in Gaullist France, where the dominant party in a multiparty parliament, associated with a powerful president, looked strong but eventually proved brittle. Theorists of democracy usually favor "hardness" for promoting broad centrist parties while still leaving voters some choice. However, theorists of democratization argue that hardness jeopardizes transition by intensifying conflict. Presidentialism in particular, through winner-take-all contests, antagonizes elites and polarizes masses, encouraging losers to reject the system. In Taiwan, so far, the emerging opposition has favored hard confrontations to mobilize the public against the incumbent regime. Nevertheless, a quick transition from soft authoritarianism to hard democracy remains unlikely.[32]

The soft tendency is toward ideological confusion, institutional autonomy, and political inclusion. Voters support a welter of discordant but mostly minor parties. There may be little relation between electoral outcomes and governing personnel or government policies, because elites negotiate coalitions between parties. In exchange, incumbents include both the ostensible opposition and their constituents in both policy formation and policy benefits. This soft tendency predominates in continental systems, particularly Italy. It also appears in strongly statist postwar Japan. Theorists of democracy sometimes deplore softness for its apparent power instability and policy immobilism. However, theorists of democratization argue that softness facilitates transition by obscuring divisive issues. Parliamentarism in particular, because no significant party is likely to lose all its seats, promotes elite reconciliation and mass acceptance, encouraging support for emerging democracy. In Taiwan, so far, the ruling establishment has employed soft strategies for defusing opposition and diffusing favors. A slow transition from soft authoritarianism to soft democracy appears most likely.

Pace of Transition

Some already scheduled events impose some temporal discipline on future developments—triennial parliamentary elections, quadrennial executive elections, and the reversion of Hong Kong to the PRC in 1997.[33]

Parliamentary elections should promote democratization, slowly but stably. The KMT has scheduled complete reelection of central representative bodies for the regular triennial central elections of late 1992, if not before. This will strengthen the function of parliament, encourage the assertiveness of Nationalist parliamentarians, and increase the leverage of the DPP. However, it is unlikely to deprive the Nationalists of a parliamentary majority, something that would probably take many elections if it occurs at all. The 1992, 1995, and 1998 parliaments will be legally democratic, but politically they will still be overcoming the legacy of authoritarianism. It was only in the 1989 parliamentary elections that the DPP first fielded serious candidates in most of Taiwan's multimember constituencies. It will take the DPP a long time to mobilize the personnel and resources to contest, let alone win, a majority in most constituencies, against entrenched KMT incumbents, in localistic contests.

A significant aspect of transition will be the choice of electoral system used. Continuing the present system would help the KMT maintain about 60 percent of votes and seats, but would also perpetuate its reliance on local factions. It would help the DPP maintain at least 30 percent of votes and seats but hinder its exceeding 40 percent. Supplementing the present system with a separate one for maintaining some mainland representation would solve a big problem for the KMT while creating few problems for the DPP. Some Taiwan scholars favor abolishing the present system in favor of single-member majoritarian elections for most seats, supplemented by letting the major parties allocate the remaining seats to whomever they wish. The number of seats for each party would be proportional to their share of the popular vote in the majoritarian elections. This would help the KMT disengage from local factions and give it seats for mainlanders. It could either make or break the DPP: one-on-one contests could mobilize a higher proportion of the vote behind DPP candidates, but the majority requirement could deny more of them victory.

Executive elections should promote democratization, rapidly but riskily. The next presidential elections are in 1996 and 2002. Lee Teng-hui has said that he will not run again for president in 1996, evidently to prove the disinterestedness of any reforms he proposes. Lee has endorsed a National Affairs Conference recommendation that the public be given a larger role in selecting future presidents. This could mean anything from the Nationalist party consulting public opinion polls, to linking the votes of National Assemblymen to public mandate, to shifting from indirect to direct election. Most people thought the National Affairs Conference wanted direct election. But that would require the Nationalist party to give up its secure hold on the most important office in the system, and would require the National Assembly to amend the Constitution to relinquish its own power to elect the president. The DPP is eager for a one-on-one direct presidential contest in 1996, but it is not obvious why the KMT would give them that chance. As noted above, the KMT has promised to resume elections for the mayors of Taipei and Kaohsiung, and begin elections for the governor of Taiwan province, at the next regular local executive elections in 1993. These executive contests, and those in 1997, have dual significance: they will test the staying power of the DPP in local politics, and they will prepare DPP presidential candidates.

The 1997 reversion of Hong Kong to the PRC could either promote or retard democratization in Taiwan, probably in no simple way. Hong Kong's reversion is widely regarded as a test of the terms on which Taiwan will eventually relate to the PRC—people in Taiwan do not want to negotiate with the PRC for at least several years after 1997, to see how Hong Kong does under PRC control. The PRC may claim that implementation of what it regards as a satisfactory solution for Hong Kong requires Taiwan to negotiate sooner not later. If PRC elders take a hard line toward Hong Kong, it will strengthen consensus that Taiwan is a separate political community that should avoid political involvement with the PRC. However, such PRC harshness may polarize Taiwan between extremists about how to maintain Taiwan's autonomy. Nationalist conservatives will say it shows that democratization must go slow, opposition radicals that Taiwan should renounce any possible political association with the PRC once and for all. If PRC youngsters take a soft line toward Hong Kong, it will perpetuate disagreement on Taiwan about whether Taiwan can combine autonomy with some form of political association with the PRC. However, such PRC restraint may strengthen the plausibility of moderate measures—centrists can argue that democratization is safe and independence unnecessary. In either case the PRC may attempt a more active role in Taiwan's domestic politics, increasing past efforts to affect them by loudly and threateningly proclaiming its demands.

There are other prerequisites for further democratization in Taiwan that have no definite schedule and therefore provide not temporal discipline but temporal latitude and excuse for delay. A supranational prerequisite is that everyone involved achieve some working compromise about Taiwan's external status. This may well involve different interpretations of the same language rather than actual agreement about Taiwan's identity. A national prerequisite is decline of the dependence of the mainlander minority on the Nationalist state so that mainlanders feel secure under rule by the majority Taiwanese. Objectively this condition appears already largely fulfilled. Subjectively, however, it may not, and the opposition might be wise to provide necessary assurances. A subnational prerequisite, mentioned above, is that consultative practices between state and society under soft authoritarianism prove able to manage continuous social change, building confidence that they will continue to do so under democracy. Whether this condition will be met, only the 1990s will tell.

Balance of Parties

The comparative literature has counterintuitive implications for the question of how party politics will evolve in Taiwan during transition. Most people would expect that, starting from one-party-dominant authoritarianism, Taiwan would be likely to end up with one-party-dominant democracy. But recent comparative literature argues that this has not been the most frequent outcome elsewhere. This finding may not predict the outcome in Taiwan, but it does suggest some probabilities. It is easier to suggest which segment of the political spectrum is likely to prevail than it is to suggest which parts of what parties will occupy what segment. Already in 1990 some were predicting that the KMT would soon break up into conservative and progressive parties, with the progressives perhaps joining with DPP moderates in a new centrist party. I consider this unlikely because both the KMT and the DPP are worth more to their members as wholes than as parts.[34]

First, although the KMT is likely to remain strong through the 1990s, in the long run continued dominance by a previously authoritarian party of the center-right is unlikely. In the course of transition, the political agenda moves on from ideological-political issues, in which parties of the center right have the advantage, to socioeconomic issues, in which parties of the center-left have the advantage. This is true even when the rightist party correctly expresses the nationalistic sentiments of the public. Continued domination would be even less likely for a KMT in Taiwan that affirms a mainland-oriented nationalism and denies a Taiwan-oriented nationalism. Under democracy, if the KMT cannot downplay the issue, it may have to convert to Taiwan-oriented nationalism.

Second, even starting from authoritarian dominance, after democratization, dominance from either right or left has been rare. Historically what has been more frequent is competition or stalemate. It is from learning to live with each other that the operative rules of a new democratic regime emerge. In any case, equal competition is the most likely prospect for the middle run, say from the mid-1990s to the middle of the first decade of the next century.

Third, if in the long run under democracy there is a successor dominant party, it is likely to be a party of the center-left—that is, one that responds to the socioeconomic demands unleashed by transition. This raises the question of who in Taiwan will be the real party of the center-left. One tends to think of the DPP as populist, but that is because it championed Taiwanese nationalism in the political-ideological phase. Socioeconomically, the progressive party could be not the DPP but the KMT. In 1990 the DPP remained caught between its reliance on Taiwanese capitalists for funds and on Taiwanese workers for votes. Meanwhile the KMT had already begun fielding social-democratic programs.

Types of Democracy

A final question is the particular form of democracy toward which Taiwan might evolve. Arguably there are three basic alternatives: Japanese fiduciary statism, American interest pluralism, and European consultative elitism. In Japanese fiduciary statism, the public entrusts a dominant party with long-term rule but expresses popular sovereignty by increasing and decreasing that party's majority. In American interest pluralism, particular publics actively intervene in the policy process through their individual congressional representatives to pursue their conflicting short-term interests, and the long-term welfare of society is assumed to follow automatically as a result. In European consultative elitism, different publics express their interests through consociational groupings, corporatist associations, or political parties, entrusting their leaders to compromise those interests for the long-term good of society. In Taiwan, the present fiduciary statism might slip toward interest pluralism, with some form of consultative elitism providing a compromise.[35]

Given external constraints, the Chinese in Taiwan may not be free to choose any political system they might prefer. Nevertheless, political culture remains an influence. One suggestive formulation holds that all cultures have both dominant public and secondary private values. Japanese are collectivist and cooperative, both publicly and privately. Americans are individualistic and competitive, both publicly and privately. Chinese are publicly collectivist and cooperative, but privately individualistic and competitive. Thus on the one hand Chinese find congenial a benign authoritarianism that gives strong public expression to collective ideals, as could also Japanese fiduciary democracy. On the other hand, Chinese relentlessly pursue their private interests. Previously in Taiwan this has been possible through economic competition or political connections. In the future, however, it may increasingly take the form of political lobbying through public groups, as in American interest democracy.[36]

Japanese fiduciary statism is what progressive Nationalists would like to install and what, if the economy remains strong, the public may be content to accept. A transition from soft authoritarianism to fiduciary democracy might require only minor procedural changes—either a premier responsible to a parliamentary majority or direct election of the president. Also, that transition could be relatively easy if it did not entail much substantive change—a tolerant polity and developmentalist economy would remain in place. Economically, postwar KMT authoritarianism in Taiwan, like postwar LDP democracy in Japan, has involved a developmentalist transnational elite that engineered an internationally competitive economy that produced high returns to domestic masses. Therefore urban white- and blue-collar workers, who were under-represented in the ruling establishment, remained content with virtual representation (elites acting on publics' behalf) rather than actual representation (publics acting on their own behalf). However, the American support and global demand that produced such high economic returns are gradually deteriorating. On the one hand, a fiduciary politics that maximizes national economic competitiveness becomes all the more valuable, as economic officials and business leaders on Taiwan emphasize. On the other hand, interest democracy expressing mass concerns becomes all the more attractive, as social groups in Taiwan already demand. In short, it will be more difficult for the KMT to do in the future what the LDP has done in the past.[37]

American interest pluralism would not be impossible in Taiwan, perhaps as a breakdown from either fiduciary or consultative forms. Indeed some people fear that in the early 1990s such a breakdown is already occurring, as democratic participation overwhelms authoritarian autonomy and parliamentary politics threaten to take on some of the directionlessness of the US Congress. However, the recent comparative record suggests that such interest-based systems are not internationally competitive, and most people in Taiwan know this. Also, interest democracy would entail a more drastic change in political economy than fiduciary democracy—more protectionism, more subsidies, more entitlements, and more deficits. Finally, it might involve a more frankly selfish public politics than the affirmation of collective ideals to which Chinese are accustomed.[38]

European consultative elitism may provide the compromise needed by these conflicts within both sociocultural ideals and political-economic exigencies. The fact that elites negotiate policy may salvage some of the economic competitiveness and collective ideals of fiduciary democracy. The fact that mass organizations express public demands may satisfy the participation demands and competitive individualism of interest democracy. European consociationalism, in particular, accommodates the kinds of ethnic conflicts over economic security and cultural policy that may arise in Taiwan. Of course, if some form of consultative democracy evolves in Taiwan, it will be distinctly Chinese. As always, Chinese will display a greater sense of the tension between social ideals and practical realities than Westerners. The leaders of mass organizations will remain more collectivist in public, and the members more individualist in private, than their European counterparts. A higher proportion of both elite initiatives and mass responses will work around the system rather than through it. Nevertheless, elite consultation would be there to handle any remaining problems.[39]

The cosmopolitan Chinese in contemporary Taiwan are groping toward more participation in their government. What they can attain will depend on the particular conjunctures that occur of the general processes outlined above. What they do attain will depend on the myriad ingenious initiatives and adaptations of Chinese political actors. In any case, like authoritarianism in Taiwan, democracy in Taiwan will be not only distinctively Chinese, but also distinctively Taiwanese.

Notes

1. Dankwart Rustow, "Transitions to Democracy," *Comparative Politics* 2 (April 1970), 337–363. Samuel P. Huntington, "Will More Countries Become Democratic?" *Political Science Quarterly* 99 (2) (Summer 1984), 193–218. Guillermo O'Donnell, Philippe C. Schmitter, and Laurence Whitehead, eds., *Transitions from Authoritarian Rule*, 4 vols. (Baltimore: Johns Hopkins, University Press, 1986). Larry Diamond, Juan Linz, and Seymour Martin Lipset, eds., *Democracy in Developing Countries*, 4 vols. (Boulder, Colo.: Lynne Rienner Publishers, 1989/1992). On national identity as a prerequisite for democratization, see Eric A. Nordlinger, "Political Development: Time Sequences and Rates of Change," *World Politics* 20 (1968), 494–530. Leonard Binder et al., eds., *Crises and Sequences in Political Development* (Princeton, N.J.: Princeton University Press, 1971).

2. The empirical basis for this characterization of Taiwan politics, and others throughout this chapter, is twenty years of following Taiwan politics, through both periodic visits and Taiwan periodicals. On Taiwan as an authoritarian regime, see Edwin A. Winckler, "National, Regional and Local Politics," in *The Anthropology of Taiwanese Society*, edited by Emily Ahern and Hill Gates (Stanford, Calif.: Stanford University Press, 1981), 13–37. Edwin A. Winckler, "Institutionalization and Participation on Taiwan: From Hard to Soft Authoritarianism?" *China Quarterly* 99 (September 1984), 481–499. Yangsun Chou and Andrew Nathan, "Democratizing Transition in Taiwan," in *Asian Survey* 27 (3) (March 1987), 277–299. Hung-mao Tien, *The Great Transition: Political and Social Change in the Republic of China* (Stanford, Calif.: Hoover, 1989), particularly 1–16. Tun-jen Cheng, "Democratizing the Quasi-Leninist Regime in Taiwan," *World Politics* 41 (4) (July 1989), 471–499. Edwin A. Winckler, "Political Transition on Taiwan," in *Guide to Asian Case Studies in the Social Sciences*, edited by Myron Cohen (New York: East Asian Institute, Columbia University, 1991). Edwin A. Winckler, "From Authoritarianism," in *Constitutional Reform and the Future of the ROC*, edited by Harvey Feldman and Andrew Nathan (Armonk, N.Y.: Sharpe, 1991).

3. The body of this chapter follows the outline of a piece written in fall 1987 and published as "Taiwan Politics in the 1990s," in *Taiwan in a Time of Transition*, edited by Harvey Feldman (New York: Paragon, 1989), 233–274. The present chapter has been completely updated and revised. Most of the introduction and conclusion, relating the Taiwan case to transition theory, is entirely new. I thank Tun-jen Cheng for his acute comments on this version.

4. Guillermo O'Donnell and Philippe C. Schmitter, *Tentative Conclusions About Uncertain Democracies* (Baltimore: Johns Hopkins University Press, 1986).

5. O'Donnell and Schmitter, *Tentative Conclusions*.

6. Donald Share and Scott Mainwaring, "Transition from Above: Democratization in Brazil and Spain," in *Political Liberalization in Brazil*, edited by Wayne A. Selcher (Boulder, Colo.: Westview, 1986), 175–215. Donald Share, "Transitions to Democracy and Transition Through Transaction," *Comparative Political Studies* 19 (4) (January 1987), 525–548.

7. Aristotle, *The Politics of Aristotle*, translated by Ernest Barker (New York: Oxford University Press, 1958). Recent work has only begun to examine the contradictory effects on transition of prior authoritarian performance.

8. Juan Linz, "Non-competitive elections in Europe," in *Elections Without Choice*, edited by Guy Hermet et al. (New York: Wiley/Halstead 1978), 36–65. Winckler, "Institutionalization and Participation on Taiwan."

9. Juan Linz, "Totalitarian and Authoritarian Regimes," in *Handbook of Political Science*, vol. 3, *Macropolitical Theory*, edited by Fred I. Greenstein and Nelson W. Polsby (Reading, Mass.: Addison-Wesley, 1975), 175–411. Amos Perlmutter, *Modern Authoritarianism: A Comparative Institutional Analysis* (New Haven, Conn.: Yale University Press, 1981). Alfred Stepan, "Paths Toward Redemocratization: Theoretical and Comparative Considerations," in *Comparative Perspectives*, vol. of *Transitions from Authoritarian Rule*, edited by O'Donnell, Schmitter, and Whitehead.

10. Laurence Whitehead, "International Aspects of Democratization" in *Comparative Perspectives*, edited by O'Donnell, Schmitter, and Whitehead, 10–19. Ralph Clough, *Island China* (Cambridge, Mass.: Harvard University Press, 1978). Edwin A. Winckler and Susan Greenhalgh, eds., *Contending Approaches to the Political Economy of Taiwan* (Armonk, N.Y.: Sharpe, 1988). Tien, *Great Transition*, 216–248.

11. Diamond, Linz, and Lipset, *Democracy in Developing Countries*. Arthur Lerman, "National Elite and Local Politicians in Taiwan," *American Political Science Review* 71 (1977), 1406–1422. Tien, *Great Transition*, 17–42. Edwin A. Winckler, "Roles Linking State and Society," in Ahern and Gates, eds., *Anthropology of Taiwanese Society*, 50–86.

12. Susan Greenhalgh, "Networks and Their Nodes: Urban Society on Taiwan," *China Quarterly* 99 (September 1984), 529–552. Susan Greenhalgh, "Families and Networks in Taiwan's Economic Development," in Winckler and Greenhalgh, eds., *Contending Approaches*, 224–245. The pitfalls of an overly abstract concept of culture are illustrated by uncharacteristic lapses in the work of two great observers of politics and China. In an otherwise magisterial survey, Samuel Huntington doubted that Taiwan would democratize because it has a "Confucian culture" (Huntington, "Will More Countries Become Democratic?"). Conversely, in an exploration of Asian political culture, Lucien Pye also argued that "Confucianism" impedes democratization, then, to handle the Taiwan exception, he claimed that Confucian authoritarianism has diminished in Taiwan. *Asian Power and Politics* (Cambridge, Mass.: Belknap Press of Harvard University Press, 1985), 232–234.

13. Charles Tilly, *Coercion, Capital and European States, AD 990–1990* (Oxford: Blackwell, 1990). Edwin A. Winckler, "Mass Political Incorporation, 1500–2000," in Winckler and Greenhalgh, eds., *Contending Approaches*, 41–66. Chiao-chiao Hsieh, *Strategy for Survival: The Foreign Policy and External Relations of the Republic of China on Taiwan, 1949–79* (London: Sherwood, 1985). Ying-mao Kau, "Beijing's Campaign for Unification," in Feldman, *Taiwan in a Time of Transition 1988*, 233–274. Ying-mao Kau, "Taiwan's New Foreign Policy Strategy," in *Beyond the Economic Miracle*, edited by Denis Fred Simon (Armonk, N.Y.: Sharpe, 1991).

14. Giovanni Arrighi, ed., *Semiperipheral Development: The Politics of Southern Europe in the Twentieth Century* (Beverly Hills, Calif.: Sage, 1985). Frederic Deyo, ed., *The Political Economy of the New Asian Industrialism* (Ithaca, N.Y.: Cornell University Press, 1987). Tun-jen Cheng and Stephan Haggard, *The Politics of Adjustments in the East Asian NICs* (Berkeley, Calif.: Institute of International Studies, 1987). Winckler and Greenhalgh, *Contending Approaches*. Stephan Haggard and Chung-in Moon, eds., *Pacific Dynamics: The International Politics of Industrial Change* (Boulder, Colo.: Westview, 1989). Stephan Haggard, *Pathways from the Periphery* (Ithaca, N.Y.: Cornell University Press, 1990). Bruce Cumings, *Industrial Behemoths: The Northeast Asian Political Economy in the Twentieth Century* (in preparation).

15. Alex Inkeles, "The Emerging Social Structure of the World," *World*

Politics 27 (July 1975), 467–495. Leo Lee, organizer, conference on *Cultural Change in Contemporary Taiwan* (Chicago: University of Chicago Press, August 1988). Stevan Harrell, organizer, conference on *Cultural Change on Postwar Taiwan* (Seattle: University of Washington, April 1989).

16. W. Howard Wriggins, *The Ruler's Imperative: Strategies for Political Survival in Asia and Africa* (New York: Columbia University Press, 1969). Robert Silin, *Leadership and Values: The Organization of Large-Scale Taiwanese Enterprises* (Cambridge, Mass.: Harvard University Press, 1976). Lloyd E. Eastman, "Social Traits and Political Behavior in Kuomintang China," in his *The Abortive Revolution: China Under Nationalist Rule, 1927–1937* (Cambridge, Mass.: Harvard University Press, 1974).

17. James A. Gregor, Maria Hsia Chang, and Andrew B. Zimmerman, *Ideology and Development: Sun Yat-sen and the Economic History of Taiwan* (Berkeley: Institute of East Asian Studies, University of California, 1981).

18. Amos Perlmutter, *Modern Authoritarianism: A Comparative Institutional Analysis* (New Haven, Conn.: Yale University Press, 1981), 89–135. Barry Rubin, *Modern Dictators* (New York: New American Library, 1987). On the tension between presidentialism and parliamentarism in Chinese constitutionalism, see Ch'ien Tuan-sheng, *The Government and Politics of China* (Cambridge, Mass.: Harvard University Press, 1961), and Andrew Nathan, *Chinese Democracy* (New York: Knopf, 1985). On Chiang Kai-shek, see Brian Crozier, *The Man Who Lost China* (New York: Scribner, 1976). On Chiang Ching-kuo, see Chiang Nan (Henry Liu), *Biography of Chiang Ching-kuo* (Los Angeles: American Tribune, 1984) (in Chinese).

19. Jack Goody, ed., *Succession to High Office* (London: Cambridge University Press, 1966). Hugh D. Baker, *Chinese Family and Kinship* (New York: Columbia University Press, 1979).

20. Samuel P. Huntington, *Political Order in Changing Societies* (New Haven, Conn.: Yale University Press, 1968). Winckler, "Institutionalization and Participation on Taiwan."

21. Alfred Stepan, *Rethinking Military Politics: Brazil and the Southern Cone* (Princeton, N.J.: Princeton University Press, 1988). F. F. Liu, *A Military History of Modern China* (Princeton, N.J.: Princeton University Press, 1956). Edwin A. Winckler, "Elite Political Struggle, 1945–1985," in Winckler and Greenhalgh, eds., *Contending Approaches*, 151–171. Hsiao-shih Chang, *Party-Military Relations in the PRC and Taiwan: Paradoxes of Control* (Boulder, Colo.: Westview, 1990).

22. Giovanni Sartori, *Parties and Party Systems* (New York: Cambridge University Press, 1976). Hung-mao Tien, *Great Transition*, 64–104, 195–215.

23. Chalmers Johnson, "Political Institutions and Economic Performance: A Comparative Analysis of the Government-Business Relationship in Japan, South Korea and Taiwan," in *The Political Economy of the New Asian Industrialism*, edited by Fred Deyo (Ithaca, N.Y.: Cornell University Press, 1987). Thomas Gold, *State and Society in the Taiwan Miracle* (Armonk, N.Y.: Sharpe, 1986). Alan P. Liu, *Phoenix and Lame Lion: Modernization in Taiwan and Mainland China, 1950–1980* (Stanford, Calif.: The Hoover Institution, 1987). Winckler and Greenhalgh, *Contending Approaches*. Chien-kuo Pang, *The State and Economic Transformation: The Taiwan Case* (Ph.D. dissertation, Department of Sociology, Brown University, 1988). Tien, *Great Transition*, 105–138. Robert Wade, *Governing the Market: Economic Theory and the Role of Government in East Asian Industrialization* (Princeton, N.J.: Princeton University Press, 1990).

24. Samuel P. Huntington and Joan Nelson, *No Easy Choice: Political*

Participation in Developing Countries (Cambridge, Mass.: Harvard University Press, 1976).

25. Myron Weiner and Ergun Ozbudun, eds., *Competitive Elections in Developing Countries* (Durham, N.C.: Duke University Press for the American Enterprise Institute, 1987). Tien, *Great Transition*, 139–161, 162–194. Edwin A. Winckler, *The 1989 Taiwan Elections: What They Mean and How They Work* (New York: The Asia Society, 1989). Edwin A. Winckler, "The 1989 Taiwan Elections: A Preliminary Post-Election Assessment" (Paper presented at the April 1990 Chicago meetings of the Association for Asian Studies).

26. Philippe C. Schmitter and Gerhard Lehmbruch, eds., *Trends Toward Corporatist Intermediation* (Beverly Hills, Calif.: Sage, 1979). Harmon Ziegler, *Pluralism, Corporatism and Confucianism: Political Association and Conflict Regulation in the United States, Europe and Taiwan* (Philadelphia: Temple University Press, 1988). Tien, *Great Transition*, 43–63.

27. Robert A. Dahl, ed., *Regimes and Oppositions* (New Haven, Conn.: Yale University Press, 1974), particularly the chapter by Linz. Peter Moody, *Opposition in Post-Confucian Society* (New York: Praeger, 1988). Kay Lawson and Peter H. Merkl, eds., *When Parties Fail* (Princeton, N.J.: Princeton University Press, 1988). Cheng, "Democratizing the Quasi-Leninist Regime in Taiwan." Mau-kuei Chang, "Partisan Preferences in Taiwan," in *Taiwan: A Newly Industrialized State*, edited by Hsin-huang Hsiao, Wei-yuan Cheng, and Hou-sheng Chan (Taipei: Department of Sociology, National Taiwan University, 1989).

28. Hill Gates, "Ethnicity and Social Class," in Ahern and Gates, eds., *Anthropology of Taiwan Society*, 241–281. Marshall Johnson, "Ethnicity, Power and Markets: The Changing Social Division of Labor in Taiwan," in Simon, ed., *Beyond the Economic Miracle*. Chang, "Partisan Preferences in Taiwan."

29. Osvaldo Sunkel, "Transnational Capitalism and National Disintegration in Latin America," *Social and Economic Studies* 22 (1973), 132–176. Hill Gates, *Chinese Working Class Lives: Getting by in Taiwan* (Ithaca, N.Y.: Cornell University Press, 1987). Chang, "Partisan Preferences in Taiwan." Sheu Jia-you, "The Class Structure in Taiwan and Its Changes," in Hsiao et al., eds., *Taiwan*.

30. Myron L. Cohen, *House United, House Divided: The Chinese Family in Taiwan* (New York: Columbia University Press, 1976).

31. Enrique A. Baloyra, ed., *Comparing New Democracies* (Boulder, Colo.: Westview, 1987). Giuseppe Di Palma, *To Craft Democracies: An Essay on Democratic Transitions* (Berkeley: University of California Press, 1990). Terry Lynn Karl, "Dilemmas of Democratization in Latin America," *Comparative Politics* 23 (1) (October 1990), 1–21. Nathan, *Chinese Democracy*. Edwin A. Winckler, "To Democracy," in *Constitutional Reform and the Future of the ROC*, edited by Harvey Feldman and Andrew Nathan (Armonk, N.Y.: Sharpe, 1991).

32. G. Bingham Powell, Jr., *Contemporary Democracies: Participation, Stability and Violence* (Cambridge, Mass.: Harvard University Press, 1982). Arend Lijphart, *Democracies: Patterns of Majoritarian and Consensus Government in Twenty-One Countries* (New Haven, Conn.: Yale University Press, 1984). Juan Linz, "Democracy: Presidential or Parliamentary. Does It Make a Difference?" (Workshop paper) (Washington, D.C.: Woodrow Wilson International Center for Scholars, 1985). Sidney Tarrow, "Maintaining Hegemony in Italy: 'The Softer They Rise, the Slower They Fall!'" in *Uncommon Democracies: The One-Party Dominant Regimes*, edited by T. J. Pempel (Ithaca, N.Y.: Cornell University Press, 1990), 162–188.

33. Albert O. Hirschmann, "Latitudes and Disciplines," in his *Development Projects Observed* (Washington, D.C.: Brookings Institution, 1967).

34. Giuseppe Di Palma, "Establishing Party Dominance: It Ain't Easy," in Pempel, ed., *Uncommon Democracies.*

35. See references given in Note 32. Also, David Held, *Models of Democracy* (Stanford, Calif.: Stanford University Press, 1987).

36. Florence Kluckhohn and Fred Strodbeck, *Variations in Value Orientations* (Evanston, Ill.: Row, Peterson, 1961). Edwin A. Winckler, "Statism and Familism on Taiwan," in *Ideology and National Competitiveness: An Analysis of Nine Countries*, edited by George Lodge and Ezra Vogel (Boston: Harvard Business School Press, 1987), 173–206.

37. Approving is Gerald Curtis, *The Japanese Way of Politics* (New York: Columbia University Press, 1988). Critical is Gavan McCormack and Yoshio Sugitomo, eds., *Democracy in Contemporary Japan* (Boulder, Colo.: Westview, 1986).

38. Theodore Lowi, *The End of Liberalism: The Second Republic of the United States* (New York: Norton, 1969/1979) argues that intra-elite deals are subverting US ideals. For a summary of Lowi's analysis of US politics, first introduced in 1964, see his "Four Systems of Policy, Politics and Choice," *Public Administration Review* 32 (3) (July/August 1972), 298–310.

39. Arend Lijphart, *Democracy in Plural Societies* (New Haven, Conn.: Yale University Press, 1977). Peter J. Katzenstein, ed., *Between Power and Plenty: Foreign Economic Policies of Advanced Industrial States* (Madison: University of Wisconsin Press, 1978), 295–336. Peter J. Katzenstein, *Corporatism and Change: Austria, Switzerland and the Politics of Industry* and *Small States in World Markets: Industrial Policy in Europe* (Ithaca, N.Y.: Cornell University Press, 1984 and 1985). Joseph LaPalombara, *Democracy Italian Style* (New Haven, Conn.: Yale University Press, 1987).

About the Contributors

(In chapter order)

Samuel P. Huntington, Department of Government, Harvard University.

Tun-jen Cheng, Graduate School of International Relations and Pacific Studies, University of California, San Diego.

Stephan Haggard, Department of Government, Harvard University.

Hung-mao Tien, Department of Political Science, University of Wisconsin.

Hsin-huang Michael Hsiao, Institute of Ethnology, Academic Sinica.

Ping-lung Jiang, Department of Political Science, National Chengchi University.

Wen-cheng Wu, Department of Political Science, Soochow University.

Constance Squires Meaney, Department of Political Science, Mills College.

Alexander Ya-li Lu, Department of Political Science, National Taiwan University.

Fei-lung Lui, Graduate Institute of Public Administration, National Chengchi University.

Fu Hu, Department of Political Science, National Taiwan University.

Yun-han Chu, Department of Political Science, National Taiwan University.

Andrew J. Nathan, Department of Political Science, Columbia University.

Edwin A. Winckler, East Asian Institute, Columbia University.

Index

About the Book

In the 1980s, after more than three decades of single-party authoritarian rule, the Kuomintang (KMT) initiated a gradual process of political liberalization in Taiwan and an expansion of democratic politics. This volume places Taiwan's experience with political liberalization in comparative perspective.

The authors address a number of issues that are peculiar to the consolidation of democracy in Taiwan, including the nature of relations between indigenous Taiwanese and Mainlanders, the changing role of the KMT, and the country's international political status as a divided nation. They also, however, explore the more general factors that have influenced the democratization process.